and I

Psychology and Policing
in a
Changing World

Wiley Series in

The Psychology of Crime, Policing and Law

Series Editors

Graham Davies
University of Leicester, UK

and

Clive R. Hollin
University of Birmingham, UK

The Psychology of Interrogations,
Confessions and Testimony
Gisli Gudjonsson

Children as Witnesses
Edited by Helen Dent and Rhona Flin

Paedophiles and Sexual Offences Against Children
Dennis Howitt

Psychology and Policing in a Changing World
Peter B. Ainsworth

Psychology and Policing in a Changing World

Peter B. Ainsworth
University of Manchester, UK

JOHN WILEY & SONS
Chichester · New York · Brisbane · Toronto · Singapore

Other Wiley Editorial Offices

John Wiley & Sons, Inc., 605 Third Avenue,
New York, NY 10158-0012, USA

Jacaranda Wiley Ltd, 33 Park Road, Milton,
Queensland 4064, Australia

John Wiley & Sons (Canada) Ltd, 22 Worcester Road,
Rexdale, Ontario M9W 1L1, Canada

John Wiley & Sons (SEA) Pte Ltd, 37 Jalan Pemimpin #05-04
Block B, Union Industrial Building, Singapore 2057

Library of Congress Cataloging-in-Publication Data

Ainsworth, Peter B.
    Psychology and policing in a changing world / Peter B. Ainsworth.
      p. cm. – (Wiley series in the psychology of crime, policing, and law)
      Includes bibliographical refeences (p.   ) and index.
      ISBN 0-471-94225-1 (case). – ISBN 0-471-95607-4 (pbk.)
      1. Police psychology. 2. Law enforcement – Psychological aspects.
  3. Police. I. Title. II. Series.
  HV7936.P75A56 1995
  363.2'01'9—dc20
                                               94–41820
                                                 CIP

British Library Cataloguing in Publication Data

A catalogue record for this book is available from the British Library

ISBN 0-471-94225-1 (cased)
ISBN 0-471-95607-4 (paper)

Typeset in 10/12pt Century Schoolbook by Vision Typesetting, Manchester
Printed and bound in Great Britain by Bookcraft (Bath) Ltd

This book is printed on acid-free paper responsibly manufactured from
sustainable forestation, for which at least two trees are planted for each
one used for paper production.

To
Genevieve Emily Ainsworth

About the Author

Peter B. Ainsworth was born in Blackburn, Lancashire. On leaving school he joined Blackburn Borough Police as a cadet, and then became a police constable with the Lancashire Police. In the early 1970s he started to attend nightschool classes and began to realise the implications which psychological theories can have for police work. After being seconded to Lancaster University, where he studied Psychology and was again able to demonstrate how theories could be applied in a practical way, he took up a scholarship to study psychology and sociology at Colorado University, USA. While there he saw at first hand some of the ways in which psychology has been applied to policing in North America. On his return to England Peter started work on his PhD, which examined cooperation between the police and social workers. In 1978 he was appointed as a lecturer in the Department of Social Policy and Social Work at Manchester University, a position which he still holds. Throughout his time at Manchester he has continued his interest in police work and psychology, often teaching psychology directly to police officers, and has carried out relevant research in the field of applied psychology. His previous book on the subject of psychology and policing was well received and did much to persuade an initially sceptical police audience that psychology was relevant, applicable and useful to everyday policing.

Contents

Conclusion   243

Series Preface

The Wiley series in the Psychology of Crime, Policing and Law will publish concise and integrative reviews in this important emerging area of contemporary research. The purpose of the series is not merely to present research findings in a clear and readable form, but also to bring out their implications for both practice and policy. In this way it is hoped that the series will not only be useful to psychologists but also to all those concerned with crime detection and prevention, policing and the judicial process.

As Peter Ainsworth emphasises, psychology and policing enjoy a common interface which is only now being addressed with the energy and commitment it deserves. Inevitably, the perspectives which psychologists and police officers bring to mutual problems is somewhat different and relationships in the past have sometimes been marked by a degree of mutual antagonism. Today, as Ainsworth illustrates, in many areas, relationships between police and psychologists are marked by a high degree of cooperation and mutual respect. This applies not merely to high-profile activities like offender profiling and interviewing techniques, but more mundane issues of police selection and training and the evaluation of performance. This process has been much accelerated by the rapid increase in numbers of police officers who have obtained undergraduate or higher degrees in psychology and have brought their skills to "the job".

Ainsworth's book is divided into three parts. The first part, dealing with 'the police and the public' looks at the way concepts, theories and techniques developed by psychologists can be put to use in understanding the range of problems police officers encounter in their everyday duties. Studies of policing demonstrate that police officers spend a considerable portion of their time not in headline grabbing activities such as car chases and arrests but in dealing with members of the public, sometimes in stressful circumstances. There is thus a great deal of emphasis on communication skills as well as the more obvious issues of interviewing and interrogation.

The other two parts of the book break new ground in looking at how psychology is being applied within the police service itself. Part II looks very much at police organisation. Like many other public services world wide, the British police have had to justify themselves and introduce audits of their efficiency and effectiveness. Ainsworth provides some useful insights into how psychology is assisting this process of changing the police culture through its role in recruitment, training and the detection of offenders. Part III discusses the relationship between the police and society at large. The media's interest in crime seems insatiable and Ainsworth illustrates how psychology can be used by the police to get across a fairer perception of the job they do and the problems they face. Recent changes in family and criminal law mean that police officers must work more closely than ever before with other state agencies such as social work departments. The problems of these changing relationships and the tensions that must be resolved are thoroughly and frankly explored.

As an ex-police officer, who trained as a psychologist and who now teaches within a university department with a focus on social policy, Peter Ainsworth is uniquely qualified to discuss this range of issues. This book should be essential reading both for police officers who wish to know more about what psychology has to offer them and for psychologists who are interested in how their science is being pitted against crime.

GRAHAM DAVIES
CLIVE HOLLIN

Preface

Interest in the police and their work continues to attract a great deal of public attention. Barely a day goes by without the media having at least one story about crime and the police. Police officers themselves are very much in the spotlight, their actions being scrutinised by an ever more demanding public. Stories of malpractice cause great concern, but the whole ethos of policing is now being examined closely. The ever increasing crime rate causes a great deal of anxiety and people are beginning to ask why the police are not more effective in catching criminals. For their part the police would say that they have very limited resources and yet are expected to tackle a wide range of duties which grows daily.

If the public are showing a continued interest in the police, then so too are academics. In the 1960s and 1970s it tended to be sociologists who conducted participant observation studies with the police. These studies were written up and published, and were often highly critical of police actions. However, at the same time, psychologists were starting to bring their research findings out of the laboratory and into the everyday world. As a former police officer who went on to study psychology, it seemed very obvious to me that a great deal of psychology was highly relevant to the training and day-to-day working of the police. I subsequently spent some time in the United States and there saw police forces which were much more open about their duties, and far more likely to accept inputs from academics, especially psychologists. Interest in academic subjects came much more slowly to the British police service, but there were signs in the 1980s that British forces were beginning to see the value of subjects like psychology. Police officers have a great sense of humour and I recall how one officer, when asked what he thought psychology was, said "Psychology is getting people to do what you want them to do without them knowing you're doing it"! I have searched in vain for an academic source for this quote, and believe it is original.

Of course police officers have a habit of reinterpreting information so that it suits their purposes. The week after I had given a lecture on non-verbal communication, a detective on the course came in and told me how useful he had found the information. He then told me how he had been interviewing a suspect who was denying the charge against him, and the detective started to tell the prisoner about non-verbal communication. He made a fist and started to push it into his other hand with some force. The prisoner appeared to get the message and, without the detective saying another word, confessed. I did begin to wonder whether all that research had really been carried out with such a result in mind!

The publication of my previous volume (Ainsworth & Pease, 1987) aroused sufficient interest to convince me that many police officers did see the value of psychology. That book was very much an introductory text designed to appeal to an interested but initially sceptical audience. Since its publication, both psychology and policing have moved on. Policing is still the difficult job it always was but, as we will see in this volume, priorities and responsibilities have started to change. Psychology has also embraced new concepts, theories and ideas, and has tried to show itself to be relevant to a true understanding of human behaviour.

This book reflects some of these changes. The content is considerably different from the previous volume and deals with areas which are of concern in the mid 1990s. It is hoped that this volume will further convince police officers of the value of psychology to their work. Many old-time police officers may well stick to their views that "outsiders" can add nothing to the knowledge base that the police themselves have built up. But the newer generation of young officers are likely to be less sceptical, and will at least listen to messages from those outside the organisation. It seems a very long time since, as a young and enthusiastic police constable, I was told by my Superintendent that "If you can prove that you've forgotten all that rubbish you've learnt at University then we might consider you for promotion". I hope that that officer has long since retired and has been replaced by one who does not take such a blinkered view about the knowledge that is required to make a good and successful police officer today.

Acknowledgements

As with any undertaking of this nature there are a large number of people who have contributed to the end product. Unfortunately it is not possible to name all of them individually. However I would like to thank my wife, family and friends who have stuck by me during the time when "the book" seemed to be my only topic of conversation, and when I became grumpy and irritable because of my inability to write more quickly! I would also like to acknowledge the contribution of the many police officers with whom I have come into contact, most recently Barry, Bill and Karen from Cumbria. They have helped me to understand some of the very real difficulties facing police employees in the 1990s.

I would particularly like to thank Graham Davies for his patient reading of each chapter, his encouragement, and his constructive criticism of my writing. I hope that the book is all the better for the inclusion of many of his suggestions. I would also like to thank Ken Pease for reading the manuscript at very short notice, and providing further comments and advice. I am also grateful to Chris Hitchen for providing me with much relevant material on the police and for her comments on drafts of various chapters. I would also like to thank Jackie for tidying up the mess that I made of the manuscript, and for helping me whenever I needed to ask yet another stupid question about word processors! Finally I would like to thank John Wiley & Sons for giving me the opportunity to show how psychology can be of value to policing in the 1990s.

Introduction

Police forces throughout the world are currently undergoing fundamental and significant changes. They are being asked to respond to an ever growing list of new demands and responsibilities, and to become more efficient and effective. The police service in Britain has never before come under such close scrutiny and questioning. There are currently major debates over the role of the police; their efficiency and effectiveness; and, in some forces, their honesty and integrity. At the time of writing this Introduction, the British police service is starting to come to terms with the Sheehy Report (1993), which has recommended sweeping and dramatic changes to the organisation of the police service in the United Kingdom. There are already objections being raised to the introduction of "League Tables" for police forces, which will focus on clear-up rates and other measures. At the same time politicians are questioning the true reason for the apparent shift of control over the British police from local to central authority.

Recently there have been some celebrated cases of people released from prison after many years, their convictions having been quashed following evidence of police malpractice. The West Midlands Serious Crime Squad was disbanded following a number of such cases. The Police and Criminal Evidence Act (1984) produced far more safeguards for accused people, though the introduction of the Act has led to many other difficulties for the police service itself (see Irving & McKenzie, 1989; Gudjonsson, 1992). Not least of the problems has been the increased paper work and administration, leading to low morale among officers.

In Britain, there is growing concern over the use of firearms by criminals. Britain remains one of the few countries where most police officers are not routinely armed. There are, however, an increasing number of incidents to which armed police officers are sent, and there have been a small number of cases where armed officers have shot and killed both suspects and innocent bystanders (see Waddington, 1988).

Incidents involving the police are constantly in the media. There are few other professions which come under such close scrutiny, and whose actions are so closely reported, analysed and criticised both in the press and on television. In some cases this constant examination has resulted in the police service closing ranks and becoming suspicious of any outsiders. One measure of this is the difficulty which researchers increasingly face in gaining access to police forces. There is also an air of secrecy which surrounds routine police practice and even training (see Chapter 8).

However, most members of the public feel they already have a good insight into how the police service operates. It is rare for an evening's television viewing to go by without the appearance of at least one programme concerned with the police. The focus of these programmes has, however, changed over recent years. Whilst the British police have been trying to play down the image presented in *Dixon of Dock Green* 30 years ago, many other images have now emerged which might inform public opinion (see Reiner, 1994). As well as the fictional detective series (e.g. *Inspector Morse*) there are an increasing number of drama series dealing with the day-to-day work of the police (e.g. *The Bill*) and even with some of the politics of the police role (e.g. *The Chief*).

It seems that there are no longer any taboos when it comes to television series on the police – one of the most controversial recent programmes (*Between the Lines*) dealt with the way in which the police investigate complaints against their own officers. It is hard to imagine that such a series would have even been dreamt of 10 years ago. Apart from these fictional accounts, there are an increasing number of documentaries which analyse in great detail the many facets of police work. Indeed, with the exception of politics, the police service seems to be the documentary makers' favourite subject (see Hurd, 1979; Sparks, 1992). Of course the media would not devote so much coverage to the police service if they did not believe that the public wanted to see programmes dealing with this subject. The viewing figures of some of the more popular fictional series suggest that there is a fascination with some aspects of police work, and with crime in general (see Sparks, 1992). The popularity of British programmes about the police is mirrored in many other countries. For example *Hill Street Blues* and *NYPD Blue* have become well established favourites in America.

There is a risk with such popular fiction in that if these programmes are not truly representative of what police work involves, the public will be labouring under a considerable misapprehension. Simplistic depictions of any role can lead to inappropriate stereotyping and misattributions (see Chapter 4). Television programmes may well lead to the public having unrealistic expectations of what the police can do. This in turn leads to dissatisfaction when the reality is confronted.

Sociologists were among the first academics to take an interest in the police service. Through participant observation studies they were able to give interesting insights into the day-to-day workings of the police, in both the USA and Britain (see e.g. Bittner, 1967; Chatterton, 1979). It is only more recently that psychologists have started to take an active academic interest in the police organisation. With an increasing wish to apply the results of laboratory-based studies (see Anastasi, 1988) came a growing interest in the criminal justice system in general (see e.g. Konecni & Ebbesen, 1982), and in the police service in particular. As in many areas, the United States led the way in first recognising the value which psychology might have for the police service. Psychology became an important and integral part of the training of most police officers in America in the 1970s and '80s and it was common for the larger departments to employ their own psychologists to deal with a range of issues from stress counselling to appraisal and training (see Brown & Campbell, 1993; Blau, 1994).

The police service in Britain was rather more reluctant to bring in outsiders to the training situation, and when psychologists were asked to make an input on basic training courses, their material was hardly ever tested in the formal examination process (see Chapter 8). The Metropolitan Police changed their initial training course considerably in 1981 to include a significant input of "Human Awareness Training" (Bull & Horncastle, 1988). A substantial amount of this could loosely be described as "basic psychology". The 1980s also saw the appearance of the first two British books dealing with psychology and police work (Bull, Bustin, Evans & Gahagan, 1983; Ainsworth & Pease, 1987). The early 1990s have seen further advances in the integration of the two fields. Manchester University has, since 1990, offered an MA in police management, whose syllabus includes a not insubstantial amount of psychology. The University of Portsmouth (in cooperation with the Metropolitan Police) has embarked upon a bold programme incorporating a Certificate, Diploma and Degree in Police Studies. The latter courses include modules on the psychology of the criminal justice system, and the psychology of police work.

It is against this background that the present volume makes further progress in linking psychology and police work. It covers much recent research in some of the areas already identified in previous books on the subject. It also identifies a number of key new areas in which psychology can usefully be applied to police work. This book is designed to be of interest and value both to serving police officers and to those who wish to gain a better understanding of the interrelationship between academic and applied psychology, and the day-to-day work of the police officer. Its primary target being serving police officers, it is written using many examples taken from routine police work.

The book is divided into three sections. Part I deals with "The Police and the Public" and will concentrate on psychological concepts and how they might be applied to policing. Chapter 1, "Dealing with Individuals", examines the nature of interactions between the police and members of society, and considers how such interactions might affect images of the police service. Chapter 2, "Interviewing, Evidence and Credibility", covers the way in which witnesses are interviewed, and looks at techniques such as the Cognitive Interview which may enhance the information obtained from witnesses. Chapter 3, "Interrogations and Confessions", looks at the way in which the police might interrogate suspects, and considers how officers might best avoid eliciting false confessions. Chapter 4, "Dealing with Groups", examines how social psychologists have added to our understanding of group processes, and looks at the implications for police officers. Chapter 5, "Violence and Reaction", deals with an area that seems to be attracting more and more concern in recent years. This chapter will describe what psychologists have discovered about violence, and how the police can best understand aggressive and hostile individuals. Chapter 6, "Dealing with Specific People", follows on from the previous chapter, and looks at how groups such as, for example, the mentally ill or drug abusers can best be dealt with by the police.

Part II, "The Police as an Organisation", starts to consider the police organisation itself and looks at applications of psychological research. Chapter 7, "Psychological Testing and Police Selection", will bring together the topics of psychometric testing and police selection. Chapter 8, "Training and the Police Culture", will look at the effects of training and the impact of the police organisation on the individual officer. Chapter 9, "Efficiency, Effectiveness, Quality and Change", looks at the way in which the police service has come to terms with such issues as efficiency and effectiveness, and whether it is possible to evaluate police performance in a systematic way. Chapter 10, "Police Science and Forensic Psychology", looks at recent advances in crime analysis, offence behaviour and offender profiling.

Part III, "The Police and Society", looks at the police service and its interactions with other organisations. Chapter 11, "The Police and the Media", examines the interrelationship between these two bodies, and whether the public's perceptions of the police could be improved through better use of the media. Chapter 12, "The Police and other Agencies", looks at the way in which the police work with other groups such as Social Services, and considers whether such relationships could and should be improved. The Conclusion will draw together the strands introduced in this volume and examine the possible future of links between the police service and academic psychology.

PART I

The Police and the Public

CHAPTER 1

Dealing with Individuals

"Another situation we had. This guy approached a bunch of officers on the street and he was real upset. He wasn't mad at the police – just life in general – and he was screaming and yelling and everybody was trying to get him to quiet down. Well, it was raining at the time, and one of the officers had glasses on, and they were getting all wet, so the officer took them off. Well, as soon as he did this the man stepped back and assumed a combative stance. Because he figured when a guy takes off his glasses he's getting ready to fight. And the whole situation got farther out of hand than it should have." (Quoted in Stratton, 1984, p. 58)

As the above example demonstrates, interactions between the police and the public are fraught with potential difficulties and dangers. This chapter will start to examine the nature of police–public interactions. In a world where members of the public are becoming less accepting of the police role, an understanding of interpersonal perception is vital if the nature of interactions is to be improved. In this chapter we will examine the use of stereotypes and the way in which we attribute causes to behaviour, and will examine Social Identity Theory as an explanation of hostility between groups.

Being able to deal with other people in a professional and effective way must be a priority for any public organisation. Perhaps nowhere is this better illustrated than in the police service. Having an interest in, and being able to deal with others has been identified as a primary quality required of any police officer (see Ainsworth, 1993). Whilst many commercial organisations have been quick to recognise the importance of their public image, organisations such as the police service have not always acknowledged how important image can be. As discussed in the Introduction, many members of the public will already have a stereotyped image of the police officer, perhaps based on television programmes. For many others, their entire perception of the police service can be affected by one short encounter with a police officer.

It can take only one brief negative interaction to produce a negative image of a whole group of other people. From that moment a person's entire perception of every other member of that group will, to some extent, be clouded by their previous experience. This applies equally to police officers' perceptions of identifiable groups, and the public's perceptions of police officers.

STEREOTYPES AND THE CLASSIFICATION OF OTHERS

A great deal of human life involves interacting with others. Most of the time people do this by responding to others in predetermined stereotypical ways. Defining somebody as "old", "black", "adolescent" or "junkie" allows a person to put others into pre-existing categories, and respond to them in well rehearsed ways (see Aronson, 1992). Stereotyping is one way in which humans can deal with the complex crowded world around them. By using stereotypes people do not have to spend hours finding out about each new person whom they meet. Once others have been categorised, it allows the observer to make predictions about their attributes, personality, and even their behaviour. They are able to do this by referring to their existing knowledge base of others who are in the same category. Stereotyping has been described as a way of taking "cognitive shortcuts"; i.e. stereotypes allow people to draw quick conclusions about others, without spending too much time gathering information about what each new person is like.

It is difficult to imagine how life would be possible if people did not use some sort of classification system when they met new faces. However, the danger is that when a new person is encountered, humans respond only to the stereotype, not to the person themselves. A recent advertisement highlighting the plight of disabled people in Britain showed a woman sitting in a wheelchair. The slogan read, "They only see the wheelchair, not the person". This does seem to provide a very apt example of how stereotyping works. Try as people might, it is difficult for them to respond just to the person (who in this example happens to have a disability) rather than to the disability itself. When people meet someone such as this, their attention tends to become focused on the main distinctive characteristic which the person possesses – in this case the fact that they are in a wheelchair. A human's classification system means that they may well simply label them as "a disabled person", and ignore the fact that this is an individual with a distinctive personality. It is not uncommon for people to speak more slowly or more loudly to a person in a wheelchair, assuming that their physical disability extends to more than an inability to use their legs. Some interesting work by Robert Sommer (1969) showed that people tended to interact at a greater distance when talking to others who supposedly were prone to epileptic fits. Whilst a fear of the condition of epilepsy might account for such a finding, it is difficult to explain why the same finding (of greater interpersonal distance) was also applied to someone who had apparently had a leg amputated.

When people meet someone with a facial abnormality it is hard to look beyond this salient characteristic to find out more about the person. Simon Weston was a British soldier who received severe facial burns during the Falklands War. He has since become something of a celebrity, with media appearances and the writing of a book. One frustration which he often expresses concerns the difficulty which he has in making people listen to what he is saying, rather than looking at his scars. Human beings do tend to be drawn towards any feature that stands out as being unusual or different. Psychologists have demonstrated how people have a tendency to concentrate on one salient characteristic of another when they are trying to attribute a cause for the other's behaviour (see e.g. Fiske & Neuberg, 1990). This is just one example of how attributions might be biased, and is a topic we will return to later.

The above examples provide quite dramatic evidence of the way in which the perception and classification of others works. People often look for one salient feature in the other person, and then use that feature to allow them to categorise (or stereotype) the other. Whilst this may be understandable in the case of a disabled person, it is interesting to ask whether the same rules apply to others who do not have one such outstanding feature. If the observer is white, and has had little direct contact with black faces, he/she will tend to be drawn by the colour and features of a new black face. The individual will also tend to fall back on his/her stereotyped view of "black people". Once again the danger is that the person will respond to "the black face" rather than the person behind it. Even if the person has had little direct contact with such groups, he/she may well have a view of what characteristics should be associated with the person. In most cases, this image will have been built up through discussions with relatives, colleagues or friends, or will have been formed by images presented in the media. Television is a very powerful medium by which people build up images of others. In the same way that members of the public build up images of the police from media presentations (see Reiner, 1994) so police officers may well build up images of other occupational groups through hearsay, rumour, during training or fictionalised television accounts. Both sociologists and psychologists have carried out extensive research on the way in which certain groups are portrayed in the media. This is a topic to which we will return in Chapter 11.

When discussing identifiable "groups" we tend to think immediately of racial or ethnic groups. However, it may also be appropriate to consider occupational groups. People already have images in their head when occupations such as bank manager, traffic warden, or accountant are mentioned. The same is also true in the case of police officers, especially those in uniform. For most members of the public, the uniform itself will be the most salient characteristic, rather than the person inside it. People will invariably respond to the uniform in some way or other. Some will respond negatively, some positively. For the fearful woman out after dark, the sight of a police uniform may well be reassuring; for the young drunk resenting authority, it may be seen as threatening or constraining. It is all too easy for a police officer to confuse respect (or disrespect) for the authority of the uniform with personal respect or disrespect.

Let us consider for a moment the ways in which police officers might respond to a motorist whom they stop for a minor traffic offence. In situations such as this, the police officer has considerable discretion in deciding whether to report the motorist for prosecution. Instead of prosecuting, the officer may simply caution the individual, and warn him or her of the consequences of any future offence. What factors might be important in the officer's decision? The seriousness of the offence will clearly be influential, as will be whether or not the officer's actions are witnessed by others (either other members of the public or colleagues). But perhaps the major influence will be the motorist him or herself, or at least how they are perceived by the officer. Classifying the motorist is, for the police officer, something which will come early on in the interaction. Indeed an initial impression may have already been formed based on the type of car being driven. If the person appears to be genuinely sorry for the offence, shows great deference to, and respect for the officer, then he/she is less likely to be reported. By contrast, the motorist who challenges the officer's version of events, or his or her authority, will be less likely to be dealt with informally or sympathetically.

STEREOTYPING AND THE USE OF DISCRETION

Decision-making and the use of discretion by police officers has been examined by both sociologists and psychologists. Sykes, Fox and Clark (1976) carried out some early research with officers in the USA. They established that there are a number of formal and informal criteria used in making decisions. Although not all criteria were applicable in every single case, there was invariably a sequence in which the factors were considered. For example, "perceived seriousness" was usually the first consideration, followed by departmental policy, then the demeanour of the person, and finally safety. This early work and much subsequent research has shown quite clearly how factors other than the offence itself can lead to the use of discretion (see e.g. Dix & Layzell, 1983; Stradling, Tuohy & Harper, 1990).

Discretionary judgement, whilst covered briefly at the Training School, is affected primarily by operational experience, and the attitudes and values expressed within the police subculture. In this way norms of behaviour are established, and each new recruit is expected by the subculture to follow the (unofficial) line when using their discretion. A police officer may well be asked by colleagues to justify his/her actions, and may be ridiculed if the group considers that an action (or the rationale for it) is inappropriate. Thus the police officer's interactions with others will be influenced by the images and stereotypes which are held in respect of that group. Not only will the subculture within the organisation teach the new officer how to deal with members of each group, it will also explain how to recognise members of different groups, and how to classify them accurately. Here we are talking not just about different ethnic groups, but more subtly different "types". Amongst these allegedly identifiable types would come "trouble-makers", "wise guys", "hard men", and so on.

Stradling, Tuohy & Harper (1990) and Tuohy, Wrennall, McQueen and Stradling (1993) have carried out some interesting work examining the use of discretion. Taking the hypothetical case of a motorist being stopped for a traffic offence, they have been able to vary the circumstances in each case and to examine how and why decisions to prosecute are made. (It must be acknowledged that in reality the decision to prosecute does not lie solely with the individual officer, but depends also on senior officers and the Crown Prosecution Service.) Stradling's earlier work established that there were a number of identifiable criteria which British police officers used in deciding whether to report an offender, or whether to use their discretion. Tuohy's recent article has established that different factors come into play, depending on the length of service which the officer has. For example, subjects who were just starting their police training were more likely to be influenced by an "in-group/out-group factor" – i.e. there was a high positive loading on items sympathetic to the person's membership of the police (e.g. the motorist is a local magistrate) and a high negative loading on items opposed to the subjects' in-group membership (e.g. "the motorist shows a marked anti-police attitude"). A second though less important factor referred to "special cases" (e.g. where the driver was an old person with little money, or where it was 3 a.m. and there was little traffic on the road). Finally there was a category labelled "costs and benefits" (e.g. the person is a police informer, or the officer is about to go off duty). The subjects who were tested after one year's experience in the police service showed a different pattern from that of the new recruits. For them, the most important criterion was "special cases" (e.g. a commercial traveller who would lose his job if booked, or a foreign tourist who was unfamiliar with British traffic laws). The other items identified by the first group were also mentioned by the second group, though their importance relative to the other factors was different.

This work seems to suggest that for the new recruits, solidarity and status are important elements in the decision-making processes (see Fielding, 1988). Thus officers' decisions of whether or not to prosecute were influenced heavily by factors which challenged their authority or their membership of an important group. The second group was significantly less likely to prosecute on these items, instead allowing "special cases" to primarily influence their judgement. Tuohy notes that the police officers surveyed appear to be going through an important period of "identity transformation" during which their individual ideology is reconstructed in organisational terms. This is an important notion which will be considered in more detail in Chapter 8.

SOCIAL IDENTITY THEORY

Some of the above findings can be explained with reference to Tajfel's Social Identity Theory (Tajfel & Turner, 1986). For any group whose authority, status and role is challenged frequently, solidarity with other in-group members becomes increasingly important. Tajfel has shown how an increase in in-group identification can lead to increasing derogation of out-group members. In other words, as the group's identity is challenged by outsiders, so solidarity within the group increases. This gives in-group members more of a sense of identity. Conversely, members of other groups begin to be seen in more negative terms, and are criticised, insulted, or even harassed. Social Identity Theory thus has important implications for a group such as police officers, and goes some way to explaining some of the abuses of power which have been identified in recent history. Social Identity Theory has received a great deal of attention from European psychologists over recent years, and will be discussed further in Chapter 4.

ATTRIBUTION THEORY

Earlier in this chapter we discussed how people might come to attribute a cause for another's behaviour. Attribution theory has become one of the most widely researched areas in social psychology in recent years, and some of its implications will be discussed here.

Whenever an event occurs people try to understand it by deciding on a probable cause. If there is a riot on a hot summer's evening, a police officer may well decide that it is because of the heat. If a woman is involved in a car accident, the investigating police officer may believe that the accident can be explained by the fact that women are just bad drivers. The point is that people make a causal attribution for virtually every situation which they come across in their lives. People spend little time thinking about events that are mundane and predictable – they feel they already know why things happen and their attributions occur almost automatically. But the more unusual and bizarre the event, the more humans puzzle over it and try to work out just how it happened. Fritz Heider, who started much of the work on attribution, suggests that humans are "naïve psychologists". Just as professional psychologists try to understand human behaviour, so do all humans, but in a more naïve or less systematic way. A psychologist may try to understand behaviour by carrying out carefully controlled experiments in the laboratory. Research carried out in such a scientific way allows psychologists to develop theories of behaviour and offer explanations for the actions of people. Non-psychologists may also build up theories of human behaviour, but without the benefit of scientific rigour or statistical analysis. People go through life learning from experience, and building up many of their own "theories" of human behaviour. Provided that the theories are accurate, they can prove a very useful way of making sense of a complex world. Unfortunately much of the work on attributions shows how they are often biased, prejudiced and inaccurate!

Let us take an example. A person is walking down the street and sees someone trip on the pavement and fall flat on their face. The observer's reaction may well be to laugh at the clumsiness of this poor stranger, and to label them a clumsy or stupid person. But is this fair? Have they carefully examined the situation and circumstances to ensure that their explanation for this event is appropriate? Of course in most such cases people would not even bother – they would be happy to carry on their lives having explained this event to their own satisfaction, content in the view that some other people are basically just clumsy. But what if the same situation occurs but with oneself as the person tripping? Would we similarly account for the event, or would we try to find an alternative explanation? Whilst some people would resign themselves to the fact that they are simply clumsy, most people would seek out another reason for the behaviour, and preferably one that didn't make them appear clumsy or foolish. They might well look for a broken paving stone and point to that; they might explain to any onlookers that they have just bought some new shoes which have very slippery soles. If you are a police officer reading this, imagine your embarrassment if you were in uniform at the time and your trip was witnessed by large numbers of others! The point is that people would try to offer an explanation for their own embarrassing behaviour, which blamed some *external* factor. This contrasts sharply with the previous situation where people assume that the reason for someone else's clumsiness was *internal*, i.e. they are just that sort of person.

The above example shows one way in which the attributions that people make for behaviour can be biased or unfair. People are often mistaken when they assume that another person did what they did just because they are that sort of person. However, they rarely stop to question their assumption or go on to check out whether their theories are correct. In fact people's attributional bias may well become a self-fulfilling prophecy. Perhaps another example will make the point.

Suppose a police inspector is conducting interviews for a job in the organisation. One of the candidates to be interviewed is a woman. The inspector does not think of himself as sexist, but at the back of his mind is a nagging suspicion that the job could be better performed by a man. (The job of police officer or special constable may be a very appropriate example in this case.) During the interview the inspector may feel that the woman does not perform very well and the decision is made not to appoint her. Asked to justify his decision, the inspector points to her poor performance in the interview. Subsequently he appoints a male applicant instead. When further pushed as to why the female applicant did not do well at interview, the inspector may well put it down to her gender, and her inability to cope in such stressful situations. The interviewing officer may go home that evening satisfied with his choice for appointment, and further convinced that women really are not as suitable – the interview just offers further proof of this.

But might this not simply be a case of a self-fulfilling prophecy? The inspector might simply have produced the result that he wanted by his own actions. Did he, for example, ask all candidates the same questions, and in the same way? Did he do as much to put the female candidate at her ease as he did the male candidate? Did he appear more aggressive in one interview than another? Most people would prefer not to admit to such matters, even if they had, preferring instead to account for the woman's non-appointment as due to internal factors – she just didn't have what it takes. (The classic case of the person who says "I'm not prejudiced but . . . " and then goes on to derogate and stereotype some other group.) If the boot were on the other foot, and we were the unsuccessful candidate, would our explanation be the same? The reader can answer that question for him or herself, though psychological research suggests that in most cases people are much more likely to explain their own failures by reference to factors outside their own control.

Offering external reasons for their own failures allows people to preserve their integrity and self-respect. Similarly, in explaining their successes by pointing to their own abilities (i.e. an internal reason), people build up their ego and gain self-confidence. Psychologists have in fact identified a continuum along which people vary according to how they attribute outcomes. This is referred to as the *locus of control* (Rotter, 1966). At one extreme are people who score highly in terms of *external* locus of control, i.e. they believe that they have little direct control over their own fate, and are carried down the river of life by a strong current which they are powerless to divert or control. At the other extreme are people who believe that they are totally in control of their own destiny, i.e. they have a high *internal* locus of control. Research has shown that the latter group are more likely to be successful in their quests in life, though liable to be more severely affected by an event which threatens their sense of control. In reality, many people do not fall into one extreme or another, but rather somewhere in the middle. They believe that there are some things over which they do have control, and others over which they do not. The dimension is, however, an interesting one to bear in mind when considering how and why people make attributions for events. A highly religious person may, for example, believe that everything that happens does so because it is "God's will". A person who believes in the supernatural may well explain events by reference to "some invisible force". By contrast, the scientist (or psychologist) may well search for a logical and more tangible explanation whose existence can be easily demonstrated.

The above examples show some ways in which people make attributions for events that occur. Attribution research suggests that people tend to use different explanations for their own behaviour than for that of others. The suspect in the police station who is asked to explain why he smashed the shop window may put it down to his drunkenness – he would not see himself as a vandal, but as someone who was not in control at the time, and just did something stupid because of too much alcohol. Another person walking past the same smashed shop window might well assume that it was smashed intentionally by some hooligan who was just "that sort of person". When trying to determine an appropriate sentence, judges and magistrates often have to decide whether an internal or external cause is the best explanation for an offender's behaviour. Whatever conclusion they reach will clearly have profound consequences for the offender. It is not uncommon for courts to ask for Social Enquiry Reports (now pre-sentence reports), or even psychiatric evaluations when a person has committed some offence which defies obvious explanation (i.e. where it is difficult to attribute a logical cause for the behaviour).

Attribution research has thus been able to show how people try to explain events, and how these attributions can be biased and unfair. The research goes some way towards explaining and understanding the behaviour of others, and indeed of ourselves, when we are searching for an explanation for any event. The work seems to show that the process is not as simple as it first appears. When trying to understand or explain the behaviour of others people should thus bear in mind that biases do occur. Some of the more important ones can be summarised as follows.

1 People tend to overreact to the most salient stimulus in another person, and pay little attention to other factors.
2 When observing others, people underestimate the extent to which their behaviour is caused by external factors.
3 When explaining their own behaviour, people overestimate the contribution of external factors.
4 People show consistent motivational bias, i.e. they look for explanations which are self-serving.
5 People often believe that they have more control over events than they actually do have.

Clearly attribution theory has a great deal to offer in terms of explaining how people try to make sense of their social world. If people (especially police officers) are made aware of the common biases in their own and other's attributions of behaviour, misunderstandings are made less likely and effective communication more probable.

SUMMARY

This chapter has examined the importance of interactions with others, and has explained how stereotypes are formed and used. It has considered some of the factors which result in certain other people being treated in unfair ways. It has also considered the way in which people attribute causes to events, and how such attributions can be biased. A number of these issues will be discussed further in Chapters 4, 6 and 8.

FURTHER READING

Harvey, J. H. & Weary, G. (1989) *Attribution: Basic Issues and Applications*. San Diego, CA: Academic Press.
Jones, E. E. (1990) *Interpersonal Perception*. New York: Freeman.

CHAPTER 2

Interviewing, Evidence and Credibility

> "We then started interviewing 'Kate'. . . . We started at eight o'clock on a Saturday morning and I worked until seven o'clock that night, which is an awful long time with a child. We had lots of breaks. It took me all that time just to get seven pages out of her . . . I had to come back on Sunday. I got about sixteen pages in the end, but it took me four hours to get one page out of her on the Sunday, because that was the bit where it actually happened . . . I'd say 'Kate, you've got to get this done' . . . Even by the time I'd got the full statement and heard the story about seven or eight times, it still made me want to cry." (Metropolitan WPC, quoted in Graef, 1990, p. 171)

This chapter deals with the important issue of how witnesses should be interviewed. As the above quote demonstrates, interviewing victims and witnesses can at times be harrowing and difficult. Interviewing is an area which has received considerable attention from psychologists in recent years, in particular in relation to the Cognitive Interview Technique. In this section appropriate and inappropriate techniques for witness interviewing will be discussed, and an extensive review of the Cognitive Interview Technique will be presented.

Following any incident the police will try to ascertain exactly what happened. In most cases, the police will not have been present during the incident, and so will have to rely on others to fill in the details. As discussed in Chapter 1, a police officer may well arrive at the scene with certain assumptions about what probably happened. If it is in a certain area, the officer may have fixed notions about the people who live there, and so will make assumptions about the causes of any trouble. The officer may arrive at the scene of a traffic accident and, seeing that one of the drivers is a young man, decide that the accident was probably caused by inexperience or fast driving. As we saw in Chapter 1, the attributions an officer makes about how a particular event happened can be affected by a large number of factors. However, once the attribution has been made that will tend to cloud any subsequent information. Notwithstanding this point, the police will need to obtain information from as many witnesses as possible, and to gather all available evidence. There may be more than one officer sent to the scene, depending on the type of incident, and its seriousness. For example, if a suspicious death is reported, there will be a set procedure which must be followed. The role of scenes of crime officers has expanded rapidly in the last 10 years, in an attempt to gather more information and evidence.

INTERVIEWING OF WITNESSES

Until relatively recently, the police service has not paid a great deal of attention to the manner in which witnesses should be interviewed. Whilst most officers, especially detectives, will have received some training in the interviewing of suspects, less time will have been spent on learning the techniques which could help to get the best information from witnesses and bystanders. This may appear surprising to the non-police reader, especially in the light of the Rand Corporation study (1975) which showed that the principal determinant of whether or not a case is solved is the completeness and accuracy of the eyewitness account. In most incidents, the taking of a statement from a witness is not seen as the first priority, there being more pressing needs. In reality this means that many witnesses are interviewed hours or even days after the occurrence. However, one consistent finding from psychological research is that the time gap between taking in and subsequently recalling that information significantly affects memory accuracy and completeness.

Many police officers will take the view that there are good witnesses and bad witnesses, and that any difference in the quality of their statements can be put down to the individual witness rather than the interviewing technique used. In other words (and to illustrate material introduced in Chapter 1) police officers will make an internal attribution when explaining the good or bad performances of witnesses. However, over the last 10 years the way in which witnesses' accounts are solicited has received increasing attention from psychologists. In this chapter we will start to look at some of the research which psychologists have carried out in the area of witness statements, and to relate this to everyday police work.

Bias in Question Format

Psychologists' renewed interest in this area stemmed primarily from recent work by a number of researchers in both Britain and the USA.

Perhaps Beth Loftus has done more than most to draw attention to the importance of the way in which witnesses are questioned. In her early work she was able to demonstrate that the wording of questions was crucial in determining the level and accuracy of eyewitness accounts. The current volume will not review comprehensively the work of Loftus, though the interested reader may like to consult other sources (see e.g. Loftus, 1979). Nowhere are her findings better illustrated than in the study which examined the estimation of vehicle speeds, and the subsequent wording of questions (Loftus & Palmer, 1974).

In this experiment, subjects watched a film of a traffic accident and then answered a number of questions. Some subjects were asked "About how fast were the cars going when they smashed into each other?", whilst others were asked "About how fast were the cars going when they hit each other?" The question which contained the word "smashed" elicited a far greater average estimate of speed (40.8 m.p.h.) than the sentence containing the word "hit" (34 m.p.h.). This was a revealing result in itself, though a follow-up provided a further interesting finding. One week after viewing the film, the subjects were recalled to the laboratory and asked a series of additional questions. (This without being allowed to see the film again.) Among the questions posed on this second visit was "Did you see any broken glass?" In reality there had not been any broken glass shown in the original film. However, a significant number of witnesses reported having seen broken glass, and those who had previously been asked the "smashed" question were more than twice as likely to report having seen the (non-existent) broken glass. In this case, it appears that the original memory had been contaminated by words like "smashed" being used in the first questioning. Some of the witnesses may have assumed that if cars "smashed" into each other there was likely to be broken glass around.

This dramatic example helped to produce a large amount of further research into the area of eyewitness testimony, and its possible inaccuracy. The research has also led to one of the more productive areas in terms of interactions between psychologists and those involved in the criminal justice system. Here, psychologists were not carrying out "theoretical" laboratory-based research with little obvious practical relevance, but were instead examining real problems with great practical significance – in this case how important the wording of questions can be. Whilst many of the early experiments still did use laboratory-based studies, it was quickly found that the results could be translated into the "real world" of witness interviewing. Prior to this work, a police officer who wanted to know about memory processes and who turned to psychology for help, may well have come away confused and disappointed. Psychology in the 1960s and 1970s was dominated by memory research which did not address the day-to-day difficulties of memory. However, when Ulrich Neisser, the founding father of cognitive psychology, spoke out against laboratory-based studies, and in favour of more applied work, the seeds were sown for a change in memory research. The fact that there have now been a number of international conferences on *Practical Aspects of Memory* also shows that psychologists are genuinely interested in addressing "real world" problems in their research. In fact there is an ongoing debate amongst psychologists concerning the extent to which laboratory-based studies are replicable in the outside world (see e.g. Yuille, 1986).

The Wording of Statements

As mentioned earlier, until very recently police officers did not receive a great deal of training in the taking of witness statements. What advice was given was concerned with the police officer obtaining a statement in a form which the court required, rather than in a form which would yield the most accurate information. Let us consider the following two opening paragraphs of witness statements.

> *Statement 1*
> Well I was just coming down the road and the red car there pulled out without looking and hit the other bloke.

> *Statement 2*
> At 9.30 p.m. on Monday 12th July 1993 I was driving my Ford Escort saloon along Bridge Street in the direction of the town centre. As I approached the junction with Dover Street I saw a red Vauxhall Cavalier registration number B408 ODX coming towards the junction at about 40 m.p.h. The Cavalier didn't stop at the Give Way sign, but just pulled straight out into the main road and collided with a green Lada, registration number DCP 136Y. Both cars sustained considerable damage in the impact.

What is the connection between these two statements you may ask? This hypothetical example tries to illustrate how a witness's first statement may well bear little resemblance to the final article which appears in the file. The majority of witnesses will have had little experience of giving statements before, and will therefore have little idea of what is required. By contrast, the police officer may well have taken many statements before and knows exactly what the courts require. Knowing that Statement 1 is too vague and incomplete, the officer may well attempt to modify it significantly so that it eventually takes on the appearance of Statement 2. It is almost as if the officer has a template in his or her head which dictates how all statements should appear. It is amazing how many witness statements start off with:

> At........... on .... I was on.............when I saw ....travelling
> along ....in the direction of......

Are we to believe that most witnesses do describe events in the form illustrated above? In fact it appears that most witnesses do not. Their initial response to the prompt "Tell me what happened" will tend to be more in the form described in statement 1 above. They will, however, try to help the police officer by allowing him/her to reword the statement into a more acceptable form – after all the police officer must know how these things have to be done. Although in theory witnesses have a free choice as to whether they write the statement themselves or allow the officer to write it for them, in practice over 90% of witness statements are written down by the officer, and then signed by the witness. One might naïvely suggest that witnesses should not sign a statement which contained words which they did not use. The reality would seem to be that most witnesses are prepared to sign a statement which may contain few of the words they used originally when asked to "Tell me what happened". They may well refuse to sign a statement which contains gross inaccuracies, but will happily sign something written in "court language".

Of course, there may be nothing wrong with this. After all the police officer has a job to do, and part of that job will be to produce statements which the court will find helpful, and which are not full of ambiguities. The final version will simply be an expanded and more informative version of what the witness said originally. But it may not be so simple. The final version of the statement may well be the result of a question and answer session between the interviewing officer and the witness (see Tulving, 1983). The questions asked will fit the template described above and the end result will be a statement which is helpful to the court, and which is clearly written. There are, however, a number of potential problems, mainly concerning the choice of words. Let us go back to the example from Loftus's work cited above. It would appear that a police officer who asks "How fast were the cars going when they collided with each other?" may obtain a different answer than if he/she asked the question "How fast were the cars going when they smashed into each other?" Any question about broken glass or the amount of damage sustained may similarly produce differing results. As has been argued elsewhere (Ainsworth & Pease, 1987) the criminal justice system appears to have either naïve or unrealistic expectations of a witness. The system seems to believe that a witness can appear in court many months after seeing an incident, and report the facts accurately and fully. It is assumed that the witness will be able to tap into the original memory and ignore any subsequent information – including the type of question they were asked by the police officer. This is seriously at odds with what has emerged from recent psychological research in the area (Wells & Loftus, 1984).

The overall and consistent finding from the many years of research is that a witness's memory is malleable, unreliable and incomplete. The large number of research studies carried out by Beth Loftus and colleagues has shown just how difficult it can be to return to an original memory once subsequent information about that incident has been encountered. Whilst there has been an academic debate about whether the original memory is actually lost (or simply unobtainable), the fact remains that witnesses' memories are quite easily altered by subsequent misleading information, or even by the form of questions used. Let us consider a couple of examples:

"How fast was the yellow car travelling before the smash?"
"How slowly was the yellow car travelling before the impact?"

Both these might be reasonable questions for a police officer to ask of a witness when taking a statement. Neither would be considered leading questions. (A leading question is one in which the answer is implied by the question, for example "The car was travelling at 40 m.p.h. wasn't it?") However, it is possible that the witness would produce a different answer depending on how the question was worded. Estimating speed accurately is something that most witnesses have difficulty with. In such cases they may well latch onto any "hints" given by the interviewing officer (even subconsciously). As was seen in the Loftus experiment described above, witnesses' answers can be affected by the form of questioning used. Not only that but having been "helped" in this way, the original memory trace may well be altered, perhaps permanently. It may then prove almost impossible for the witness to return to the original uncontaminated memory. The less sure a witness is, the more likely it is that their memory can be altered. And even a witness's level of confidence in their own accuracy can be increased by the form of questioning. A witness who is casually informed that their version of events confirms what others have said is likely to go away more confident in their testimony than if they were led to believe that their statement was at odds with other evidence.

Police officers should thus be aware of the impact that their form of questioning can have on a witness. Whilst it is easy to see how questions can distort memory, it is more difficult to be precise about how questions can be asked in a more neutral (i.e. less suggestive) way. Returning to the previous example, it is easy to see how using the words "fast" or "slowly" in the question can affect estimates of speed. However, coming up with a form of questioning which is completely value free proves to be rather more difficult. (E.g. asking *what speed* was the vehicle travelling may conjure up an image of "a speeding car".) Those involved in teaching police officers how to take witness statements should be aware how subtle variations in question format can affect responses. They should also be aware that, once altered, it can prove difficult for a witness to be able to recover the original, uncontaminated memory. Whilst interviews with suspects are now routinely tape recorded, in most cases the same procedure has not been advocated for the taking of victim or witness statements. If this were done routinely, psychologists would be able to point out how the form of questioning may have affected the eventual version of events. There is one set of witness interviews which are now routinely recorded, these being interviews with children in cases of alleged sexual abuse. The taking of statements from children poses additional difficulties, and the reader may wish to bear in mind that in a number of cases where prosecutions have failed, this has been because of the interrogative techniques used by those questioning a child.

Obtaining Accurate and Complete Accounts

Police officers are understandably keen to learn of any method which will allow them to obtain more information from a witness. Their wish to achieve this may have been bolstered by those psychologists who have suggested that far more information is stored in memory than can be accessed at any one time. There are a number of reasons why this might be, including:

1 The original incident proved to be so traumatic that the person finds it too painful or disturbing to recall.
2 The witness feels that some details are so trivial that they do not bother to think about them.
3 The witness does not use the best or most appropriate retrieval methods when trying to recall details of the incident.

In those cases suggested in (1) above, psychologists might advocate the use of some form of relaxation to allow the witness to recall the events without the ensuing trauma. Recognising this, victims of serious sexual assaults are now taken to special suites for interview, rather than to a cold and uninviting police station interview room. Hypnosis has also been used as one method of eliciting more information, although this technique is itself fraught with great potential difficulties. (In fact a number of states in the USA do not allow witnesses who have been hypnotised to subsequently give evidence in court.) Whilst under hypnosis, the witness may well produce more information, but this information may not be accurate. There are a number of myths that surround the use of hypnosis. One is that hypnosis works like some kind of truth drug, in that witnesses always tell the truth when hypnotised. Witnesses can in fact be just as wrong when under hypnosis as they can when in a non-hypnotised state. However, the main problem with using hypnosis is that it is all too easy to "lead" a witness. We have already seen from Loftus's work how witnesses can be misled by certain forms of questioning. When under hypnosis (a state in which the subject is more susceptible to the influence of the hypnotist) it is even easier to lead the witness, albeit inadvertently, and to produce a distorted account of events. After hypnosis, it is more difficult for the witness to separate out those bits of the story which are from the original memory and which are merely confabulation (see Orne, Soskis, Dinges & Orne, 1984).

Recently, a way of interviewing witnesses has been developed which is claimed to improve the amount of information a witness can produce, but without this leading to a decrease in the accuracy of additional information. This is known as the Cognitive Interview Technique (Fisher & Geiselman, 1992). It has been developed primarily to address those difficulties outlined in (2) and (3) above, and is one of the best illustrations of how the fruits of psychological research can be applied to a real world problem.

THE COGNITIVE INTERVIEW TECHNIQUE (CIT)

The Cognitive Interview is a technique which has been developed to assist witnesses to recall as much information as possible from their memory. It does not rely on procedures such as hypnosis, but rather uses knowledge gained in the psychological study of cognition to address the question of accurate and complete recall by witnesses. The primary developers of this approach have been two American psychologists, Ronald P. Fisher and R. Edward Geiselman. In the introduction to their book dealing with this topic, they confess to coming across the technique quite inadvertently. Both were aware that they were often able to help friends whose temporary lapses of memory had led to difficulties, such as people who had misplaced their car keys, or forgotten a friend's name. In retrospect the authors came to realise that "many of the techniques we used to prompt memory came directly from the scientific, laboratory research we lectured about in our college classrooms" (Fisher & Geiselman, 1992, p. vii). Since the early development of the technique, the authors have worked closely with police forces in America, both in training individual officers, and in interviewing a number of witnesses themselves.

Fisher and Geiselman are very bullish about the CIT. In the introduction to their book they claim:

> "experimental tests of the Cognitive Interview showed it to increase substantially the amount of information gathered in many different settings. It worked with student and non-student eyewitnesses; it worked with novice and experienced investigators; it worked with criminal and civil investigations; it worked in the laboratory, and more important, in the field, with actual victims and witnesses of crime." (Fisher & Geiselman, 1992, p. 5)

For those accustomed to tentative conclusions from psychological research these are surprisingly strong claims, perhaps more akin to the claims made by washing powder companies in television commercials! However, the CIT is now used extensively by police departments in the USA and is now starting to be used by some British police forces (George, 1991). In the study in Britain by George it was claimed that after training, detectives elicited 55% more information than before training. Fisher and Geiselman also claim that the technique is preferable to hypnosis, as it does not evoke the same increased susceptibility to leading questions, and does not require lengthy periods of training. Information elicited through a Cognitive Interview will also be more readily accepted than evidence obtained whilst a witness was under hypnosis.

Some limits to the usefulness of the CIT are acknowledged, and can be summarised as follows:

1 The CIT will be most useful in cases where eyewitness accounts make up the bulk of the evidence.
2 The CIT is designed to be used with cooperative witnesses and cannot be used to persuade the reluctant witness.
3 The CIT may take longer to conduct than the standard police interview.
4 The CIT requires greater concentration on the part of the interviewer, and greater flexibility.
5 Some interviewers consistently elicit more information than others, though all those undergoing training in CIT show some improvement.

Memory and Communication

The Cognitive Interview focuses on two major components: memory and communication. The eyewitness must firstly retrieve from their memory all the details of the event, secondly translate the memory into a form of words, and thirdly communicate the information to the interviewer. The central component of the technique is *guided retrieval*. In this, the investigator's role is seen as assisting the witness to access information already in the memory store. The successful interviewer is thus seen as a person who can quickly identify how the witness has stored the information, and can guide him/her through the retrieval process. It is interesting to note that in the CIT, the witness is seen as the dominant character in the interaction, with the interviewer taking a subsidiary role. This is in contrast with other interviews, where the detective makes it very clear that he (or occasionally she) is in charge. Although Fisher and Geiselman's book is described as a "How to do it" text (p. 7) the police reader may be slightly disappointed to learn that the technique does not involve a step-by-step guide which can be applied in all situations. Indeed the authors concede that the technique is not intended as a recipe whereby one can simply memorise a set of questions in advance. It is said, for example, that all interviews should be "highly interactive and spontaneous" (p. 16) and that "one must be flexible enough to use good judgement and change directions as unexpected conditions arise" (p. 16).

Fisher and Geiselman suggest that one should look at the interview in the same way as any other social interaction. Both the interviewer and the witness enter the situation with their own goals and expectations. The first task for the interviewer is to encourage the active participation of the witness. It is all too easy for the witness to assume that the police officer is in charge and that they can rely on him/her to dictate how things will be done. The rule is stated as follows by Fisher and Geiselman:

> "The key to effective interviewing is to convey to the eyewitness that she plays a central role in the interview and that she must take an active part in generating information." (p. 19)

One can see immediately how this might mean that the witness is less likely to be influenced in his or her answers by the form of questioning – a difficulty highlighted by Loftus in her work. This approach may at first appear as though the police officer is giving up control of the interview situation – something which many officers might see as threatening or counter-productive. However, the shift is really more of a semantic one. The interviewer can decide what questions to ask, when to terminate the interview, and so on, whilst still making the witness feel more central to the interaction.

Open-ended Questions

One way in which the interviewer can encourage more participation is by asking open-ended questions, rather than closed questions. For example the question "Can you describe his clothes?" will lead to a fuller answer than the question "What colour was his jacket?" By asking open-ended questions, the interviewer is encouraging more participation than if he/she asked a question requiring a one word answer. Police officers reading this must bear in mind a point made earlier in this chapter, i.e. that for most witnesses the interview situation is a strange and unrehearsed one. Most witnesses have not been in the position before, and will be taking their cues from the more experienced police officer. If the witness assumes that the police officer simply wants single word answers, that is probably what they will produce (see e.g. Smith & Ellsworth, 1987). The same effect can be accomplished if the interviewer constantly interrupts the witness when they are giving information. It is far better for the interviewer to allow the witness to finish their answer, pause for a moment to allow further elaboration, and then ask for clarification of points if necessary. Whilst this approach may seem a reasonable one, both Fisher and Geiselman (1992) and George (1991) point out that it is almost the opposite of what traditionally takes place during interviews. Typically police officers have tended to ask closed questions, and to interrupt frequently – indeed one study showed that police officers on average interrupt the witness only 7.5 seconds after the start of their narration (see Fisher, Geiselman & Raymond, 1987).

Dealing with Traumatised Witnesses

Whilst the techniques advocated so far are useful in most situations, it must be borne in mind that for some witnesses, providing information about an event will be particularly stressful and traumatic. Victims of serious crimes, especially those involving personal danger, may well be less able, at least initially, to tell their story. In cases such as a sexual assault, the victim will be both offended by what happened and embarrassed when asked to describe it. Following an outcry over the way in which some police officers dealt with sexual assault victims, the police are now more sympathetic to the plight of such people. Many officers do now recognise that it is not always easy for such victims to provide detailed accounts of the incident, the memory being simply too painful or embarrassing. A recent British television programme (*Panorama*, 26 July 1993) highlighted the difficulties faced by rape victims. In one telling moment, a victim described how she felt as though she had been raped three times: once by her assailant, then by the medical examiner, and finally by the trial process.

In such cases, it is essential that the interviewing officer spends some time building a rapport with the victim. The provision of a less formal interview room, the presence of a sympathetic female officer, perhaps even the absence of any male officers, may all help to make a female rape victim feel slightly more comfortable. Even then, some time will need to be spent in developing a trusting and non-judgemental interaction. Fisher and Geiselman advocate two techniques which can be used: personalising the interview, and communicating empathy. In the former of these, it is suggested that an officer should try not to give the impression that "this is just another case" and the victim is just the latest in a long line of people adding to the officer's workload. As in most interactions, there will be a tendency for each party to respond to the other in predetermined stereotyped ways (see Chapter 1). The victim may be seen as just another unsolved case by the officer, whilst the officer may be seen by the witness as simply a representative of an authoritative organisation. Anything that can be done to break down these stereotypes may well prove beneficial. The officer may, for example, introduce her/himself by name – perhaps even including a first name. The victim might also be referred to by name – either first or second name, depending on which makes the victim feel more comfortable. These might appear to be trivial matters, but are the first step towards personalising the interview and establishing a good rapport between interviewer and victim.

Communicating empathy with a victim is another important ingredient. Victims need to feel that the interviewing officer does understand just how she/he is feeling and that this is not just another case like so many others. It is difficult to advocate one simple technique for communicating empathy, though with training and practice police officers are more likely to be able to achieve this objective. A starting point is for the officer to try to imagine the scenario from the victim's point of view, even though this may not always be easy. For example a male police officer may have difficulty in fully understanding the feeling of violation which a female rape victim may be experiencing. Simple statements like "I can understand how difficult this must be for you" will communicate empathy, as will an apparent sympathy for the victim's suffering. If appropriate, the officer may identify with the victim's suffering by explaining how they felt when they were a victim. Fisher and Geiselman suggest that the interviewer should also avoid making judgemental comments or being confrontational. Any apparent inconsistencies can be clarified at a later point.

The techniques advocated above are designed to elicit more information from a witness through the development of an appropriate interaction between the parties. The cynical police reader may interpret this as just "being nice to a witness" though there is much more to it than that.

Psychological research has shown that people are more likely to produce accurate and full accounts when they are made to feel more relaxed, and have a good rapport with the interviewer. There can of course be other spin-offs. For example a witness who is treated courteously and sympathetically will be more likely to be willing to appear in court. The same witness is also more likely to have a positive view of the police, and to be more willing to help in any future cases. Compare this with a witness who is treated unsympathetically and comes away from the interaction feeling a failure, and feeling that they have been ridiculed by an unsympathetic and uncaring officer.

An interviewer who is able to gain the confidence of a witness (as outlined above), is also more likely to be able to diminish the effects of anxiety. Hardened police officers who have dealt with many victims of violence may be prone to forget just how stressful such events can be for the individual concerned. If the event itself has provoked anxiety, then any subsequent recall will similarly affect the individual's level of stress. Psychologists have often demonstrated how too much stress can interfere with the memory processes. In fact it has been suggested that arousal affects memory in a curvilinear fashion (the Yerkes–Dodson Law). If people are insufficiently aroused by an event, they will pay it little attention, and it will not tend to make a lasting impression. Conversely, if the event is too arousing, people will be so agitated as to be incapable of taking in information accurately. As mentioned above, the amount of arousal at the time of recall will also affect accuracy and completeness. A witness who is half asleep and bored by the interview will recall less than one who is alert and attentive, whilst the witness who feels extremely tense when asked to recall the event will also tend to leave out some details. Of course a witness's level of anxiety can, to some extent, be controlled by the interviewer. The problem of anxiety and recall can be illustrated by the example of the examination candidate who can remember facts before entering the examination room, and immediately after leaving, but cannot remember details when highly aroused in the exam room itself.

Reducing Anxiety and Stress

It has been shown that anxiety and stress can all too easily interfere with accurate recall (see Loftus, 1979; Peters, 1988). One of the primary objectives for a successful interviewer is thus to be able to reduce or overcome the anxiety which a witness or victim is feeling. There is however one dilemma for the investigator here. Whilst it may be desirable for the interview to be conducted as soon as possible after the event, this will be the time when the witness is still in a state of shock, and their memory may well be less clear. Fisher and Geiselman suggest that one way of overcoming the effects of anxiety is to reassure the victim. Victims may well feel embarrassed that they are reacting so emotionally to the event, and this itself may interfere with recall. Anything that the interviewer can do to reassure victims that their reaction is normal and understandable will help to placate the situation. Similarly, the interviewer can acknowledge that some anxiety will be aroused by recall of a traumatic event, but can reassure the victim that the trauma will not be as great as the original event, and suggest that now the person is in a better position to control the intensity of the reaction. A technique that is used by some therapists is for a victim to tell the story as if it were happening to someone else, i.e. tell it in the third person. Latts and Geiselman (1991) and Reisser (1980) suggest that this method is particularly appropriate for rape victims, and may also be beneficial for child victims of sexual assault. Whilst this could be a useful technique, it might be open to legal challenge.

Clinical psychologists are well versed in the use of relaxation techniques as a means of countering anxiety. People who are experiencing phobias can be trained how to relax, and can then transfer this skill to the anxiety-producing situation (see Wolpe, 1969). Whilst it would be inappropriate for police interviewers to spend long periods teaching appropriate relaxation techniques, there are some measures which would have a calming effect, including:

1 Providing a soothing environment. A noisy sterile police interview room with uncomfortable chairs will do little to calm a troubled witness. Conversely, a relaxed atmosphere can be communicated by a relaxing environment.
2 Encouraging the witness to try to relax before any questions are asked. Fisher and Geiselman advocate encouraging the witness to take a few deep breaths as a way of calming down. Other common techniques used in therapy might also be appropriate, for example, imagining a pleasant and peaceful scene which has a soporific quality.
3 Reassuring the witness that the interview is not some kind of test on which their performance will be evaluated. There is a subtle dividing line here between letting the witness feel important and central to the interaction, and putting pressure on the person by comments such as "You're our last hope – we're really relying on you". Witnesses who are made to feel some kind of failure will tend to increase their level of anxiety, which is counter-productive.
4 Adopting a relaxed and patient approach on the part of the interviewer. To some extent, a witness's feelings may come to match those emanating from the other person in the interaction (see e.g. Schachter,

1959). If the interviewer appears nervous, then this will to some extent affect the witness and add to his/her anxiety level. The interviewer should also acknowledge when the witness is becoming very anxious (for example when describing the more harrowing details of the incident), and give sufficient time for the witness to calm down before proceeding. Fisher and Geiselman suggest that the interviewer should leave the most stressful questions till the end of the session, thus ensuring that most details will already have been elicited before anxiety levels start to rise.

5 Gentle encouragement and reinforcement of witnesses, so that they get the message that they are doing fine, and that their answers are genuinely of interest. The interviewer should avoid passing judgement on each answer as it appears (for example by pronouncing one answer correct or by giving another an amused look) but can still calm the witness by making them feel their story is of value. The interviewer should also be aware that some of the questions may be too difficult for the particular witness, and if necessary a more simplistic question format should be used.

Eliciting Suppressed Information and Looking for Consistency

It is acknowledged that some witnesses may suppress information when being interviewed. This might be because the person feels the point is trivial or irrelevant, or because the information appears to contradict some other statement. The former of these problems can be overcome to some extent by the interviewer encouraging the witness to report everything, no matter how unimportant it appears. However, the second problem is slightly more complex.

Humans like their behaviour to be consistent and are uncomfortable when they realise that their actions are inconsistent. Festinger (1957) has suggested that when people realise that there is an inconsistency in their actions, or between their attitude and their action, a tension is generated. He referred to this feeling as Cognitive Dissonance. Festinger argues that dissonance is an unpleasant state which people will try to avoid, or will try to remove or reduce once it is encountered. Thus people may change their attitude so that it becomes more consistent with their behaviour, or may try to deny some previous statement or action.

The reason why this might be important in the current context is that a witness who recognises an inconsistency in his/her story may well feel uncomfortable, and be motivated to reduce the dissonance aroused. They may thus change an earlier part of their story, or may choose not to mention a detail because it is inconsistent with something mentioned previously in the interview. Whilst the interviewing officer may understandably be keen to avoid giving the defence barrister ammunition in the form of inconsistencies in a statement, Fisher and Geiselman suggest that inconsistencies should not be challenged immediately during the interview. The inconsistency may be a simple error which can be clarified at a later point, or may actually be a misunderstanding on the part of the interviewer. By immediately challenging inconsistencies, the interviewer may well put the witness on the defensive, and discourage him/her from providing more information. Alternatively, the witness may well invent non-existent details in order to save face. Fisher and Geiselman even go so far as to suggest that the assumption that "inconsistency means inaccuracy" (see e.g. Bailey & Rothblatt, 1971) may not in fact be true. They point out that there is actually very little experimental evidence to verify this belief, and one recent study (Fisher & Cutler, 1991) found little evidence to support the assumption.

Other advice which is offered by Fisher and Geiselman to assist witnesses in giving statements includes:

1 Using relative rather than absolute judgements. It is acknowledged that most witnesses are not skilled in giving exact height, weight, size, and so on and therefore it may be better to provide some kind of reference point. For example, "Was he taller than average?" "Was he bigger or smaller than you?"
2 Recognition vs recall. A common finding from psychological research is that people are generally better at recognising something that they have seen before, than they are at describing it accurately. Bearing this in mind, the interviewer may wish to provide some props. For example, "Was the gun like this, or more like that?"
3 Use of non-verbal methods. Although the witness may have to answer questions verbally, the words then being written down, some witnesses may be able to demonstrate some details more easily than they can describe them. For example, the witness may demonstrate through gestures how the robber walked, or may be able to show the interviewer how far away from the robber he was standing.

Whilst most police officers are used to describing the physical properties of vehicles or describing facial features, they should be aware that most members of the public are not, and so they should be given every opportunity to provide descriptions using any method which the witness finds helpful.

Retrieval Techniques

We will now examine some retrieval techniques advocated under the auspices of the Cognitive Interview. The four major tenets are:

1 *Recreating the context of the original environment.*
2 *Using focused concentration.*
3 *Encouraging multiple retrieval attempts.*
4 *Using varied retrieval techniques.*

Recreating the Context

Whenever a person witnesses an event, the context of the incident will affect the way in which the memory is stored. Such factors as the person's mood at the time, whether they were rushing somewhere, who they were with, will all have an effect on the memory for the event. Fisher and Geiselman suggest that because context is such an important factor in the memory trace, it also plays a crucial role in determining what type of retrieval technique is likely to be the most successful. In essence they suggest that recall of details of the incident can be enhanced by recreating the original context at the time of the interview. This can be achieved by either requesting the witness directly to think about the context, or by asking specific questions which will force the witness to think about this aspect. This should be done before any specific questions are asked, the witness being given sufficient time to recreate the context. Witnesses who are unclear about how to recreate the context can be asked such questions as "How were you feeling then?" or "What was on your mind at the time?"

Recreating the context can be particularly useful when a witness feels that he/she did once have a particular detail in the memory, but cannot recall it now. By going back through the incident, including discussing feelings, it is more likely that the witness will be able to recall the missing detail. A similar technique is advocated where a witness knows that prior to the interview he/she had been successful in retrieving the memory, but is having difficulty recalling it now. Fisher and Geiselman suggest that getting witnesses to think back to the occasion when they did successfully recall the detail (i.e. reinstating that context), can lead to a successful recall. An interesting example of context reinstatement is provided by Fisher and Geiselman (1992, p. 102). In this example, a witness remembered that she had made a conscious effort to memorise the registration number of a car, but was now unable to recall it. Encouraging the witness to think about why she tried to memorise the number, and how she achieved this at the time, produced a successful result. In this example, the witness remembered that the registration number reminded her of her previous address. Recalling that this was how she had tried to memorise the number meant that she was able to go back from her old address to recreate the registration number. The researchers were particularly pleased with this result as the original sighting of the car had been some 12 months earlier, and previous attempts to elicit the registration number from the witness had proved unsuccessful. Whilst this anecdotal evidence does not guarantee that the technique is infallible, it shows how important context reinstatement can be.

Focused Concentration

Fisher and Geiselman suggest that witnesses store both general and highly detailed information in their memory store. They suggest that witnesses store information in both a *Concept* code and an *Image* code. They take the view that these two are different modes of coding information, though acknowledge that not all psychologists agree with such a distinction (see Kosslyn, 1981; Pylshyn, 1981).

The job of the interviewer is to extract as much detailed information as possible from the image code. In order to retrieve information in this way, the witness will need to be encouraged to concentrate a great deal. It is suggested that the following statement should be used in order to facilitate concentration.

> "I realise that this is a difficult task, to remember the details of the crime. All of the details are stored in your mind, but you will have to concentrate very hard to recall them. You have all the information, so I'm going to expect you to do most of the work here. I understand that this might be difficult, but try to concentrate as hard as you can." (p. 103)

Having succeeded in achieving this focused concentration, the interviewer's task is then to maintain this level of diligence. It is all too easy for the interviewer to disrupt concentration even by non-verbal communication. Interviewers are often unaware of just what they do during an interview. As with many other aspects of training, a police officer who sees a videotape of her/himself is more likely to be able to pick out any annoying or distracting habits, and to be able to eliminate them. Other sources of distraction should also be eliminated as far as possible, for example, other people entering the room, or noise from a police radio.

Multiple Retrieval Attempts

Memory retrieval can be compared with a search process. If a person misplaces something, he/she may well start on a quick search of the most likely places where the item may have been put. If the first search proves unsuccessful, then further attempts may be made, in some cases going over the same ground but more thoroughly. Fisher and Geiselman suggest that this same idea is appropriate in the case of a witness searching for information in their memory. Witnesses may well be reluctant to make more searches, and so may need to be encouraged and motivated by the interviewer. Some of the techniques mentioned above (e.g. not interrupting the witness) may also encourage further searches.

The point about many of these techniques is that they are geared towards getting the most information possible from the witness, through both verbal and non-verbal methods. These can be very subtle, but nonetheless effective. For example, the interviewer who allows a silence at the end of a witness's sentence can encourage more information than one who immediately jumps in with another question. Of course the use of such techniques is only appropriate where the witness has more information to give. There is a danger that an interviewer who constantly pushes a witness for more information may encourage the witness to guess or fabricate. As discussed earlier, this has been a particular problem when using hypnosis with a witness (see Orne, 1979). The social interaction encouraged in the Cognitive Interview may also cause a situation where the witness wants to please the interviewer, and so may try to produce the answer which he/she perceives the interviewer to want. At present there is little evidence to suggest that this does happen, though the interviewer should be aware of the potential danger of pushing a compliant interviewee (see e.g. Gudjonsson, 1992).

One memory problem identified by psychologists some time ago is the so-called "tip of the tongue" phenomenon (Brown & McNeil, 1966). Most people will have experienced this state, when a name or some other detail is on the tip of one's tongue, but cannot be recalled at that instant. People are usually certain that they know the word, and in some cases can say how many letters there are in the word, or what it begins with. Experience suggests that if people stop trying to recall the information it will come to them some time later. Fisher and Geiselman suggest that this is an appropriate strategy in the interview situation, and the interviewer should move on and then return to the elusive detail later.

Varied Retrieval

When asked to describe what happened, witnesses will invariably tell their story in chronological order and from their own perspective. Fisher and Geiselman suggest that some benefit can be gained by asking the witness to try to retrieve the information in a different sequence or from a different perspective. The technique of asking witnesses to recall the events again, but in reverse order, often provides additional information (see Burns, 1981; Geiselman, Fisher, MacKinnon & Holland, 1986). In particular, peripheral details of certain actions are often recalled which may, for example, help the police to draw comparisons with other crimes. As an interesting aside, the technique of reverse recall is also claimed to be a useful technique when interviewing a reluctant suspect. It appears that asking a suspect to do this can produce a breakdown in a well rehearsed but fabricated story (Geiselman & Callot, 1990). It should be stressed that at present there is little experimental evidence to support this assertion, though it is an interesting notion, worthy of further research.

In addition to asking a witness to recall events in a different sequence, the Cognitive Interview Technique suggests that a witness should be asked to try to describe how events would appear from another person's viewpoint. This stems from the view that a witness will tend to recall events only from the way in which they affected him/herself. For example, the witness may choose not to describe an assailant's gun, because she was not threatened by it directly. However, when asked to describe events from the perspective of the building society cashier, the witness may well retrieve stored information about the gun.

Two further notes of caution should be mentioned here. Firstly, pushing a witness who is unclear about details to provide information from another's perspective may simply produce fabrication, i.e. the witness may well say what they *imagine* the other person would have seen. The second note of caution concerns interviews with children. Because of their level of cognitive development, children have great difficulty in seeing things from another's point of view. Jean Piaget established many years ago that children are essentially egocentric, and tend to view the world only from their own point of view. Thus being asked to see things from another's viewpoint would be impossible, and might result in the child fabricating evidence to try to please the interviewer.

A final way in which enhanced retrieval may be produced is through the probing of different sense modalities. Most witnesses will rely almost entirely on their visual sense when describing what happened. However, if an interviewer fails to ask questions about other information, then valuable details may be lost. Whilst it is true that people do rely on visual perception a great deal, auditory, olfactory, and tactile information may also be taken in. On prompting, the witness may recall that the offender was wearing a particularly distinctive aftershave, or did not appear to have bathed or used a deodorant for some time. The witness may not be able to describe visually the assailant's clothing, but may remember that when he grabbed her, his sweater appeared to be made from Angora wool. Identification by voice is at an early stage of investigation though when asked, a witness may recall that the person's voice had a distinctive lisp or unusual accent. Recall of such information may prompt further information from other sense modalities. For example, when recalling the person's voice a witness may remember that, at the time, he/she thought that the voice didn't really go with the face (i.e. it challenged a stereotype). By exploring this aspect, more information about the person's face may then be produced.

Most of the above techniques are geared towards improving recall in general, though Fisher and Geiselman suggest techniques to retrieve specific details. They suggest that there are two underlying principles to be considered when trying to elicit specific details. These are:

1 Knowledge about an event is represented as a collection of attributes.
2 The various attributes about an event are associated, so that activating one attribute may stimulate other attributes.

(Fisher & Geiselman, 1992, p. 113)

It is thus suggested that an interviewer should probe the various attributes of, say, a name or registration number, and by eliciting one attribute, others may follow. For example, a witness may recall that one assailant referred to another by name, but he cannot remember the actual name. The interviewer may ask questions like "Was it a very common name or an uncommon name?" "Was it a nickname or a first name?" Fisher and Geiselman suggest other ways in which attributes can be examined, including scrutinising contextual and subjective properties of the item.

The remainder of Fisher and Geiselman's methods are summarised in their recent work. In particular, the use of witness-compatible questioning, techniques to probe both image and concept memory codes are discussed. Police officers may also find the sample interviews (with analysis) and the suggested sequence of the procedure useful.

SUMMARY

This chapter has attempted to introduce the reader to the importance of the way in which witness interviews are conducted. It has attempted to identify some of the potential pitfalls, and to offer advice on some ways in which interviewing techniques can be improved. The Cognitive Interview Technique has been spelled out in some detail as an example of how psychology can be applied to the very real issue of witness interviewing.

Throughout this chapter we have been discussing interviews with adults of normal levels of intelligence. One of the fastest growing areas of psychological research has been concerned with interviews with children (see Dent & Flin, 1992). Interviews with children and with adults with learning difficulties pose their own problems, of which interviewers should be aware (see Gudjonsson, 1992).

FURTHER READING

Fisher, R. P. & Geiselman, R. E. (1992) *Memory-Enhancing Techniques for Investigative Interviewing*. Springfield, IL: Charles C. Thomas.
Gudjonsson, G. (1992) *The Psychology of Interrogations, Confessions and Testimony*. Chichester: Wiley.

CHAPTER 3

Interrogations and Confessions

"In November 1993 George Heron was cleared of the murder of a seven year old girl in North East England. He had made a confession to the police, but the trial judge, Mr Justice Mitchell, ruled that this was inadmissible. He attacked what he called 'oppressive' tactics used by the police in eliciting the confession. Heron claimed that he made the confession only after four days of intensive interrogation, and after the police had also arrested other members of his family. He claimed that he only confessed in order to put a stop to the police actions. This was not the first case of its kind. A year earlier, the Appeal Court had quashed the convictions of the so-called Cardiff Three for the murder of a prostitute in 1990. The Appeal Court judges were said to be 'horrified' at the 'travesty of an interview' in which the police obtained a confession. The Lord Chief Justice, Lord Taylor, said 'Short of physical abuse, it is hard to conceive of a more hostile and intimidating approach by officers to a suspect'."

As the above cases show, the subjects of interrogations and confessions have received extensive coverage in the last few years. Indeed a previous volume in this Wiley series has dealt exclusively and extensively with this area (Gudjonsson, 1992). There have been a number of high-profile cases in recent history where miscarriages of justice have occurred, some of which have led people to question the role of the detective conducting interrogations. Whilst many years ago a confession might have been seen as absolute proof of a person's guilt, recently the way in which confessions are obtained has been examined more closely. In addition, the status of a confession as accepted proof of guilt has come under increased scrutiny. Part of the problem with confessions stems from the fact that most people, including police officers, find it hard to accept that anyone who is genuinely innocent would make a confession. Most people would like to think that if they had been accused unfairly, no amount of pressure would make them confess to something that they had not done. However, as we shall see later, the pressures which may be exerted on a suspect mean that some innocent people, especially certain vulnerable groups, could be persuaded to confess to something which they had not done. In this chapter we will start to look at the dynamics of the interrogation situation, discuss how false confessions might be avoided, and consider ways in which interrogations might be conducted in a more ethical but effective way.

There appears to be a polarisation of views as to the real purpose of the interrogation of a suspect. The police have traditionally seen their role to be that of obtaining a confession from someone who is "obviously guilty" but is at first reluctant to admit such guilt. After all, the police officer might reason, the person would not have been arrested if he or she was not guilty. The interrogation is thus seen by the police as a way of "cracking" a person in order that he/she will confess and thus be more likely to be convicted. For members of the public, interrogation may be perceived somewhat differently. It may be viewed more as a way in which the police get to the truth – where the innocent are eliminated and the guilty are identified. A number of writers have suggested that pressure on the police to obtain convictions, and thus improve their clear-up rates, means that attempts to elicit confessions assume a high priority. Indeed great respect is accorded to any officer who is capable of persuading a reluctant suspect to "cough". It is somewhat ironic that at a time when some coercive police interrogation techniques are being questioned, the British government is considering introducing league tables which may put further pressure on the police to obtain confessions in order to improve their clear-up rate (see the Sheehy Report, 1993; Chapter 9 this volume).

The reality of interrogations is often somewhat different from that portrayed in fictional accounts. For example, the situation where a figure such as Inspector Morse uses his brilliant skills to persuade a reluctant suspect to admit all, is actually not as common as might be assumed. In one study (Baldwin, 1990) researchers found that in only 20 out of 600 cases did suspects change their story over the course of an interview or series of interviews. In fact Baldwin is quite dismissive of the mystique and mythology which the police culture gives to the skills which the good detective is assumed to possess. It could, however, be suggested that as Baldwin examined mainly the formal tape-recorded interviews, he missed previous informal conversations where a suspect had changed an original story.

Interrogations are in some ways similar to witness interviews (which were discussed in the previous chapter). Indeed, many of the factors identified previously are also important in the interrogation situation (e.g. establishing rapport, asking appropriate questions, listening attentively). Moston (1991) suggests that the distinction between interviewing and interrogation is an arbitrary one, and uses the term "investigative interviewing" to cover the interviewing of both witnesses and suspects.

Swanson, Chamelin and Territo (1988) suggest that there are four commonly recognised objectives of the interrogation process, namely:

1 To obtain valuable facts.
2 To eliminate the innocent.
3 To identify the guilty.
4 To obtain a confession.

Many of the difficulties with interrogations arise because police officers have concentrated on the fourth of these, whilst neglecting the other three (see Baldwin, 1993).

ATTRIBUTIONS AND INTERROGATIONS

In the first chapter we discussed the notion of *attribution* and the ways in which people explain why and how events occur. Let us consider for a moment a person who has been arrested on suspicion of having committed a crime. There is insufficient evidence to guarantee a conviction, and so additional evidence is sought, in the form of a confession. The police officer assigned to the case may well enter the interrogation room with certain assumptions. Perhaps the most important one is that the suspect is "obviously" guilty, otherwise why would he/she have been arrested and brought to the police station? Whilst the presumption of guilt is understandable if there is overwhelming evidence against a person, some recent research has suggested that there might also be an assumption of guilt in many cases where the evidence is less than strong (Stephenson & Moston, 1993, p. 35).

If the suspect protests his/her innocence, this may be interpreted as simply an attempt to avoid being sent to prison. If the suspect appears nervous, then this might be assumed to indicate guilt – the fear of being found out producing the nervousness. But might not a suspect who was wrongly accused of a crime also show signs of nervousness? The point is that whatever the suspect does, this may be seen as confirming a view that the interrogating officer already has, i.e. that the person is guilty. In psychological terms the interviewing officer is simply trying to make a confirmatory attribution.

In one study (Moston, Stephenson & Williamson, 1992), police officers were asked about their attitudes and assumptions about the suspect just prior to an interview commencing. It was found that in about three-quarters of the cases, the interviewers were already "sure" of the suspect's guilt. Furthermore, in about 80% of the cases, the stated aim of the interview was seen simply as being to obtain a confession. The "assumption of guilt" was particularly strong when the suspect had previous convictions.

The use of interrogations varies, and often depends on the strength of other evidence which already exists. For example, Moston found that when there was strong evidence against a suspect, some 92% were charged, irrespective of whether or not they made an admission. For cases where the evidence was only moderately strong, some 87% were charged when they did confess, compared with 45% when there was no confession. There was a further interesting finding concerning the "right to silence". In Britain at the current time, a suspect is cautioned to the effect that "you do not have to say anything unless you wish to do so, but whatever you say may be given in evidence". However, if the suspect chooses to exercise the right to silence, the prosecution cannot draw attention to this during the trial (though at the time of writing the British Home Secretary has proposed a removal of this provision). Interestingly, Moston found that when suspects did use their right to silence they were more likely to be charged than if they had denied the accusation during interrogation. (Some 58% of suspects who used their right to silence were charged, compared with 45% of those who chose to deny the charge.) It would appear that the police make different assumptions about what the use of silence implies than would a court. For many police officers the use of the right of silence is seen as further evidence of guilt, though it is not entirely clear why this should be. Throughout this process police officers are making judgements about guilt and innocence. Once the judgement has been made and the label applied, it is then difficult for any subsequent events to be seen with a completely open mind.

Labelling can have a very powerful effect on the way in which we attribute causes to behaviour. Nowhere is this better illustrated than in a study carried out by Rosenhan (1973). Rosenhan had a number of normal people gain admission to mental hospitals by claiming that they were hearing voices. All were admitted to the hospitals, nearly all with a diagnosis of schizophrenia. There are many interesting findings which emanated from this research, but for present purposes we should consider just one, i.e. the way in which the pseudo-patients' perfectly normal behaviour was reinterpreted because they had the label "schizophrenic" attached to them. For example, the pseudo-patients made notes about what went on, and this behaviour was recorded by the staff in the form "Patient is exhibiting writing behaviour". A perfectly normal behaviour, in this case writing something down, was reinterpreted as somehow being symptomatic of the illness that the patient had.

Rosenhan's study provides many other interesting examples of how behaviour is reinterpreted so that it fits the original diagnosis, rather than being taken at face value. Even a relatively normal upbringing was reinterpreted as being abnormal so that it fitted the label.

The reason that these findings are important is that the reinterpretation of behaviour following labelling may also be found in the case of a suspect in the interrogation situation. In other words, any behaviour which might be considered normal if exhibited in the outside world may be interpreted as a sign of guilt when displayed in the interrogation room. A person who is guilty might well appear nervous, might get angry, might break down in tears, might demand to be left alone; but so might an innocent person. Most police officers have not themselves had the experience of trying to persuade an accuser that they really are innocent (except perhaps in cases where the officer is facing a disciplinary charge). It is thus not surprising that they have little sympathy for someone who continues to protest his/her innocence. In the same way that everything that Rosenhan's pseudo-patients did was reinterpreted, so whatever the innocent suspect does or says may be construed in such a way that it is seen as proof of guilt. One should perhaps bear in mind a suggestion by the eminent social psychologist Elliot Aronson that "people who do crazy things are not necessarily crazy" (Aronson, 1992).

In discussing interrogations, Swanson et al (1988) suggest the following:

> "Religious statements such as 'Honest to God' and qualified answers to questions beginning with such phrases as 'to be perfectly honest' are potential indicators of deception and should be pursued by the attentive interrogator." (p. 214)

But might the innocent person not use such phrases as ways of emphasising that he/she really is telling the truth?

There is an assumption made by many officers that it is "obvious" when someone is lying or has something to hide. Often these beliefs are encouraged by colleagues who pass on tips to younger officers suggesting that there are easy ways to pick out a liar. This is in conflict with a great deal of psychological research which suggests that the detection of deception is not so straightforward (see e.g. Miller & Stiff, 1993; Vrij & Winkel, 1993).

A recent article in *Police Review* entitled "Spotting A Liar" illustrated the assumptions that might be made by police officers. In this article, the author (a Cambridgeshire detective) states that: "powers of lie detection are usually instinctive, based on years of experience, but the techniques can be learned" (Oxford, 1991, p. 328).

The article suggests that the interrogating officer "needs to be able to turn himself into a human polygraph" (p. 328). This statement may be particularly worrying for those psychologists who already have serious doubts about the validity of so-called scientific polygraph tests! Oxford goes on to say: "The experienced interrogator . . . has an armoury of lie-detecting tactics to spot those who are hiding their guilt."

The article then identifies a large number of ways in which lies can supposedly be detected. It would not be appropriate to list all of these, but a couple of examples will illustrate the potential problem.

> "A delayed response can often betray a lie. Especially in long and complex interviews, suspects need time to invent a plausible answer . . . The suspect might begin his reply with such phrases as 'If I remember correctly' or 'Now let me think'. Some of these apparently innocent expressions can say more about the suspect than he would wish." (Oxford, 1991, p. 328)

Throughout the article there is an assumption that most suspects are not truthful: "Suspects usually lie to avoid guilt or criminal proceedings" (p. 328). Any detective reading Oxford's comments may well assume that if their version of events differs from the suspect's, there is only one reason – the suspect is lying. The possibility that the person is not agreeing with the officer because he/she really is innocent, and that the detective is wrong is hardly considered. A further example will illustrate the point.

> "'I know what you are saying but . . .' is another favourite, but an innocent person has no need to show he understands the question before he gives an answer . . . When the suspect is normally fluent, but suddenly begins to stutter and stammer, he can be indicating that he is unable to think up lies quickly enough." (Oxford, 1991, p. 328)

The point about all these assertions is that the comments may well apply to a lying suspect, but may equally well apply to a perfectly innocent person – especially one who is beginning to realise that a totally false version of events is being taken seriously by the interrogating officer, regardless of the repeated attempts to protest (genuine) innocence. A final example highlights the potential danger.

> "Both the innocent and the guilty will be nervous, but the guilty person's nervousness is often more physical, reflected in excessive perspiration, . . . nervous laughter, yawns or sighs. Efforts to hide guilt often cause problems with the adrenal system." (Oxford, 1991, p. 329)

All of the symptoms described above are recognised signs of stress. However, there are few psychologists who would support the assertion made by Oxford that the anxiety of a guilty person can be differentiated from the anxiety produced in an innocent person wrongly accused. Perhaps this article reflects the differences of approach between the "science" of policing and the "science" of psychology. Whereas the former may be content to rely on anecdote and experience, the latter would investigate the issue by means of carefully controlled studies, the results of which would be analysed statistically. Whilst the latter method produces its own difficulties (in particular the problems of external validity) the police method is in danger of merely producing a self-fulfilling prophecy. For example, the police officer chooses not to believe the suspect, applies pressure which leads to a confession, which in turn leads to a conviction. The police officer thus has "proof" that he/she was right all along – otherwise the person would have been acquitted. Of course innocent people never get convicted, do they?

We can see that there are a large number of difficulties associated with the interrogation process, not the least of which is differentiating the truly innocent from the guilty. At the heart of the problem is the interrogation process itself. For anyone who has not been in this situation it is difficult to appreciate just how powerful an influence the process of interrogation can be. Indeed as attribution research has demonstrated consistently, people underestimate the powerful force which situations can apply on individuals. A number of well known social psychological studies have demonstrated that people do often take courses of action which seem totally incomprehensible at the time. For example, it is inconceivable that 38 people would watch a person being murdered and yet do nothing about it. Yet this did happen in New York in 1964 when Kitty Genovese was attacked near her own home. Her assailant took more than 30 minutes to kill her, and it was later established that some 38 people had witnessed the attack. However, none of the witnesses went to her assistance nor even called the police. In this case their inaction was explained by reference to situational forces rather than apathy (see Latané & Darley, 1968).

The point is that situational forces are much more powerful than people assume, and there is a folly in always blaming the person concerned when bizarre things happen. To some extent people make internal attributions about another's bizarre behaviour because by doing so they can convince themselves that they would never do such a thing. If someone does confess to a crime, it is assumed that it is for an internal reason (i.e. he/she really is guilty) rather than for an external reason (e.g. the suspect found the interrogation so stressful or coercive that they would say or sign anything just to get out of there). One could perhaps draw parallels with some of the less reputable time-share companies who persuade significant numbers of people to purchase a time-share which they cannot afford and do not want. When people hear of others being "conned" in this way, the tendency is to assume that they must be weak. By doing so they convince themselves that they would never fall for such a ploy.

It was pointed out in Chapter 1 that one of the fundamentals of attribution theory is whether people make an internal attribution or an external one. In other words, whether people assume that the reason for a person behaving in a particular way was because of something within that person, or was a function of the situation. Let us take an example from one of the more infamous experiments in American social psychology. Suppose you were asked the question "Would you be willing to give another person an apparently fatal electric shock, just because someone told you to?" Most people who have been asked this question answer with a very firm "No". But suppose you were told that a number of people had administered the shock, how might such behaviour be explained? When informed of such apparently surprising results, most people make reference to some *internal* factor, such as that the sort of person who did this must be sadistic, uncaring, cruel. In other words they would look for an explanation for the behaviour within the individual him/herself, rather than considering the pressures exerted by the situation. (The interested reader should see Milgram (1965) for a fuller account of this experiment.) In the experiment quoted here, almost two-thirds of the subjects were prepared to give what could have been a fatal electric shock (Milgram, 1965).

This example shows just how powerful *situational* factors can be in influencing behaviour. Yet, as attribution research has shown, humans consistently underestimate the power of these forces, and overestimate the influence of internal factors. (This has become known as the Fundamental Attribution Error, its influence being so pervasive and rudimentary.) Social psychology is laden with examples of similar findings, where people do things which at first appear inexplicable, but which make a little more sense once the powerful situational forces are taken into account. For example, inhumane treatment of prisoners by guards has been explained by reference partly to situational factors (Zimbardo, 1966). The mass suicide of almost 1000 people can also be better understood when we consider the powerful situational forces at work (see Osherow, 1988).

Such examples have implications for the situation encountered in police interrogations. Denial of the persuasive properties of interrogation can lead anyone, including police officers, to conclude that only a guilty person would really confess. Being deprived of one's liberty, being made to feel that one has little control over one's immediate fate, being pressurised by an authority figure, being told that one's situation is hopeless; these and many other factors can have a profound effect on even the most determined suspect. As long ago as 1908, Munsterberg pointed out that a false confession may in fact be a "normal" phenomenon triggered by unusual circumstances.

Ekman (1985) has carried out some interesting work on lies and the presumption of guilt. He refers to what he calls the "Othello effect" (because of similarities to the dilemmas faced by this Shakespearean character). This suggests that the more accusations are put to a person, the higher will be their level of stress. These higher levels of stress will in turn lead to more signs which will be interpreted as guilt by the interviewing police officer. The final consequence of this will be a greater (but mistaken) certainty of guilt!

INTERROGATION METHODS

In Britain there have been a number of recent changes in legislation which mean that interrogations are now carried out somewhat differently from 15 years ago. The most important changes were those brought in under the Police and Criminal Evidence Act (PACE), 1984. Irving and McKenzie (1989) have carried out some research examining the effects of this legislation on police practice in the interview room. The main changes that were identified following the introduction of the Act included a dramatic fall in the number of manipulative and persuasive tactics used by detectives. For example, in 1979 some 165 tactics were used on the 60 suspects whose interrogations were observed. By 1986 (following the introduction of PACE) the number of tactics used had fallen to just 42 in the 68 cases observed. Interestingly, when observations were made just one year later, the number of tactics used had risen to 88, though this was still significantly below the 1979 level. The rise between 1986 and 1987 was partly explained by a relaxation of the strict adherence to PACE's provisions which had immediately followed its introduction. Despite the somewhat confusing results produced by Irving and McKenzie, it does seem obvious that the introduction of PACE had a dramatic effect on the techniques used by interrogators, at least in the less serious cases.

Of all PACE's provisions the introduction of the tape recording of interrogations perhaps produced the most dramatic changes. It is interesting to note that most police officers were very much against this provision when it was first suggested, but after seeing it in practice, they became much more enthusiastic. In particular, tape recording removed the possibility of a suspect being able to deny what had been said in the interview room, and meant that claims of "undue pressure" or inducements could be refuted by an examination of the tape recording. Of course audio tape recording is not perfect and may not pick up things like threatening non-verbal communication. Tape recording has meant that the exact tactics used by the police can be analysed and, in some cases, questioned in court.

Williamson (1990) has provided further evidence of the way in which police interrogation has been affected by the provisions of PACE. He points out that the police now use more professional and less coercive tactics in their questioning of suspects. He also supports the findings of Irving and McKenzie that PACE has resulted in fewer interrogations at night, fewer repeat interrogations, and more ready access to a solicitor. However, Williamson's work does raise other causes for concern. In particular, his findings suggest that most English police officers still do not believe that innocent suspects could or would make false confessions, nor that some types of people are particularly vulnerable to the sort of questioning which is traditionally used in interrogations.

Moston (1990) has carried out extensive work on interrogations in Britain. He supports previous research in recognising how the tape recording of interviews has had a marked effect on the way in which interrogations are conducted. Prior to tape recording, contemporaneous note-taking was used to record both questions and answers. One effect of this was that the interrogation process was stilted and disjointed. The writing down of each word gave a suspect ample time to think how he or she wanted to answer the question. By contrast, tape-recorded interviews were more likely to resemble a normal conversation, without time to carefully consider each question and answer. Moston analysed over 400 recorded police interrogations conducted by London Metropolitan Police detectives. He found that the interviews invariably began in one of two ways, i.e. *inquisitorial* or *accusatorial*. As one might expect, the inquisitorial style was used to gather general information, whereas the accusatorial was aimed primarily at obtaining a confession. Which technique was chosen depended partly on the interviewer's skill, but also on the assumptions which the interviewer made about the suspect's likely guilt.

When it was used, the inquisitorial style of questioning was employed at the beginning of a session in order to establish rapport and to get to know the suspect's typical way of behaving to non-threatening questions. In effect the officers were establishing a baseline by which to measure the suspect's responses to later questions. However, Moston found that this style of questioning was rarely used. It was much more likely that the officer would use an accusatorial (or confrontational) questioning style. In other words, the purpose of the interview was not to establish what had happened, but rather to attempt to obtain a confession. The accusatorial style generally took one of three forms. Firstly, there might be a direct accusation where the interviewer asks the suspect simply "Did you commit this crime?" Secondly, the officer might present the suspect with the evidence that has been amassed against him or her and ask for an explanation – in effect inviting a confession. Thirdly, the interviewer might use what Moston calls "supported direct accusation", which is in effect an amalgamation of the first two, and is often the most successful strategy in eliciting a confession. However, whilst the third method is most likely to elicit a confession from the guilty, it might also produce a false confession, especially from a suggestible or compliant suspect. The other danger with this tactic is that the suspect is given information about the crime at the start of the interview, and may later simply repeat what he/she was told earlier. Ironically, this might serve to convince the interviewing officer that the person must be guilty because he/she seemed to know so much about the details of the crime!

Moston's conclusion is that the manipulative form of interrogation used at the time of Irving and McKenzie's initial study in 1980 has now been replaced by a more confrontational form whereby suspects are immediately accused and informed of the evidence against them. By doing this, the detectives are trying to elicit incriminating evidence directly from the suspect, rather than simply trying to obtain information. Once again, whilst this tactic is understandable and appropriate for a reluctant but ultimately guilty suspect, it is a less appropriate strategy for identifying those who really have been falsely accused.

Moston has also examined what case characteristics are linked with the likelihood of confession. He identified three important factors:

1 When there was strong evidence, confessions were more likely.
2 With increasing offence seriousness, suspects were less likely to reply to an accusation, and more likely to use the "right to silence".
3 Admissions were less likely when the suspect received legal advice.

Interestingly, some other factors (e.g. the sex and age of the suspect, criminal history, and offence type) were not associated with the likelihood of confession (Moston, Stephenson & Williamson, 1992, 1993).

Earlier it was suggested that if suspects resist attempts to persuade them to confess, this might be explained by reference to the fact that they had a great deal to lose if they did admit the offence. In other words resistance is seen as an act of self-protection. However Shepherd (1993) has suggested that there are other plausible explanations for why resistance is encountered. His view is that police officers, by their own actions, are more likely to produce resistance – the exact opposite of what they are trying to achieve. He points out how the introduction of

PACE alienated police officers who wished to conduct interviews. Some police officers perceived that the regulations embodied in PACE imply that individual officers cannot be trusted to carry out interrogations in an appropriate way.

Shepherd suggests that a suspect's use of the right to silence or a simple "no comment" can in some cases be made more likely by the actions of individual officers. It is further argued that an officer's ability to cope is threatened by such tactics, which may lead to a worsening of the interaction between suspect and interviewing officer. For example, the presence of a solicitor during interrogations is seen as a negative factor by police officers. The perception is that the solicitor will hinder the investigation and make it less likely that the suspect will confess. There is thus antagonism towards legal representatives and a general air of unhelpfulness and suspicion. However, Shepherd points out that the antagonism towards the solicitor may be construed by him/her as indicating that there really is not a strong case against the suspect. The solicitor may thus advise the client not to answer the questions – the exact opposite of what the police officer was trying to achieve. Shepherd cites this as an example of a self-fulfilling prophecy, leading to further antagonism against legal representatives. Shepherd is even more scathing of the competence of some officers, stating:

> "It is all too clear that too many officers embark upon investigative interviews ill-informed and ill-prepared – psychologically and practically – to a degree which predestines the emergence of resistance and prejudices their prospects of coping with it." (Shepherd, 1993, p. 6)

Shepherd argues that resistance should not be viewed as though it automatically proves the guilt of the suspect. He suggests that most police officers recognise only one dimension to resistance, i.e. willingness or unwillingness to talk. However, he argues that there is an important second dimension, i.e. ability or inability to tell. In this latter case, the suspect's resistance is born of ignorance rather than a desire to evade the question. The suspect might simply not know the answer to the question, in that he/she might have an unclear memory of exactly what did happen. Whilst police officers may feel intuitively that they can tell the difference between someone who does not know the answer and someone who is merely avoiding the question, there is, as far as this author is aware, no empirical evidence to support this view. Similarly a suspect who talks and tells the truth may act in an identical way to a suspect who talks but confabulates (see Gudjonsson, 1992).

Conversation Management

Shepherd sees the interrogation process as similar to other types of interaction (e.g. a psychiatric interview) where one needs to motivate the other to talk. He argues that consideration is a crucial element in such interactions. His position is summarised thus:

> "Consideration here means thorough commitment to the psychological and practical requirements to motivate and to facilitate talk. These requirements include: the rejection of a 'win-lose' mentality; detailed knowledge; forethought in terms of grasp of information and issues; detailed planning and detailed preparation including potential barriers to talk; and a balance of assertion and listening consistent with finding out facts and minding feelings, i.e. respect for the person, empathy, supportiveness, openness, a non-judgemental attitude, straightforward talk and a conversational style signalling a commitment to talk across as equals, not up-down or as pseudo-equals." (Shepherd, 1993, p. 7)

This is certainly a tall order and one which appears to be a radical departure from the way in which interrogations have traditionally been conducted. The cynical police officer may perceive the long list of dos and don'ts as going too far towards protecting the rights of the suspect, and not allowing the officer to use any form of coercion. However, the techniques outlined above, and others proposed by Shepherd as "ethical interviewing" (Shepherd, 1991) have now been adopted by many British police forces. Shepherd's belief is that many skilled negotiators know that interviewees are more likely to want to talk if the conversation is appropriately managed, and if consideration is shown to the person. In this case, the interviewee begins to think that the questioner is a thoughtful person who has planned and prepared well for the interview, and is thus more likely to cooperate. Shepherd believes that resistance is more likely to be evoked when an interviewer's technique lacks an explicit framework for managing and monitoring the exchange, and when the interview is conducted in an unprofessional way. He argues that both suspects and legal representatives will pick up on the lack of competence and assume that there is not much of a case to answer. Shepherd lists the major shortcomings of traditional interrogation techniques as follows:

1 Poor conversation management. An explicit and announced framework is essential so that both parties are clear as to the purpose of the interview. The interviewer needs to know the exact topic coverage, and the sequence of questioning; what Shepherd calls a "route map".
2 Inappropriate pacing. Shepherd identifies a tendency for interviewers to rush in immediately after a suspect's response and to quickly fill in

any silences. If the suspect does not answer, the interviewer should not be afraid of the silence, and should not be tempted to answer the question him/herself. Pauses allow time for thought and reflection and allow the interviewer a chance to compare answers with previous knowledge. Again this is in marked contrast to traditional interrogation techniques where questions are fired at a suspect in quick succession, thus supposedly denying any opportunity to fabricate a story.

3 Inappropriate forms of assertion and listening. Talking over the other person, constantly interrupting, appearing disinterested, and rapidly changing topics all serve to discourage the other from talking. Similarly, appropriate forms of listening will be more likely to produce cooperation – appearing genuinely interested will help, as will not assuming what the answer will be before it is given.

4 Inappropriate content of assertions. This is seen as perhaps the most important of all the strategies, Shepherd suggesting that "Inappropriate content of responses is the major threat to the credibility of an investigative interviewer" (Shepherd, 1993, p. 9). It is argued that no matter how socially skilled the interviewer is, he/she will never be able to overcome the hurdles of insufficient knowledge, or uncertain reliability of information. It is suggested that both the innocent and the guilty will be more likely to resist when they lose confidence in, and respect for, the interviewer.

Shepherd suggests that if used mistakenly, all of the above factors may combine to virtually guarantee that resistance is produced. His further concern for the interrogation process is eloquently stated thus:

> "To set the scene finally for the compounding and creation of resistance it only remains for an interviewer to pay scant attention to preparation – not review and memorise information, not to think of interview aids, not to attend to administration, not to ensure that interruptions do not occur, not to think through and to specify to his or her number two 'who does what', and, to round things off, to brief in a suitably terse, cursory manner those obstructive third parties – legal advisers. And for good measure, overlook to brief adequately other third parties such as parents, responsible adults and interpreters.
>
> The result? Alienation, antipathy, mistrust, loss of confidence in the interviewer and loss of interviewer credibility and loss of self-confidence. Those who could have been motivated are demotivated. Those who could have been facilitated to talk are rendered silent – the innocent frustratingly so and the guilty and those with something to hide happily so." (Shepherd, 1993, p. 9)

It remains to be seen just what the consequences of such a dramatic shift of interrogation style could be. Some police officers already see this as another nail in the coffin of their legendary powers of persuasion. Others see it as a technique which, when used, is more likely to uncover the truth, and to remove some of the suspicion of more traditional interrogation techniques. Clearly research is needed to monitor the changes that do occur following the incorporation of Shepherd's guidelines.

False Confessions and Convictions

It has been argued in the early part of this chapter that assumptions of guilt might mean that undue pressure is put on a suspect to admit to the offence under investigation. But how might this occur? Kennedy (1986) has suggested that the most common cause of false confessions is overzealousness by the police officer conducting the interrogation. Reacting to some kind of gut feeling that the person is guilty, the officer may try to browbeat the suspect into confession. Other tactics might also be used, for example, pressurising witnesses to say what the officer wants them to say. The officer may even suppress or ignore other evidence which challenges his/her assumption of guilt, or which could provide an alibi. Kennedy suggests that some officers might go so far as to conveniently "lose" documents which might be of assistance to the accused. These are serious allegations which do not relate to the vast majority of such interrogations. However, a number of recent cases in Britain show how the innocent can sign confessions which are later proved to be false. One thinks of the Guildford Four or the Birmingham Six, whose cases have been analysed by Gudjonsson (1992).

Kennedy provides an interesting example of how a false conviction can be obtained by the use of certain tactics. Whilst the case cited below did not involve a confession, it did show how innocent people could be convicted, simply because some police officers start with an assumption of guilt and then try to make the evidence fit in with this view. The case is that of Noel Fellows who in 1970 was accused of the murder of a 67-year-old debt collector. Interestingly, Fellows was an ex-police officer and so presumably was familiar with police procedures. At the time of his arrest he was working as a taxi driver. The main evidence against Fellows was that his mother-in-law's name was in the debt collector's notebook. In addition, a witness reported seeing the victim getting into a taxi on the day he was killed. The police interrogated Fellows for 6 hours, but he still maintained his innocence and did not confess. It is then reported that the police "persuaded" a witness to state that Fellows had a grudge against the debt collector – in fact the accused had never even met the victim. Perhaps most worrying about the case is the fact that the police appear to have suppressed information that proved that the accused was working at the time of the murder, and so could not have committed the offence. Documents which could have proved this went missing so that the accused's alibi could not be proved.

Fellows was convicted of manslaughter and was sentenced to 7 years imprisonment. Several years later the real murderer was apprehended, and Fellows's conviction was quashed. This case is cited not as a way of portraying the police service as dishonest, but rather as an example of how an assumption of guilt, made at an early stage of the investigation, can cloud judgement of all subsequent evidence. Police officers are not unusual in exhibiting the human desire to make their behaviour appear consistent. Once a course of action has been decided upon there is a strong tendency to stick to that path, despite subsequent contradictory notions. Psychologists have suggested that people strive for cognitive consistency or balance in their thoughts and actions. People feel uncomfortable when faced with the fact that two sets of actions are inconsistent, or that an action is contradictory to a belief which they hold. Festinger (1957) has suggested that humans faced with such inconsistency experience what he calls cognitive dissonance. This is an unpleasant state which people are motivated to reduce. Thus the person who chooses to smoke cigarettes despite knowing that this is likely to cause serious illness experiences dissonance. The person may well try to reduce this unpleasant feeling by such statements as "Well not everyone who smokes dies". Or "Well I'm going to die anyway so I might as well enjoy the cigarettes". In other words people strive to ensure that there is no inconsistency between their thoughts and their actions. Relating this to the Fellows case cited earlier, one can imagine that police officers in the case had a mind-set or schema which led them to search for any clues that would confirm the original assumption of guilt, and to ignore or even conceal evidence which would have led them to question the original decision that Fellows was guilty.

Although Fellows did resist attempts to make him confess, in his account of his experience (Fellows, 1986) he gives a graphic account of the pressure which he felt when being interrogated. He describes how the forcefulness of questioning led to intense emotional upheavals:

> "He started shouting and banging his fist on the table. By this time fear had totally engulfed me and I just broke down. I could not control my emotions. As I tried to fight the tears back, they just kept on flowing. Deep shock set in and I was inwardly fighting to get words out of my mouth." (p. 15)

Remember the emotions expressed above are those of an innocent man who was trying to convince his interrogators of this innocence. One wonders what a detective following Oxford's advice would have made of such behaviour. It is easy to see how this display of emotion might have been interpreted by Fellows's interrogator as the actions of a guilty person trying hard to conceal his guilt. Despite the pressure exerted, Fellows did not confess and interestingly feels that if a person really were innocent they would not confess. He says: "This approach certainly worked to raise the level of fear within me, but if you are innocent, how can you confess to something you haven't done?" (Fellows, 1986, p. 18). Perhaps Fellows's personality or his previous experience as a police officer enabled him to stick to his story despite the pressure. But not all suspects are as resilient, and a number do bow to the pressure and confess falsely.

Of course some individuals confess falsely, without any pressure being applied upon them. After details are announced of some major crimes, police interview rooms contain a collection of individuals who want to claim credit for the crime, and of course want the notoriety which would accompany this. In a bizarre way it is one method by which a person can enhance their self-esteem. Kassin and Wrightsman (1985) note that after the Lindbergh kidnapping some 200 different people confessed to the crime. Whilst desire for fame may be the main reason why people confess, others might do so in order to get rid of guilt feelings which they are experiencing. Gudjonsson (1992) makes the important point that this guilt might relate to an actual previous wicked act or an imagined one. Indeed some personality types may well carry round with them general and all-embracing "guilt complexes". These may predispose the individual to confess to any number of crimes in order to remove some of the heavy burden of guilt.

A third reason why people might confess falsely occurs when individuals confuse fantasy with reality. Whilst this state is more likely to be found in people with severe mental illness (e.g. schizophrenia) it may also be found in a mild form in others who do not have an obvious mental disorder. One need only bring to mind how dreams can be confused with reality, at least for a short period, to imagine how some people could have difficulty in disentangling imagined events from real ones.

There is a fourth reason why people might confess, i.e. in order to protect the real perpetrator. This is by no means unusual, especially where one member of a family lies in order to protect another. Providing that the false confessor knows enough about the case, it will be difficult for the police to identify all the instances where this form of deception takes place.

However, the more worrying cases (at least in terms of the reputation of the police) are those where a person confesses falsely because of the pressure exerted on him/her. Gudjonsson (1992) refers to these as *coerced-compliant false confessions*. Here the person may confess in order to end the stress and ordeal of interrogation, or in order to be released from police custody. Whilst the suspect might realise that a confession could have serious long-term consequences, the need to escape from the situation he/she is currently enduring is more pressing and demands more immediate action. To put it another way, the short-term gain (temporary escape from the interrogation) is preferred to the longer term problems which a confession might subsequently cause. The suspect might in any case convince him/herself that the confession can be retracted later and the truth be proven.

A second type of false confession is referred to as *coerced-internalised false confessions*. These involve cases where a suspect may come to believe the version of events provided by the police, and come to believe that he or she really did commit the crime – despite having no actual memory for the event. Gudjonsson and MacKeith (1982) suggest that this arises from a "memory distrust syndrome" – suspects feel that they cannot rely on their own memory and so start to believe externally generated versions of events. (In this case, the version given by the interrogating officer.) This could occur because the person is suffering from amnesia, or where the intake of alcohol or other drugs has interfered with memory processes. A similar problem is found with so-called false memory syndrome. This can occur in a particularly suggestible witness, or with children, and has also been demonstrated in particular when people are under hypnosis (see Orne, 1979). A person (especially one in a hypnotic state) can be persuaded to believe that something which has not in reality occurred did take place. In one recent case, it was claimed that a psychotherapist "planted" a memory for childhood sexual abuse in a patient, although such abuse had not in fact taken place. Once a suggestion has been accepted, it can prove virtually impossible to convince the person that what they recall is in fact a false memory.

There is a second, and perhaps more worrying form of the "memory distrust syndrome". This is where a suspect does initially have a clear memory of what happened, but becomes persuaded by a skilful interrogator that they should question their original version of events. Their original (and correct) memory thus becomes replaced by a version of events which has been put forward by the interrogating officer. The reader may find it hard to believe that this could actually be done if the suspect started off with a clear memory for events. However, it would appear that such "thought reform" can be produced if enough confusion and self-doubt are produced in the mind of the suspect (see Gudjonsson, 1992).

The coerced-compliant suspect may retract his/her confession as soon as the pressure of the situation is removed. However, things are more complex and difficult in the case of a coerced-internalised confessor. The point about any internalised belief is that it becomes part of the person's belief system and is thus less easily altered. Research by cognitive psychologists has shown that when an original memory has been distorted by a subsequent (and perhaps misleading) version of events, it is very difficult to return to the original memory (see e.g. Loftus, 1981). In other words retrieval of the original uncontaminated memory trace is almost impossible. Clearly the implications of this situation are very serious. The person may come to accept a version of events that is considerably different from reality. Here again pressure towards achieving behavioural consistency may further come to persuade the person of their guilt. In terms of Bem's Self-Perception Theory (Bem, 1972), the person may well think "Well I did confess so I guess I really must be guilty".

Ofshe (1989) has made a study of this type of false confession. He notes that the essential ingredients are the production of self-doubt and confusion by the interrogator, and an alteration in the suspect's perceptions of reality. To achieve this, the interrogator must firstly convince the suspect that there is irrefutable evidence that he/she did commit the crime. Secondly, the interrogator must provide a good and valid reason why the person has no memory of having committed the crime. Ofshe describes the way in which this type of confession can be produced. This can be summarised as follows:

1 The interrogator constantly and confidently asserts his/her belief in the suspect's guilt (e.g. "Look we all know you did it . . . ").
2 The suspect is prevented from communicating with anyone who could be an ally and challenge the notion of guilt. Additionally, the suspect is not made aware of any evidence which might challenge the interrogator's version of events.
3 The interrogation takes a long time and is conducted with a high level of intensity and tension.
4 The interrogator constantly tells the suspect that there is good scientific evidence to prove his/her guilt.
5 The interrogator constantly draws attention to any memory difficulties which the suspect has shown, or suggests that the person is suffering from a mental disorder which has led to memory loss.
6 The interrogator insists repeatedly that the suspect must accept the interrogator's version of events.
7 The interrogator arouses fear in the suspect's mind as to the consequences of continued denial.

Ofshe points out that many of the techniques described above are those used by trained interrogators in the USA. The worrying aspect is that while the techniques will produce confessions, it is impossible for the interviewing officer to identify which of these confessions are in fact false. Ofshe's small study of people who had made this type of confession found that none of them could be described as mentally ill. However, he does point out that certain types of people are likely to be more susceptible to this form of interrogation. Specifically, people who trust those in authority, who lack self-confidence, and who are highly suggestible, are most likely to succumb. However, Ofshe makes the point that whilst this type of person is more likely to confess falsely, and to do so quickly, others who are subjected to the above techniques for a long period may also confess.

SUMMARY

We have seen in this chapter some of the ways in which interrogations are conducted. We have drawn attention to the techniques used by the police and others to elicit confessions. We have also drawn attention to the dangers of a presumption of guilt. This can have far reaching consequences for all subsequent interactions between suspect and interrogator. The way in which false confessions may be elicited has also been examined. It remains to be seen whether initiatives such as those brought in under PACE, and the ethical style of interviewing advocated by Shepherd have an effect on the rates of confession – both true and false.

FURTHER READING

Gudjonsson, G. (1992) *The Psychology of Interrogations, Confessions and Testimony*. Chichester: Wiley.

CHAPTER 4

Dealing with Groups

"The trouble is, Joe Public doesn't take us for a person, they take us for a uniform. My answer whenever I get involved with somebody . . . is 'What have I ever done to you? . . . You've never met me before. You don't know who I am'." (WPC quoted in Graef, 1990, p. 41)

"Is it down to us to make people realize the person underneath? We can, but wouldn't it be nice if the media turned round and said: 'Hey people out there, OK you get the bad coppers, but underneath that uniform in a lot of circumstances there is someone who will deal with your problems. Don't look just at the uniform, look at that person and how that person deals with you.' Wouldn't it be nice for that to be published?" (WPC quoted in Graef, 1990, p. 42)

In this chapter we will start to look at how an individual's behaviour is affected by membership of groups. This is seen as one of the cornerstones of social psychology. Humans are generally thought of as social animals, choosing to live with large numbers of others. Groups can serve a number of different functions for the individual, some positive and some negative. However, the "rewards" of group membership can also involve a "cost" to the individual, in terms of giving up some aspects of individuality. The two quotes at the beginning of this chapter make that very point. This chapter will examine the functions which groups serve for the individual, and examine how groups give individual members a sense of identity – but at the expense of demanding conformity and compliance. It will also take a brief look at how social psychology can help in understanding the ways in which juries make decisions.

When talking of group membership, many different "groups" would be included. If a person is asked to describe him/herself the reply will invariably contain aspects of group membership – the person will give their age, sex, race, and many other details which help to identify the individual. We have already seen in Chapter 1 that group membership is one of the ways in which humans classify other individuals; membership of a certain racial group for example helps people to put others into a pigeon hole and react in a predetermined way. At some times group membership is even more important – such as in times of stress and anxiety, or when a person feels threatened. One need only think of the way in which ethnic groups in Bosnia became more solid in face of the threat from opposing groups.

Members of the police service are often perceived as members of a closely knit group or subculture which relies on other members of the group for support and identity. When under threat (e.g. from proposals outlined in the recent Sheehy Report) the group shows even more solidarity and unites behind a common barrier to oppose the threat from outside. Long-established rivalries between different ranks, different branches of the service, or different police forces are suspended when a common enemy is identified. Police officers may be no different from any other group in this respect, though role ambiguity and the danger inherent in the job may result in a heightened need for solidarity (see Chapter 8). Some recent research on stress shows that the lack of support from colleagues and others in the criminal justice system can be as stressful as the physical dangers faced in police work (see Brown & Campbell, 1993). For the outsider, "the police" would be thought of as an identifiable group all of whose members have similar attitudes – in other words most civilians will have a stereotyped view of a police officer based simply upon their membership of an identifiable group (see Simon, 1992). This is one reason why a single officer's transgressions can affect the image and reputation of a whole force. However, for the individual officer, his/her identity will be formed by reference to immediate colleagues, others on the relief, others of the same rank, others in the same department. During the miners' dispute in the 1980s many police officers were thrown together and had to work as large teams. However, officers still saw themselves as representatives of their own force, and exhibited pride in that group membership. This is illustrated in the following quote:

> "The Met used to bundle out of the van, putting bits of uniform on. We were the scruffiest cunts up there. But at the end of the day, when it came to actually doing anything, the other forces just waited for orders, whereas we waded in and dealt with it . . . We liked our reputation – I'm not sure it was 100 per cent justified, but that's what happened." (Metropolitan Police sergeant quoted in Graef, 1990, p. 68)

Groups can be used as an important form of social support. Following a disaster it is quite common for support groups to be formed in order to help the individuals whose lives have been affected (see e.g. Bromet, 1990). Families will also tend to rally round, and the unit become closer. This group support is important, and it is not uncommon for families to say that a disaster did have one good feature in that it brought together previously distant relationships. Everyday group membership also serves important functions in helping people to define their own identity. One of the first questions people ask when meeting another is "And what do you do?" This identity testing is an important way in which people define themselves and others. People who retire from a career often have great difficulty in adjusting to their new life, not least because one of the primary means of self-identity has been removed. Membership of a group called "retirees" might offer some delineation of the self, but might also have more negative connotations than a previous respected occupation. It is hard to imagine life without such opportunities for self-definition, and difficult to see how people could have a true sense of just who they are without reference to the groups of which they are a part.

But if groups do serve important functions for everyone, we should also be aware of the consequences of belonging. If membership of a group, any group, produces feelings of belonging, how does that make the person view other groups? Many psychologists hold the view that "in-group pride" comes at the price of "out-group hostility". Examples of this phenomenon can be seen in the antics of English soccer fans, or in the neighbourhood street gangs in Los Angeles. Each is encouraged by the group to be proud of his/her group identity and to be hostile towards members of other groups. There is also a tendency for people to overestimate the differences between their own group and others (see Krueger, 1992). An example from the psychological literature is used below to illustrate the tendency to favour members of the person's own group.

Duncan (1976) conducted an experiment to examine whether an action carried out by a member of one race (in this case a white person) would be perceived differently from the same action carried out by a member of a different racial group. Duncan asked his subjects (all white American college students) to watch a videotape which showed an interaction between two people. The interaction developed into an argument which became more and more heated until finally one participant pushed the other. Duncan showed the videotape to groups of subjects, though there were in fact a number of different versions of the interaction. In particular, for some of the subjects, the person who was seen pushing the other was white, and in another version he was black. Apart from this, the videotapes were identical. After viewing the interaction, Duncan's subjects were asked to describe what they had seen. They were asked to say whether the behaviour of the aggressor should be categorised as "playing around" or as "violent behaviour". The results were somewhat revealing. When the perpetrator was white, only

13% of subjects labelled his actions as "violent behaviour"; however, when the perpetrator was black some 70% chose this category. Remember that in this case all the subjects were white, and that they all saw exactly the same incident, except for the fact that the race of the aggressor was changed for different groups of subjects.

Duncan's experiment provides an interesting example of how attributions can be biased, something which was discussed in the previous chapter. It shows how the actions of members of one's own group may be perceived differently from the same actions carried out by members of a different group. This applies to almost all of our attributions, from the behaviour of "our" football team to the behaviour of members of "our" political party. Duncan's results seem merely to illustrate a process which occurs in humans' attributions of many different events. Interestingly, Duncan went further in his study. Having asked his subjects to describe the actions of the aggressor, he then asked them to explain why the person had behaved as he did. In the case of the black aggressor, subjects tended to explain it in terms of personal characteristics: "he is a violent person". In other words they made an internal attribution – the person behaved as he did because he was that sort of person. However, when those subjects who had viewed a white aggressor were asked the same question, they explained the behaviour by reference to situational factors, i.e. they made an external attribution.

It would thus appear that actions carried out by members of one's own group are perceived differently from the same actions carried out by members of another group. (One person's freedom fighter is another's terrorist.) Thus some transgressions by members of an officer's own police force may be perceived differently from the same actions carried out by a member of the public (or perhaps even by a member of another police force). Not only do people define the behaviour differently, but they also seem to offer different explanations for the behaviour, dependent upon who carries out these actions. Duncan's experiment dealt specifically with racial groups, though the same sorts of biases have been identified in many other groupings (e.g. occupation, sex, age). The police officer reading this might wish to consider whether the same action carried out by a police officer or a social worker would be perceived in the same way (see Chapter 12). Stereotypes are often built up to the point that any action by a member of another group is perceived negatively. As we will see in Chapter 12, there has often been animosity and suspicion between police officers and social workers. Each suspects the other's motives, intentions and agenda, and is likely to be wary when, for instance, disclosing information in child abuse cases (see Hebenton & Thomas, 1992; Fielding & Conroy, 1994).

However, many of these stereotypes can be challenged and broken down when a member of one group has to work with a member of the other (as in child sex abuse cases). Of course people are members of many different groups at the same time, and will behave differently according to the group with whom they are interacting. A group of male police constables may unite when discussing "the public out there", but may display different behaviour according to whether or not there are female or black police officers present (see Holdaway, 1991). What people display in such situations has been termed ethnocentrism.

ETHNOCENTRISM

Ethnocentrism essentially refers to the way in which people look inward, and see themselves or their group as the major focus of their attention. Each group tends to nourish pride in itself, and assumes itself to be superior, or at least to have some admirable qualities which others do not possess. Groups thus concentrate on, and highlight, those areas in which they are different from others. People who are male, young, violent, unemployed and have short hair, may take pride in the label of "skinhead" as it differentiates them from others who, apart from their hairstyle, share the same characteristics. Ethnocentrism appears to be a very common human trait, though for some it may be more important than for others. Some countries deliberately foster national pride whilst others are not so nationalistic. Such tendencies do of course rise when a nation is under threat or at war. Brewer (1979) studied ethnocentrism in 20 different locations around the world – from Canada to the South Pacific and West Africa. He found in every location that for the local people the "in-group" was perceived as having more positive traits than the "out-group". Ethnocentrism thus appears to be universal and, according to Brown (1986), often inevitable.

The roots of ethnocentrism can be found in individual psychology. In this case the motivating factor appears to be a person's desire to establish and maintain positive self-esteem. One of the main ways in which an individual can be proud of her/himself is by perceiving the groups to which she/he belongs as better than the alternative. Thus by emphasising the positive aspects of the in-group – and of course derogating the out-group – a person is made to feel superior. Perhaps with the exception of those who are severely depressed, people need to feel that there is always someone to whom they are superior. Prisoners may not see themselves as members of a group of which they should be proud, but even within prisons there are hierarchies established which allow each prisoner to feel some pride. For example prisoners who have committed violent acts feel superior to sex offenders. And even within the sex offenders there are subgroups – for example those convicted of sexual attacks on children are derided and have to be segregated for their own protection. In this latter case, ethnocentrism can produce hostility and violence, though this is not an inevitable outcome. Brown (1986) suggests that ethnocentrism *in itself* need not lead to aggression. He suggests that an additional factor comes into play, i.e. comparability. In this case, the groups must be similar enough that they can compare themselves with each other and decide that there is an unfair or unjust disadvantage. Thus fans of football teams in the same division, and in the same area, will show more hostility towards each other than those in different leagues or areas. Fans whose team has just lost an important divisional game against their neighbours will feel even more hatred towards the opposition than existed previously.

When ethnocentrism is combined with perceived injustice and stereotyping then intergroup conflict can result. This conflict can be played out under a series of rules (e.g. sporting fixtures between rival teams) or under less clear or unofficial dictates (e.g. fights between rival fans or local gangs). One of the best examples of this effect was demonstrated by Sherif (Sherif, Harvey, Hood & Sherif, 1961) in their Robbers Cave study. Although this research was carried out many years ago, it provides one of the best examples of how intergroup conflict develops, and we will thus examine the study in some detail.

Sherif's Robbers Cave Study

This study is unusual in the psychological literature in that it did not rely on a brief experiment carried out in the laboratory, using undergraduate students as subjects. The experiment could be more accurately described as a field study under "natural" conditions. The study was carried out using a typical American summer camp as its base. Summer camps are almost a way of life for many American children. Both boys and girls spend up to 8 weeks interacting with others and enjoying sport and other group activities. The 22 subjects in Sherif's study were 11-year-old boys who believed that they were going to spend several weeks at a summer camp in the Robbers Cave State Park, Oklahoma. In fact they did exactly that, though Sherif and his colleagues kept the boys under close observation and introduced a number of factors. In particular, Sherif introduced the factors previously mentioned, i.e. ethnocentrism, stereotyping and perceived injustice, the three components of intergroup conflict.

The boys were divided into two separate groups and the groups matched as far as possible for size, athletic ability, and so forth. The two groups were then taken to separate cabins some distance apart. Each cabin had its own facilities and could essentially be self-sufficient. At first, neither group knew of the existence of the other, and they spent their time getting to know members of their own group. Through cooperative activities, each set of boys started to develop as a cohesive unit, though there were hierarchies within each group. Each group was allowed to develop its own identity or subculture, and quite quickly different norms of behaviour developed. For one group, being tough and swearing a lot became important identifying characteristics, whereas for the other, nude swimming became an important activity. By the end of the first week, both groups had gelled well and norms of behaviour had been established. The boys were all given plain T-shirts upon which they could write the name of their group and an identifying motif. From this point on the two groups were known as "The Rattlers" and "The Eagles". Towards the end of week 1, Sherif and his colleagues allowed each group to learn of the presence of the other, though at this time there was no face-to-face contact. It was at this point that ethnocentrism started to be shown, with each group expressing suspicion towards the other. There was a development of in-group and out-group language – in other words the boys made clear distinctions between "us" and "them".

The second part of the study involved a tournament between the two groups. This stage lasted for 5 days and involved a number of competitive encounters, particularly in sporting events such as baseball and tug-of-war. The camp counsellors could also award points to each team for such factors as the neatness of their cabins. (This element was introduced in order to ensure that the contest between the two could be kept close right to the end.) The groups were told that a prestigious trophy would be presented to the winners, along with individual medals and Swiss Army knives to each member of the winning team. The losers would receive nothing. This introduced an element of "competition for scarce resources", something which Sherif believed would produce hostility between the groups.

The first contest between the groups was a baseball game which the Rattlers won. The game was played in a reasonably fair way, and there was some element of sportsmanship shown. However, after the game the losing Eagles team started to claim that the contest had been unfair because the members of the Rattlers team were bigger and older than them. In fact this was not the case but it is interesting to note how *"perceived* injustice" started to appear after only one game. When members of the Eagles found their opponent's flag flying on the sports field, they seized it and burnt it. Burning of the other group's flag is a highly symbolic gesture which demonstrates both hostility and contempt for the others, and is often seen in other spheres where there are disputes between nations or factions. When the Rattlers discovered the burnt flag, they were furious and their leader initiated a fight against their opponents which the counsellors had to break up. It is important to point out here that the actions of the groups were not suggested, initiated or encouraged by the counsellors, but developed spontaneously within each group.

The next baseball game was won by the Eagles who then derogated their opponents and decided that they should not even speak to members of the other group. From this point onwards the exact details of events became a little confused, but basically the level of animosity between the two groups grew ever stronger. After losing the tug-of-war, the Rattlers openly accused the Eagles of cheating and organised a "commando-style raid" on the others' cabin, causing considerable damage. The Eagles organised a retaliatory raid and then withdrew, armed with coshes made from rocks inside socks. At this point the counsellors considered it prudent to intervene and to calm the situation! Again we must remember that the violence and aggression shown by the groups was not suggested by the counsellors but appeared merely to stem from the competition. Eventually the Eagles won the competition and were awarded their prizes. However, that was not the end of the matter. As the winners went off to celebrate their victory the Rattlers raided their cabin and stole the prizes.

Sherif and his colleagues later interviewed the boys and found that they all showed a very high level of "in-group preference" and "out-group hostility". The boys consistently rated members of their own team as superior to those of the opposition. There were numerous personal taunts and insults directed at the opposing team. There was also clear evidence of stereotyping both of the in-group and of the out-group. Every time one team lost a contest the outcome was perceived as unfair, and anger and resentment were produced spontaneously. The reader may be questioning the ethics of this sort of study which appears to encourage youngsters to commit various criminal acts. Three important points must be made in this respect.

1 The organisers of the study did not actively encourage any of the behaviour described above. In fact they had devised a number of strategies to increase out-group hostility but these were not needed. The simple element of competition produced more resentment than had been envisaged.
2 The boys and their parents did not see anything unusual in what took place at the camp. In fact this sort of competition is quite common throughout summer camps and is often seen as the highlight of the camp experience.

3 The researchers were able to show later how the bad feelings between
   the teams could be dissipated, by both groups having to engage in
   cooperative activities. Typically, problems were introduced which
   could only be solved if both sets of boys worked together on a solution.

The Robbers Cave study thus demonstrates how ethnocentrism,
along with stereotyping and competition, can produce resentment,
hostility, and even violence. Although it was carried out using 11-year-old
American boys as subjects, the results do appear to be applicable to
many other situations where conflict is found. One need only think of the
many conflicts which erupt between different factions within a society or
between different nations, to realise how relevant Sherif's work is.

There are also a number of implications for police work in particular.
For example, the more ethnocentric the police service becomes, the more
likely it is that hostility towards other groups will be produced.
Conversely, police forces which appear to be working with other
agencies and towards a common goal, are likely to receive more
cooperation and to experience less hostility (see Chapter 12). This has
implications for many situations where police officers have to work
closely with representatives of other agencies. For example in child
protection cases or in joint initiatives with the probation service
cooperation is not always easy. Because the police service has tended to
be ethnocentric in the past, there is a legacy which makes many officers
suspicious of any "outsiders". The canteen culture of police work means
that stories about other groups will be told and retold and often
embellished in order to justify the negative views held towards other
groups. Relationships can thus become strained and common purpose
abandoned in favour of in-group pride and out-group hostility. Each
group may then be perceived as trying merely to score points off the
others, and dialogue breaks down (see Thomas, 1994). Following the
Broadwater Farm riots in Britain there was a great deal of animosity
shown by the residents towards the police and vice versa. It took a long
time and great effort to even begin to break down the barriers which had
been built up by both sides and which stifled many attempts at
communication.

The police service is by no means unique in its ethnocentrism. Many
organisations, especially commercial ones, actively encourage in-group
pride, with the concomitant out-group hostility. Distinctive uniforms
may be worn so that group members can quickly distinguish between
their own group and "the opposition". In the commercial sector, being
better than the other companies is seen as an essential element for
financial survival, and thus encouragement of in-group pride and
loyalty to the company are actively encouraged. There are various ways

in which this can be achieved – an increasingly popular method is by having working groups go off together on Outward Bound courses, where interdependence is fostered.

In the Robbers Cave study, competition between the groups was seen as a vital element in the production of in-group preference and out-group hostility. However, more recent research has begun to question whether competition is actually necessary for the production of such prejudices. In particular the work of Tajfel and Turner (1986) leads us to believe that competition is not a necessary or essential element in the production of this phenomenon.

SOCIAL IDENTITY THEORY

Tajfel's theory is perhaps best illustrated by one of his early experiments (Tajfel, 1971). In this study, groups of 14–15-year-old schoolboys were recruited. They were shown slides containing a number of dots for a fraction of a second. They were next asked to guess how many dots were contained in each slide. Tajfel then told the boys that in his experience people were either chronic *over*estimators or chronic *under*estimators. It was not that members of one group were any more accurate than the others, just that all people were either one or the other. In truth this was a deception on the part of the experimenter, and the boys were actually randomly assigned to one group or the other. The boys did, however, come to believe that their membership of one group or another was for a genuine reason. The boys were then given a second task. This was to observe another person's performance and then award points which could be exchanged for money by the person being observed. Before doing this, however, the boys were told that the other person was either an overestimator or an underestimator. In other words the boys believed that the person whose performance they were evaluating was either a member of the same group as themselves, or a member of the other group.

The results were interesting since there was a consistent in-group favouritism shown by the boys in that they consistently gave more points to the boys whom they thought were in the same group as themselves, and less to members of the other group. That such an effect could be produced by groups which had been formed only a few minutes earlier suggests that groups really are powerful agents which produce bias in the judgements people make about others. As we saw in the Duncan experiment earlier, ethnocentrism produces biases in the explanations people give for others' behaviour, i.e. they make systematic biases in their attributions. Memory can also become selective in that good actions by members of the in-group are remembered, whilst bad actions are not. Conversely bad actions by the out-group are remembered whilst good actions are not (see e.g. Howard & Rothbart, 1980).

The finding in Tajfel's studies has been labelled the *Minimal Group Effect*. Remember that the boys in his study were already members of many other groups within the school, and yet the new categorisation produced immediate favouritism effects. In fact Tajfel has shown that simply assigning people randomly to one group or another (in one case literally by the toss of a coin and then placement in the "As" or "Bs") a group preference effect is seen. The fundamental claim made by Tajfel (1981) is that whenever people are assigned to any group, they immediately and automatically think of that group as better than the alternative. The primary motivating factor here is the person's wish to achieve and maintain a positive self-image.

Thus far we have seen just how powerful groups can be in providing a sense of identity, a feeling of pride, and a feeling of superiority. We have also seen how such positive elements are countered by the negative aspects of hostility towards the members of other groups. The police service, especially if its members feel under threat, will increase its internal solidarity and look inward for support. The irony is that this will produce even more alienation from the wider society and a greater feeling of isolation. Moves towards "community policing" increase and decrease over time as fashions and perceptions change. However, true and full community policing has rarely if ever been introduced (see Friedman, 1992). Whilst John Alderson made a serious attempt to introduce some aspects of community policing to South-West England in the 1970s, his ideas and vision were never fully realised (see Alderson, 1979). Perhaps any such moves are doomed to failure given the way in which different factions will have different agendas and priorities, and given the very different views of the in-group and the out-group.

JURIES AND GROUP BEHAVIOUR

When discussing groups and group behaviour, it would be particularly appropriate to consider juries. They are after all functional groups which come together to achieve some purpose. Juries are of particular interest to both social psychologists and legal psychologists. The processes which take place within a jury room may well tell us a great deal about groups and, in particular, group decision-making. Such studies may also help us to decide whether trial by jury really should remain one of the cornerstones of a criminal justice system.

Juries have long held a fascination for legal scholars, not least for their occasionally unexpected verdicts. It is only relatively recently that psychologists have taken such a keen interest in these groups. Many of the findings from group studies in general have been applied to juries, but the distinctive and unique features of juries have in themselves been a source of psychological research. There can be few groups whose decisions have such far-reaching consequences for an individual as do those of juries. It may thus be assumed that juries' decision-making processes would have been explored extensively by those within the legal profession. It may come as a surprise to the outsider to learn that, in fact, the study of actual juries involved in real cases is extremely rare. Indeed most criminal justice systems which use trial by jury specifically ban researchers from studying juries involved in criminal cases. One British newspaper was recently prosecuted for interviewing ex-jury members after a long fraud case. In many countries jurors themselves are also barred from discussing the case with anyone other than fellow jury members.

It is for this reason that researchers have often used what are called *shadow juries* or *mock juries*. In the case of shadow juries, a researcher would pick a group of people to sit in the public gallery and shadow the real jury. They would listen to all the evidence and then retire to consider their verdict. Unlike the real jury, their discussions can be monitored closely by the researcher, and they can be asked questions about the case. In studies using mock juries, groups of people typically will read a transcript of a case, and then discuss the matter and reach a verdict. As with shadow juries, their every word can be recorded and analysed in an effort to understand decision-making processes. Such techniques may have disadvantages (the main one being that decisions made by these "juries" do not have consequences for the accused) but they do provide very useful insights. In particular they allow a researcher to vary one aspect of the case and then to test whether this makes a difference to the group's decision. We may for example want to know whether the sex of the accused makes a difference to whether he/she is likely to be found guilty. Groups of subjects could be given identical court transcripts to read and discuss, but for some groups the accused would be described as male, and for others female. If decisions were found to vary according to the sex of the offender, then further research could be carried out to establish why this occurred.

One further problem with using mock and shadow juries concerns selection. Whilst a researcher may be careful to choose a random sample to make up the alternative jury, such individuals will not go through the important procedure of challenges from prosecution or defence counsel. Recently this aspect of jury selection has attracted a great deal of attention and will now be considered.

Jury Selection

There has been a considerable amount of research in the area of jury selection (see Hastie, 1993; Wrightsman, 1991). In America, the process of selecting a jury can take many days, with each side allowed a large number of challenges to potential jurors. The original reasoning behind this idea was that it would be more likely to lead to a fair trial if the jury did not contain members who already held biased views about an issue or a certain case. However, the right to challenge has now assumed much greater significance, especially for the defence. The background, attitudes and opinions of all potential jurors are scrutinised carefully and a selection made on this basis. One can see how such a process might be important in eliminating those whose minds might already be made up about a case, but the technique is now used much more widely to select a jury who are likely to have certain attitudes – and who may thus be expected to decide on a case in a certain way. There is an assumption made that people from certain backgrounds, and with certain attitudes, will behave in predictable ways. Psychologists have long debated the question of whether one can predict behaviour from knowledge of a person's attitudes. Like many other aspects of human behaviour, the question is not so simple to answer. Whilst attitudes may well predispose people to behave in certain ways, there are a number of intervening variables which finally dictate what behaviour will be exhibited (see Ajzen & Fishbein, 1980). This aspect will be discussed later in the chapter.

Notwithstanding such difficulties, jury selection has become a very important strategy used by both sides involved in a trial. A case from the American literature provides a fascinating insight into how jury selection can be used. This case involved the trial of John Mitchell and Maurice Stans who were accused of conspiracy to impede a Securities and Exchange Commission investigation. This arose following the Watergate scandal. It is reported (see Wrightsman, 1991) that before their trial Mitchell and Stans instructed their assistants to approach some prominent psychologists to help with the selection of an "appropriate" jury. Interestingly, these researchers refused to help in this particular case, and so the defence next approached a public relations firm. This firm conducted a survey in order to give some guidance as to who would be the most sympathetic jury members. They were able to identify the sort of person who would be most biased (i.e. most likely to convict) in this particular case. The "worst" juror was portrayed as being a Liberal Democrat, well educated Jewish person who read the *New York Times* or *New York Post*. He/she would also be likely to watch television news read by Walter Cronkite (an influential media figure at the time), to be interested in political issues, and to be well informed about Watergate.

This case has been analysed in some depth by Zeisel and Diamond (1976), and their report makes interesting reading.

In the Mitchell and Stans case a panel of prospective jurors was selected which in the first instance included some 196 people! The judge in the trial immediately excused 85 of these people on hardship grounds (e.g. they had important jobs or were in poor health). On scientific grounds we may wish to question this decision as it immediately introduces possible biases in the selection procedure. Of those remaining, a further 38 were excused because they were thought to be highly prejudiced, or because they had a conflict of interest. The trial judge then excused a further 21 people so that a pool of 52 remained. Interestingly, the prosecution used only six of its eight possible challenges to jury members, and used none of the three possible challenges to "alternate" jury members. By contrast, the defence used all twenty of its permitted challenges in addition to three challenges to alternate jurors. The result of these challenges was that the defence succeeded in selecting a jury which consisted of individuals who closely matched their image of the ideal candidate. For example, whilst some 45% of the original sample of 196 people had some college education, only one (out of 12) of the final jury had. Whilst almost a third of the original sample was well informed about Watergate, only one of the final 12 could be so described.

In terms of assessing the effectiveness of jury challenges, this trial provides an interesting case study. The jury could hardly have been better in terms of meeting the criteria which the defence had specified, and so we may predict that they would be highly unlikely to find the defendants guilty. In fact the two accused were acquitted, but this by no means tells the whole story. Interviews with the jurors (something which would not normally be allowed in Britain) showed that initially eight of the twelve voted for conviction, and four for acquittal (see Arnold, 1974). Previous research has shown that when initial opinions are of this order, the defendant is highly likely to be convicted. For instance, Kalven and Zeisel (1966) showed that when there were originally between seven and eleven jury members who voted for conviction, a unanimous guilty verdict followed in some 86% of cases.

In the Mitchell and Stans trial there was a peculiar twist of fate which appeared to heavily influence the final outcome. This came in the form of an alternate juror named Andrew Choa. He was drafted onto the jury after one original member became ill several weeks into the trial. Interestingly, Choa was perhaps the least suitable person to be on the jury – at least as far as the defence was concerned. He was a well educated vice-president of a large bank who read the *New York Times* and was very well informed about Watergate. In fact the defence had originally asked for him to be removed from the panel because he was likely to be prejudiced. What neither the defence nor others involved in the case had realised, was that Choa was an ardent supporter of Richard Nixon. As such he worked hard to persuade the other jury members that they should acquit the two accused.

Choa turned out to be a very powerful persuader. He tried to convince others of his viewpoint partly by logical arguments, but he also ingratiated himself by doing things to make the other jurors' task less traumatic. For example he arranged a number of social activities to keep the jurors content while they spent many long nights in a hotel during the trial. Many years ago, Bales (1950) suggested that a group member who can combine task-oriented leadership with social-oriented leadership is the most powerful leader a group can have. Choa's powers of persuasion seemed to emulate those of Henry Fonda in the film *Twelve Angry Men*.

Perhaps this case is unusual and unrepresentative. Given that the majority of jurors had been picked because they were uninformed and not well educated, one very powerful figure may well have found it relatively easy to persuade others towards his viewpoint. The irony of the case is that a person who should in theory have been the wrong choice for the defence turned out to be its biggest ally. The case also demonstrates that selecting a favourable jury is by no means an exact science. Often personality variables can interact with group dynamics to produce an unanticipated outcome. This point is made forcibly by Kadane (1993) who says:

> "Some of the subtlety (and confusion) inherent in this selection process is revealed by the fact that attorneys from *opposing sides* of the case often *agree* on which jurors should be eliminated from the jury (for example, both defense and prosecution attorneys frequently attempt to eliminate highly educated jurors)." (Kadane, 1993, p. 233)

Kadane suggests that jury selection and decision-making are far more complex than was originally thought. He makes the point that it may be inappropriate to generalise from a small number of laboratory-based studies to all jury trials and all jurors.

The Mitchell and Stans trial raises a number of questions, not least of which is "was the jury selection fair?" It could hardly be said that the final jury was random nor was it representative of the wider society. Whilst each country (and in America each State) has its own rules as to how juries are selected, all try to ensure that no subgroup within society is under- or over-represented. However, Hyman and Tarant (1975) found that 92 federal courts in America used 92 different methods of jury selection. The issue of representativeness is a thorny problem which is hard to resolve even using legislation (see e.g. the American Jury Selection and Service Act, 1968). Such legislation did not prevent riots after the acquittal of three Los Angeles police officers following the Rodney King assault. The perception was that the jury in that case was neither representative nor fair, and this was the reason for the acquittal. In fact in the second trial which the officers faced, the case was moved to a different area partly so that a fairer (i.e. allegedly less prejudiced) jury could be selected. At the time of writing there is great debate about whether O.J. Simpson can ever receive a fair trial, given that almost everyone in America knows about the case, and will thus not approach any trial with an open mind.

The reason why criminal justice systems strive for representative juries is obvious. It is also hoped that the wider the spread of different people on the jury, the better. There is an assumption that the more heterogeneous the jury, the more likely it is that the verdict will be fair. In fact, this assumption does not rest on a great deal of empirical evidence. There are a few laboratory-based psychological studies which show that groups made up of people from different backgrounds, for example, are better at problem-solving (see Hoffman, 1965). However, it is questionable whether such findings are directly transferable to the complex processes involved in decision-making by juries.

A further problem of representativeness is the fact that in most countries, some people are excluded from jury service altogether (e.g. ex-convicts, the deaf, ex-police officers). In addition other groups can, and invariably do, claim exemption from jury duty. These include people such as doctors and dentists, but can also include mothers with young children. Whilst such exemptions are understandable, they can result in juries which bear little relation to the make-up of the wider community.

There is a second reason why juries should be seen as representative of the wider community, and this is to do with *perceived* fairness. A jury is supposed to reflect the norms of the society from which it is drawn. However, if a jury contains members of only one section of that society, then it will be perceived as unfair. For example, a jury comprised entirely of retired white males would not be perceived as fair by a young black female defendant. Devons (1978) gives an interesting example in this respect. He recounts a case where a defendant claimed that he came by an item of stolen property by "buying it off a bloke in a pub". This story comes second only to the explanation of "it fell off the back of a lorry" typically used by British thieves and receivers. However, Devons makes the point that for a middle-class jury, the very notion of buying anything from an unknown person in a pub was an alien concept to which they could not relate. A traditional male working-class jury may well have been better able to appreciate that the selling of goods in pubs is actually quite common. They may thus have reached a different conclusion about the guilt or innocence of the accused. Perhaps the fairness or otherwise of juries is an example of justice not only being done, but also being seen to be done.

Wrightsman makes a further interesting point concerning jury fairness. He says:

> "Not only do representative juries preserve the legitimacy of the legal process, but they also solidify the participants' positive feelings towards the process. If members of underrepresented groups – the poor, the elderly, black, youth – do not serve, they are more likely to develop hostile attitudes toward the legal process. Almost always, the net result of serving on a jury is an increased appreciation for the jury as a worthwhile institution." (Wrightsman, 1991, p. 255)

Whilst this is undoubtedly true, if juries are treated with the disdain which Devons (1978) describes, the experience may not be as positive as Wrightsman suggests. Devons describes how potential jurors are treated with little respect, are told nothing about what is going on, and are kept hanging around for long periods of time. They are also given very little guidance as to what is required of them. Such treatment may well produce resentment of the jury system by those treated so badly. There remains an interesting piece of research to be carried out to see whether potential jurors who are challenged and rejected – particularly if this happens more than once – suffer any loss of self-esteem, and become more hostile towards the jury system.

It is undoubtedly important that those prosecuting or defending an accused person be given the right to challenge potential jurors. Quite clearly a person who already holds deeply prejudiced views about an issue relevant to a case, should be excluded. But interestingly most jurors are rejected not because of prejudice, but for some other reason. Hans and Vidmar (1986) found in a survey in New Mexico (USA) that only about one in 20 jurors was rejected on the grounds of prejudice. In fact potential jurors can be rejected without any reason being given. The case of *Swain* v. *Alabama* (1965) established that each side may exclude a certain number of potential jurors "without a reason stated, without inquiry, and without being subject to the court's control". Some of these notions were overturned in another landmark decision, in the case of *Batson* v. *Kentucky* (1986). This decision stated that the prosecution (but not the defence) was under an obligation not to discriminate, at least on the grounds of race. Thus, in the case of a black defendant, the prosecution could not object to all potential jurors who were black, even if they believed that they would be prejudiced in favour of the defendant.

As pointed out earlier, the exact number of pre-emptory challenges allowed varies from area to area, and country to country. In America it also varies by State, and according to whether it is a civil or criminal case, and, in the latter case, how serious the crime is (see Wrightsman, 1991, p. 259).

Whilst eliminating the deeply prejudiced juror is a laudable aim for the defence, challenges can be made in the hope that the jury eventually selected will be prejudiced in favour of the defendant. In other words, in the name of establishing fairness, a jury may eventually comprise people who are biased systematically and may thus not be impartial. Trial lawyers base their choices on what may be called implicit personality theories, and rely heavily on stereotyped views of certain groups of people. We have already seen in Chapters 1 and 3 how stereotypes can affect the way that all people, including police officers and lawyers, view others in the world. This is pointedly illustrated in the following passage taken from the famous lawyer Clarence Darrow:

> "I try to get a jury with little education but with much human emotion. The Irish are always the best jurymen for the defence. I don't want a Scotchman, for he has too little human feeling. I don't want a Scandinavian, for he has too strong a respect for law as law. In general I don't want a religious person, for he believes in sin and punishment. The defence should avoid rich men who have a high regard for the law, as they make and use it. The smug and ultra-respectable think they are the guardians of society, and they believe the law is for them." (Quoted in Sutherland & Cressey, 1974)

It is hard to imagine how such a brief passage could contain any more stereotypes than this one does! Clearly Darrow had a large number of implicit personality theories, or prejudices, which guided his choice of potential jurors. The question remains, however, as to whether there is any truth at all in assumptions about how certain types of potential jurors will decide a case. We have already made the point that predicting behaviour from knowledge of such factors as personality or attitudes is not as simple a process as might be assumed.

Demographic and personality variables can affect ultimate decisions, but not in a straightforward or predictable way. For example, Penrod (1979) found that personal variables interacted with the type of trial in producing certain decisions. Similarly Simon (1967) found that the gender of jurors had some influence on decisions, though this depended on the type of crime. In Simon's research, women showed more leniency than men towards a defendant charged with housebreaking, yet were more punitive than men when the charge was one of incest. Where gender differences are found, this is often associated with the level of activity by each jury member within the discussions. For example men are much more likely to be elected foreman (and thus control the discussion) and are also more likely to be perceived as experts in such matters (see Strodtbeck & Lipinski, 1985). High socio-economic status is also associated with more of a tendency to convict defendants, though again this can interact with status within the jury. Although some slight differences have been found in respect of ethnic origin, it is difficult to disentangle this effect from other variables such as socio-economic status. There are also of course interactions, depending on the type of crime and the race of the defendant. These mean that it is inappropriate to make any generalisations as to whether jurors of one race are more lenient than those of another.

If demographic variables are not particularly useful in allowing us to make predictions, then what about personality variables? Some factors have been identified, but again no simple conclusions can be drawn based on personality alone. In some cases, the balance of evidence may be so strong in one side's favour that jurors' personality characteristics will be irrelevant to the eventual outcome. Having said that, some factors which appear to be at least relevant are as follows:

1 *Authoritarianism.* In general research has shown that jurors with high authoritarianism are more likely to convict than those with low scores on this personality measure. In fact of all the personality measures tested, authoritarianism is the best predictor of verdicts. Even here though we must treat such findings with caution. For instance, if the defendant is an authority figure himself (e.g. a police officer), a conviction is less likely by those with high levels of authoritarianism (Wrightsman, 1991).

2 *Internal vs external locus of control.* This is a personality dimension which measures the extent to which people believe that their lives are internally controlled (e.g. through skill and effort) or externally controlled (e.g. by luck, or pressure from others). Those who can be classified as predominantly internal are more likely to convict, especially if a defendant's actions are ambiguous.

3 *Belief in a just world.* Lerner (1970) established this as another dimension of personality. It is concerned with the extent to which people believe that there is justice in the world, and that people tend to get what they deserve. There are two consequences of such a view. Firstly, "innocent" victims may be seen as somehow having contributed to their own victimisation. (This is often seen in cases of rape.) Secondly, people who believe in a just world may be more punitive towards an arrogant defendant. (Saying, perhaps, "I'll teach him to be so cocky".)

We can thus see that whilst personality and demographic variables are important in affecting jurors' decisions, knowledge of such factors does not allow lawyers, or indeed psychologists, to make totally accurate predictions at the individual level. Where such factors may be important, however, is when considering the make-up of the jury as a whole. If a defence counsel can choose one or two jury members who are both sympathetic to their client and have strong personalities, then this may be an effective strategy.

There are of course a number of other factors from psychological research which are relevant when considering jury decisions (see Hastie, 1993). Some of these have been covered in a previous volume (see Ainsworth & Pease, 1987) but more recently other new factors have emerged.

Memory and Jurors

There is an assumption by the criminal justice system that when a jury is sworn in, its members will listen to each and every word in the case, remember it, and then reach an appropriate conclusion. It has been clearly established through decades of psychological research on memory processes that humans are simply not capable of such feats. Memory is selective, incomplete, and unreliable. People are simply not capable of holding massive amounts of complex information presented over weeks of a trial. For this reason, deliberations in the jury room do not appear to be a careful sifting through of each piece of evidence. Rather snippets and impressions will be recalled and discussed (see Blanck, 1993). A defendant's appearance and demeanour might be remembered whilst his/her exact words might not.

From a psychologist's viewpoint it does seem amazing that jurors are not routinely offered pen and paper to take notes; are given little or no opportunity to reread statements made by the parties in a case; are given no opportunity to ask questions of a witness or a defendant, even if this is merely to clarify a point; are expected to suspend judgement on a case until all the evidence is heard; are assumed to be able to erase from their memory a piece of information which they have heard, but which the judge has ruled inadmissible; are assumed not to be subject to the same sorts of group pressures found in all other groups.

Wrightsman (1991) puts the problem thus:

> "Deliberating juries are assumed to be decision-making groups that produce objective and fact-based outcomes. Generally ignored is the possibility that they are subject to the group pressures or irrational impulses that operate in some other groups when they make

decisions. The courts disregard the likelihood that the content of jury deliberations may be on other matters (personal anecdotes, opinions about the trial attorneys, and so on) than the evidence and the law." (Wrightsman, 1991, p. 290)

It thus seems obvious that juries will not always make appropriate or indeed correct decisions as to guilt or innocence in any particular case. Psychologists can and already do make suggestions as to how the jury's task could be made easier and perhaps more accurate. But until such time as researchers are allowed routinely to monitor jury room deliberations (and thus demonstrate unequivocally that mistakes can be and are made), it is unlikely that the legal establishment will acknowledge the need for any change to the jury system. In these days of so-called open government and public accountability, the jury must be one of the few institutions left which has such faith put in its workings, and which is kept so hidden from public scrutiny.

SUMMARY

This chapter has looked at the way in which membership of groups allows people to form a sense of identity and to improve self-esteem. However, it has been shown that membership of any group tends to produce in-group pride and engender hostility towards others who are not members of that group. We have seen how competition can in itself produce suspicion, prejudice, hostility and even aggression. We have also seen how psychological research provides interesting insights into the workings of some groups; in this case juries.

FURTHER READING

Baron, R. A. & Byrne, D. (1994) *Social Psychology: Understanding Human Interaction* (7th edn), Chapters 9, 12 & 14. Boston: Allyn & Bacon.

Hastie, R. (1993) *Inside the Juror: the Psychology of Juror Decision Making.* Cambridge: Cambridge University Press.

Stroebe, W. & Hewstone, M. (1992) *European Review of Social Psychology*, vol. 3. Chichester: Wiley.

Wrightsman, L. S. (1991) *Psychology and the Legal System* (2nd edn). Pacific Grove, CA: Brookes/Cole.

CHAPTER 5

Violence and Reaction

"They don't think about the impact of injuries. We've had blokes here – one on the other shift was a long time sick; a back injury just wouldn't let go. He'd been hit with a scaffold pole on the back of the head . . . They noticed after Toxteth that people were going sick with backache. Then they realised how many had been injured. After I was beaten up, every time I put my head back my nose hurt. Now, I won't get as close as I used to. When a bloke starts thrashing out with an umbrella, I just grab hold of him and put him on the deck, because I'm scared of getting my nose broken again. You can't help that sort of reaction." (Metropolitan PC quoted in Graef, 1990, p. 225)

Most modern societies are concerned with levels of violence and aggression. Any increase in such levels is particularly worrying for the police service – not only will police officers have to deal with a larger number of violent crimes, but they will also feel more vulnerable to attacks upon themselves. Whilst the level of violence varies significantly from culture to culture, most societies see violence as a threat and work towards reducing such levels. As we will see in Chapter 11 there is currently a perception that violence in society is becoming much worse. In this chapter we will review a large amount of literature on the causes of violence and aggression. We will consider whether it is appropriate to see aggression as an in-built human trait, or whether it is better understood as an externally stimulated drive. We will also consider whether any of the theories allow us to offer advice as to how aggression might be reduced.

The public believe that crime is rising incessantly, though in most countries the fear of crime is greater than its actual level might justify. The media bombard the public with images of a violent society, and lead people to believe that life is much more dangerous than it was only a few years ago (see Chapter 11). However, as we discussed in Chapter 1, the image portrayed by the media may not be a true reflection of the actuality. There is no doubt that violence is a very real problem in most modern societies, yet fears of such violence must be kept in perspective. One can understand why the police warn the public "not to go out until this or that offender is caught" – but such warnings further intensify the fears of an already worried population. In Britain at least it remains the case that one is much more likely to lose one's life as a result of a traffic accident than at the hands of an unknown violent assailant. Yet it is unheard of for the police service to warn the public "not to go out on the roads until this hit and run driver is caught". Violent crime is and remains a source of great concern for both the general public and the police service.

Throughout this chapter we will be discussing both aggression and violence. In everyday language the two words are often used inter-changeably, though for most psychologists the two are perceived slightly differently. As violence is even more difficult to define than aggression, many researchers have preferred to concentrate on the latter.

Like many other areas studied by psychologists, violence and aggression are terms which are easily understood, yet prove much more difficult to define accurately. Indeed researchers often assume that aggression means different things, and consequently their experiments investigate different aspects. Geen (1990), who has recently reviewed a great deal of psychological literature on aggression, suggests that a definition which provides at least a working basis can be summarised in three points.

1 Aggression consists of the delivery of noxious stimuli by one organism to another.
2 The noxious stimuli are delivered with the intent to harm the victim.
3 The aggressor expects that the noxious stimuli will have their intended effect. (Geen, 1990, pp. 3–4)

Even Geen admits that this definition may be flawed as it may not cover every possible scenario subsumed under the heading "aggression". Many social psychologists prefer the simpler definition that aggression is "any behaviour directed toward harming another living thing". In this definition, intention is seen as an important element, as is harm, though this may not necessarily be physical harm. The word violence also means different things to different people – the same act committed by different people may be defined as violence in one setting, but simply "fooling around" in another (see Chapter 4). These problems of definition must be borne in mind in the remainder of this chapter.

PSYCHOLOGICAL THEORIES OF AGGRESSION

As concern over violence and aggression has grown (see Chapter 11) so too has the amount of research trying to understand the reasons for its occurrence. There are a large number of different explanations which have been offered by psychologists and we will here consider some of the more prominent examples.

Inborn Urges or Instincts

It is interesting to speculate on whether humans are *naturally* violent and aggressive – in other words whether such tendencies are inborn. A look through any history book would tend to support such a view – no other animal on the earth inflicts such harm on members of its own species as do humans. We may be fearful of sharks and tigers yet even such animals' aggression pales into insignificance compared with the human race. Between 1820 and 1945 some 59 million people died at the hands of their fellow human beings. Since the beginning of this century almost a million American civilians have died as a result of criminal acts.

Such facts led Sigmund Freud and others to suggest that violence and aggression are in-built factors in all humans. Freud suggested that: "The tendency to aggression is an innate, independent instinctual disposition" (Freud, 1930, p. 102). Freud believed that humans have a death wish or instinct (labelled "thanatos") which is initially aimed at self-destruction. However, this urge is soon redirected in the form of violence towards others. Freud saw this as an inevitable feature of the human make-up and one which society could perhaps control, but could never eliminate. In fact Freud saw society's job as simply to channel the in-built aggressive impulses into socially accepted forms of release. Obvious examples would be violent sports such as boxing or American football, though Freud went so far as to suggest that countries may even go to war as one way of releasing built-up aggressive impulses. Freud believed that unless the forces built up by these innate powerful drives were released, they would explode in a totally uncontrolled and unpredictable way. Freud also suggested that in some cases the aggression may be directed inwards and lead to self-destructive behaviour.

Many psychologists are today sceptical of Freud's views, though there may be merit in some of what he said. The problem which modern psychologists have with Freud's views is that the methodology from which he developed his theories was somewhat suspect, and he did not carry out the carefully controlled experiments favoured by modern researchers. However, it is true that society does sanction certain forms of ritualised violence (e.g. boxing, karate, rugby, American football) and allows those who commit such violence within the rules to escape punishment. Indeed it is somewhat anomalous that a society that shows such great concern for levels of violence, offers prestige, status and money to those who are the most violent (for example the world heavyweight boxing champion). Aggression in many sports is encouraged, yet sportsmen and women are punished if their aggression spills over to other parts of their life or goes beyond the rules laid down for the game. It is not uncommon for young people who have committed violent crime to be diverted onto schemes where they can "work off their aggression" in less harmful, or at least socially approved ways.

A similar view of the cause of aggression was put forward by the ethologist Konrad Lorenz (1966). He believed that humans, like many other animals, have an in-built fighting instinct. This is necessary to guarantee the survival of the species, and is evoked whenever it seems appropriate. Ethologists believe that there are certain "releasers" which stimulate the aggressive drive. Thus an apparent attack upon oneself is responded to by a resort to aggression. Lorenz's views are interesting and may explain why so many altercations start with such phrases as "What are you looking at?" For most animals, a stare is a challenge, and humans may respond similarly to other animals to such "threats". Similarly, a person who bumps into another in a crowded pub may be challenged to a fight as this invasion of personal space is seen as potentially threatening. Men fighting over a woman may also be seen as a throwback to a more primitive time, when the choice of an appropriate mate was important for the survival of the family (see also Dawkins, 1986, for an alternative explanation). Lorenz believes that humans are more violent to their own species than other animals are, because they have not developed appropriate rituals of submission and retreat. It is also true that humans have at their disposal a very large range of potentially lethal weapons.

A somewhat similar view of aggression has been put forward by Wilson (1975) who sought to explain aggression in terms of sociobiology. Wilson believes that humans are aggressive because this is appropriate for the survival of the species. He believes that aggression served a purpose in ensuring that the fittest of the species survived while the weaker ones perished. The more aggressive members of the race are thus able to acquire more resources, to defend these, and to protect their relatives. Thus aggression is seen as almost inevitable, as a way of ensuring that only the strong survive. Perhaps these views are the origins of such expressions as "It's a jungle out there".

Whilst these theories are interesting, they are also worrying. They all suggest that violence and aggression are inevitable in humans, and society can merely try to limit the level or the circumstances of such behaviour. They may also seem depressing for the police officer, as they suggest that the police can at best try to control the amount of violence, but will always be fighting a losing battle. However, none of the theories can fully explain violence and aggression in society. For example, they find it difficult to explain different levels of violence in different societies, or different levels in the same society at different times. Freud's pessimistic view of "human nature" does not adequately explain why the vast majority of people are not violent and aggressive most of the time. Nor does it explain why men are more violent than women in most societies. Whilst the ethology studies of other animals are interesting, it is not always easy to prove that humans exhibit identical behaviour. Inherited dispositions may play some part in the production of aggression (see Rushton, Fulker, Neale, Nias & Eysenck, 1986) though the exact nature of these influences is difficult to prove.

Frustration and Aggression

A somewhat different view of aggression was put forward by Dollard and his colleagues in the late 1930s (Dollard, Doob, Miller, Mowrer & Sears, 1939). Dollard believed that frustration (i.e. the blocking of the achievement of some goal) inevitably led to the production of aggression. Similarly he believed that any aggressive act could be explained by the fact that the person committing such an act had recently experienced some degree of frustration. Taken at face value, this theory does seem to have some merit. People do get angry when they are prevented from doing what they intended to do. For example the person who is stuck in a traffic jam may curse and swear and may well threaten the source of the hold-up or even other drivers. The man who is refused a drink because the bar has closed may well lash out in a violent way. The passenger whose flight is delayed because of a bomb scare may verbally abuse airline staff. The person who enters a public phone booth only to find that the phone is out of order may well slam down the receiver and break it.

It is easy to see why such a view attracted great attention when it was first proposed. However, like many all-embracing theories, it turned out to be rather too simplistic. Whilst frustration *may* lead to aggression, this is only one of a number of possible reactions. For example, frustrated people may simply give up and resign themselves to the fact that they are not able to do what they want. Others may see the frustration as a challenge, and explore innovative ways of overcoming the problem. It is also too simplistic to assume that all aggression can be accounted for by reference to frustration. Frustration may be one reason why people become aggressive, but there are many other possible causes. The local gang leader may become violent in order to gain prestige and respect, rather than because he has been frustrated.

One reason why frustration leads to aggression on some occasions but not others, is that aggression may be an effective means of removing the frustration in certain cases. The football fan who is locked out of the game may threaten the steward, knowing that such threats may intimidate the other and thus remove the frustration. However, in other circumstances aggression may achieve nothing, and so would not be used. Aggression is also more likely when the frustration is intense rather than when it is relatively minor.

Whilst the frustration–aggression hypothesis may be flawed in its original form, some recent revisions make it somewhat more tenable. It has now been established that the more severe and arbitrary the frustration, the more likely it is to lead to aggression. There is, however, an important intervening variable, i.e. anger. It would appear that only when frustration leads to anger is it likely to produce aggression. In a similar vein, Berkowitz (1989) has suggested that frustration may simply produce increased arousal and thus a readiness for aggressive acts. Some people may then become aggressive, while others may not. An individual's personality and his/her previously learned behaviour may act as intervening variables here. Berkowitz believes that Dollard's original theory could be more accurately described as a theory of frustration–arousal–aggression.

According to Berkowitz, the presence of aggressive cues in the environment may further trigger aggressive acts. Although such cues are not always necessary, their presence increases the likelihood of aggression. Berkowitz has thus argued that the presence of weapons may elicit aggressive responses in some people (though we must acknowledge that the experiment on which such a view was based has been criticised on methodological grounds). Berkowitz's view is expressed thus: "Guns not only permit violence, they can stimulate it as well. The finger pulls the trigger, but the trigger may also be pulling the finger" (Berkowitz, 1968, p. 22).

It would perhaps be too simplistic to suggest that the massive difference in homicide rates between Britain and the USA can be accounted for by the presence of more aggressive cues (i.e. more guns) in the latter country. However, at a time when the British police service is considering arming all officers, such theories should be borne in mind. Legislators in America are also finally acknowledging the terrible toll which guns inflict on that country's young people.

One further point from Berkowitz's work is worthy of mention here. In one study, he found that people who had been angered by another were more likely to aggress against that person if he was said to be interested in boxing (as opposed to someone who was not). One wonders whether this partly explains why some people are more likely to be involved in fights than others – people with reputations are often sought out by others wishing to prove themselves. Police officers dealing with known "hard men" may also react in a more aggressive way than when dealing with others.

Social Learning Theories

As psychologists started to question the view that aggression is innate and to question whether frustration could really offer a complete explanation, a set of ideas began to emerge which were based on a somewhat different premise. Rather than assuming that humans are "naturally" aggressive, or that some inner drive leads them to behave in aggressive ways, this view held that aggression is a *learned* behaviour. Just like many other social behaviours, aggression is thus seen as originating from, for example, children watching the behaviour of others, and then imitating it. This phenomenon is known as observational learning or modelling. Much of the early work on this theory came from experiments by Bandura (1973). In his classic study, groups of small children watched an adult playing with a large inflatable Bobo doll. Half of the children saw the adult playing in a gentle way, whilst the others saw him behaving in a violent way – such as by hitting the doll. The children were then allowed to play with the doll themselves, and their behaviour was observed.

Bandura found that the children who had watched the aggressive model were consistently more aggressive than those who had watched a non-aggressive model. They were also more aggressive than members of a control group who had not watched either model. While some researchers have questioned the relevance of these studies to "real life" aggression, Bandura maintains that much aggressive behaviour can be explained by reference to learning principles. He does however make the important distinction between the *learning* of a response and the *performance* of such a response. When watching the attacks, children learn this behaviour and see it as appropriate in certain circumstances. However, in the future they may choose to exhibit such behaviour, or may decide that it is not appropriate at that time (for example if a strict parent is watching them). In this case, a second element comes into play, i.e. whether the behaviour, once exhibited, is rewarded or punished. The behaviourist school of psychology advocates that any behaviour which is reinforced will be more likely to be repeated, whereas a behaviour that is ignored (or in some cases punished) will be much less likely to be exhibited. Thus some parents will reward their child for behaving in an aggressive way, while others will try their best to eliminate such responses, by disapproval or punishment. Thus aggressive acts by boys are more likely to be accepted (or even rewarded) than the same acts committed by girls.

Television, Videos and Violence

If social learning theory is correct in seeing aggression as a learnt response, then it is understandable that people will question whether behaviours seen on television or on videos will be imitated by viewers. Debates on this issue tend to arouse great passion, with frequent calls to "clean up television" or to ban so-called "video nasties". Such calls become even more vociferous following particularly disturbing crimes, as after the Hungerford massacre in England. In this instance Michael Ryan went around the town of Hungerford shooting a number of victims almost at random (see Canter, 1994, pp. 191–193). In seeking to explain such frightening behaviour, the press latched onto the fact that the perpetrator was dressed like Rambo (a violent fictional film character played by Sylvester Stallone) and had apparently enjoyed watching the video of Rambo's exploits. It is easy to see why people adopt such ideas to explain the apparently inexplicable, though such an explanation leads one to wonder why all the other people who had watched this video did not choose to emulate Rambo's behaviour.

Another recent case in Britain involved the murder of a toddler called James Bulger by two young boys. Like the Hungerford massacre, this crime shocked the nation (see Chapter 11). The trial judge drew attention to the fact that at least one of the boys had had access to violent videos, and that this might explain the awful crime. It is not surprising that the debate over violent television and videos becomes so heated when such simplistic explanations are offered for horrendous acts.

In the academic literature there have been literally hundreds of research studies examining the apparent link between screen violence and violence in society. It is not easy for the interested reader to plough through the massive amount of data that has been generated and reach a firm conclusion. Some studies appear to demonstrate that there is a link, whilst others seem to suggest that there is not. A number of studies have even concluded that watching screen violence has a beneficial effect, through the process of catharsis. From the present author's reading of the literature it would seem reasonable to draw the following conclusions.

- Young children are more likely to be influenced by behaviour seen on screen than are adults (see Belson, 1979).
- Programmes or videos which show an aggressor being rewarded for his/her aggression may be more likely to be emulated than actions for which an aggressor is punished.
- Whilst most people do not imitate actions seen on screen (see Milgram, 1977), if large amounts of violence are observed this can have a disinhibiting effect. There is a danger that violence becomes

normalised and no longer arouses concern in those watching. Normalisation also means that each individual will be less restrained when contemplating using violence him/herself.

- Whilst watching violence may not in itself produce violent behaviour in the viewer, it may suggest new, innovative ways of inflicting pain or injury (see e.g. Ainsworth & Armitage, 1989).
- Certain kinds of screen violence committed by different people on screen may have more of an effect than others. For example violence carried out by "the good guys" appears to be more dangerous than the same act committed by villains.
- Some personality types will be affected more than others, and may be more likely to imitate actions seen on screen.

The issue of screen violence will not go away so long as society is concerned with the level of violence. However, despite the massive amount of research that has been generated, it is still not possible to make predictions about whether a certain programme will make an individual violent. Each society needs to decide for itself where to draw the line between freedom of expression and protection of its members. For example, should the authorities ban a video that is enjoyed harmlessly by 10 million people, but which affects just one person negatively? There was violence in society long before television, videos, or computer games became available, so it is perhaps inappropriate and simplistic to blame all society's problems on one such factor. It is also true that some videos (e.g. snuff movies) evoke such revulsion that most members of society would want them banned.

Individual Differences and Aggression

Whilst the previous theories go some way towards offering an understanding of aggression, they cannot fully explain why some people are more aggressive than others. We have already mentioned the fact that genetics may play some part, though it would be appropriate here to examine some relevant research in this field. In one study by Rushton et al (1986) some 500 pairs of identical and non-identical twins were given personality tests. It was found that the pairs of identical twins (who, as the name implies, were genetically identical) had much more similar personalities than did the pairs of non-identical twins. In particular, levels of aggression and assertiveness were considerably more alike in pairs of identical rather than in non-identical twins. This suggests that at least some aspects of aggressive behaviour have a genetic component.

One theory which came to prominence in the 1960s was that of the XYY genotype. The sex of a child is determined by the presence of X and

Y chromosomes in the embryo. Females are XX whilst males are XY. As work on genetics gained momentum in the 1960s, a number of genetic defects were identified. We now know for example that Down's syndrome is caused by a defect of the 21st pair of chromosomes. One other defect that was identified was that some men, rather than having XY chromosomes, were in fact XYY. In other words, they had an extra male chromosome. Given that males are generally more aggressive than females, it was suggested that any male who possessed an extra Y chromosome might well be twice as aggressive as a normal male. Early research suggested that some people who had been convicted of particularly violent crimes were indeed XYY.

As with many other simplistic theories of criminal behaviour this evidence was seen as a great breakthrough and provided a neat scientific explanation for why some people commit violent acts. Unfortunately subsequent research has not been able to prove that there is a direct link between XYY chromosomes and aggression (see Witkin, Mednick, Schulsinger et al, 1976). There is a correlation between low intelligence and XYY types, and it has been suggested that this is why such people may be more likely to end up in institutions. Although the theory has now been discredited to a large extent, it did raise a number of interesting issues. For example, if it were true that XYY genotypes were all potential killers, should such foetuses be aborted, or if born, should such people be locked up even before they commit any crime?

As psychologists and biologists discover more about the physiology involved in aggression, they have also begun to examine the brain activities of particularly violent people. It may not be appropriate to examine the exact biology involved in the emotion of aggression here, but one piece of research is particularly interesting and relevant. Pontius (1984) carried out an intensive study of eight violent male patients. In each case, some event had triggered what was described as a "seizure-like" rage reaction that culminated in particularly violent outbursts. Pontius concluded that the outburst could be explained by reference to a malfunction in a particular part of the brain; in this case the frontal lobe of the cortex. For most people the cortex exerts control over emotions (e.g. rage and anger) which arise from the limbic system. This is why when most people start to get angry, they can control the emotion to some extent, and do not give full vent to their feelings. People who have been angered by another may well *say* "I could have killed him" but know that in reality they are highly unlikely to do this, and will control their reaction. However, for Pontius's subjects, some event often triggered a memory of a previous violent reaction, and the person was unable to control the violent outburst.

Although Pontius's study may be specific to a small number of men, there is further evidence that neurological disorders may account for some forms of aggression. For example, Lewis, Moy, Jackson et al (1985) found that, because of neurological impairment, some men are much more likely to become violent when provoked than are others. These men tended to act quickly and brutally when they felt threatened, leading to quite vicious attacks. On a slightly different tack, it has also been suggested that high testosterone levels may be associated with increased levels of aggression. For example, Dabbs, Frady, Carr and Besch (1987) found that testosterone levels were correlated with the levels of violence that had been used by their sample of offenders. Olweus, Mattsson, Schalling and Low (1980) have suggested that high testosterone levels may be associated with a predisposition to aggress – but that other provocations must be encountered before this disposition produces an aggressive response. These findings have also led researchers to examine whether the taking of anabolic steroids leads to more aggressive behaviour. There is some evidence that this may well be the case, though again there are a number of intervening variables. All the studies mentioned in this section point to the role played by biochemical processes in the production of aggression. As we understand more about the brain's structure and chemistry, it is likely that there will be many more such factors identified by researchers. Having said that, it is not so clear what we should do with such information. Should we for instance test men's testosterone levels and prescribe compulsory medication to those whose levels are high?

It is also clear that personality variables account for some of the differences in rates of aggression. Hans Toch (1969) has suggested that many violent offenders are guided by "violence-prone premises" or assumptions. His work suggested that for such people, apparently innocuous interactions often resulted in violent outcomes. Whilst most people would handle minor frustrations in a constructive or resigned way, many of Toch's sample saw almost all encounters as potentially threatening. Toch suggested that there was not one type of violent man but several, i.e.:

1 *Self-image compensators*. These were people who had a very low opinion of themselves and tried to compensate for this by appearing strong and by resorting to violence.
2 *Bullies or sadists*. This group actually did enjoy inflicting pain or injury on others and in watching their victims' suffering. They always sought to gain the upper hand, e.g. by being armed.
3 *Paranoids*. These were men who were deeply suspicious of others in the world and sought to attack other people even before any major

provocation. This is what has become popularly known as "Getting your retaliation in first"!

Although Toch identified a number of distinct types of violent men he suggests that in some cases these "types" result from predominant cultural values which existed in America at the time. Many Americans do see their society as threatening and potentially harmful, with trouble lurking around every corner. (This is beautifully described in the Ry Cooder song *Down in Hollywood*.) This is not far removed from the behaviour of the paranoids identified by Toch amongst his prison population. The notion that cultures can produce their own distinct type of violent offender will be taken up in the next section.

Cultures, Subcultures and Aggression

The previous studies have pointed to individual differences in the rates of aggression. However, it is also true that some cultures as a whole show higher levels of violence than others. One need only compare crime figures for Britain with the USA to be reminded of this. Whilst such differences have been examined by sociologists and social anthropologists, it is important that such factors should also be considered by psychologists. Geen (1990) makes this point:

> "Most societies sanction violence to some degree. . . . The espousal of violence within the norms and cultural values of a society serves as still another background variable that renders aggression more or less probable when suitable provocations occur." (Geen, 1990, p. 24)

Researchers such as Mulvihill and Tumin (1969) have shown how American culture facilitates different attitudes towards violence than in other countries. The fact that the American constitution gives its citizens the right to bear arms also affects the way in which American citizens view violence.

Not only do different cultures have different levels of violence, but within each society different subcultures also vary in their expectations and actions (see e.g. Wolfgang & Ferracuti, 1967). There are many reasons why this should be. As an example, historical precedent might dictate that residents in one area take on a tough outlook, and defend themselves and their property with as much force as they feel is necessary. Subcultural norms are perhaps best illustrated in neighbourhood gangs, although even here the average level of violence varies from society to society.

Both sociologists and psychologists have studied gangs extensively and have identified a number of factors associated with levels of violence found therein. Klein (1969) suggested that such groups are most likely to form in areas where there is a great deal of social change taking place. Inner city areas in the process of redevelopment are particularly likely to produce neighbourhood gangs. It is suggested that as the normal social order breaks down, so gangs are formed which introduce new and often more violent norms of behaviour. For the young person feeling alienated from society at large, the gang provides a ready and immediate source of identity and prestige. Masculinity and toughness are often the cornerstones of such groups, so it is not surprising that violence becomes one of the primary forms of expression.

Violence in the Home

Whilst most members of the public may live in fear of an attack by a stranger, statistics show that the home can be a much more dangerous place than a dark alley. People are much more likely to die at the hands of an acquaintance or partner, than at the hands of an unknown aggressor. The close family group may provide security for family members, but can also produce irritation, conflict, and in some cases, violence. Only relatively recently have police forces in Britain been inclined to take assaults in the home seriously (see Bourlet, 1990).

The home can also be the place where norms of behaviour are established, especially in growing children. For example, parents who use physical violence in the home may simply teach a child that force is an appropriate means of resolving conflicts or settling disputes (see Patterson, 1980). There is further evidence that different child-rearing styles can produce different levels of aggression (see e.g. Loeber & Dishion, 1984). Straus (1980) has identified a number of factors which are associated with aggression in children. These include the use of physical punishment, child abuse, spouse beating, and the encouragement of aggression as normal behaviour. These factors, especially if accompanied by a high level of stress and conflict in the home, tend to produce much greater levels of aggression in growing children.

ENVIRONMENTAL FACTORS AND AGGRESSION

We have so far considered predominantly internal factors as explanations for aggression. However, in recent years psychologists have started to pay more attention to factors in the environment which may have an effect on levels of aggression. This shift of focus is important as it is often easier to modify an environment than to change ingrained modes of behaviour.

Psychology has traditionally been a science of the individual, but there is now more recognition of the fact that all behaviour is a function of the interaction between the person and their environment. Even some of the most violent people described earlier are not violent all the time. Invariably there is some factor in the environment which triggers a violent outburst, and it is this fact that has led to a more detailed examination of the external factors which might stimulate violence and aggression.

Many different environmental stressors have been identified by social and environmental psychologists. One need think only of such factors as noise, overcrowding, excessive heat, and air pollution, to realise that such conditions can often affect humans in a negative way.

Mueller (1983) has pointed out that environmental stressors produce four effects, each of which could be linked with increased levels of aggression. These are:

1 Increased arousal.
2 Stimulus overload.
3 Interference with ongoing behaviour.
4 Negative affect or mood.

Increased arousal means that people are more likely to become angry, and subsequently more aggressive. An overload of stimuli means that humans find it difficult to cope with incoming information in a calm, relaxed or objective way. They are thus more likely to snap and become abusive or aggressive towards others. Interference with ongoing behaviour may be seen as another way of defining frustration which, as we have seen earlier, may produce aggression. Negative mood means that people are more likely to be irritable and to overreact, perhaps in an aggressive way. We will next consider some of the environmental factors which have been found to affect aggression.

Noise

As more and more people crowd into large cities, it is inevitable that noise levels will rise. Factors such as transportation noise, neighbours' music, construction work, can all have a wearing effect on even the most tolerant. The main problem with such sounds is that they are uncontrollable, often unpredictable, and so make people feel helpless. Noise can be very stressful, though some people are more affected than others. Because noise is seen as a stressor, it would be reasonable to assume that it would lead to increased levels of aggression. Research evidence seems to suggest that it does, but only in certain circumstances.

Firstly, it appears that noise intensifies whatever feelings are being experienced at the time. Thus if a person is angry and prone to aggression, or is already living in a difficult environment, noise may simply intensify these feelings of dissatisfaction and produce aggressive behaviour in the individual. Secondly, noise may decrease an individual's ability to cope with frustration. Thus a person who is experiencing frustration anyway, will be even more likely to become aggressive when he/she is also living or working in a noisy environment. Noise may have an immediate effect on the individual, but it can also have a cumulative influence. The longer an individual is subjected to a noisy environment, the less able that person is to cope with other concerns. The police officer called to deal with a citizen's complaint about noise may well feel that the person is overreacting to something trivial. The officer may not immediately realise that this call for help could well stem from months or even years of exposure to unwanted sound. Disputes between neighbours can reach terrifying levels of animosity, and often stem from a long history of noise complaints.

Heat

It has for some time been assumed that heat can increase levels of aggression. One need only think of how many riots occur in the summer, compared with the winter, to conclude that temperature may well be correlated with aggression. Indeed the weather in general can have quite dramatic effects on behaviour – a sudden torrential downpour may have far more effect on an angry crowd than any number of water cannon and plastic bullets. Analyses of crime reports also suggest that crimes of violence are more common during hot weather, though it may not be appropriate to assume that there is a simple causal link here (see Anderson & Anderson, 1984).

Laboratory-based studies suggest that the relationship between heat and aggression is not as simple and straightforward as might be assumed. Studies have sometimes produced contradictory findings; whilst many showed increased levels of aggression with increased temperatures, others showed no such effect. Some researchers have even suggested that increased temperatures lead to decreased levels of aggression. It would appear that, at least in the case of laboratory-based studies, heat may affect levels of aggression, but not necessarily in a straightforward linear fashion. In some cases there appears to be a curvilinear effect, i.e. levels of aggression do increase in line with increased temperatures, but only up to a certain point. Once a critical point is reached, levels of aggression start to decline again. This could be one explanation as to why the very hottest days, or the hottest geographical areas, do not necessarily produce the highest levels of aggression.

One explanation for the sometimes contradictory findings has been provided by Baron and Bell (1975). They suggest that heat, along with other stressors, leads to increased negative affect: i.e. it produces a negative mood. During relatively modest increases in temperature, a person may well react by being aggressive towards others. However, as the temperature increases more, the heightened discomfort may instead motivate the person to try to escape from the aversive environment. Whether or not a person becomes more aggressive may also be related to the presence or absence of other stressors in the situation.

This area is one in which laboratory-based studies do not always confirm other data (e.g. archival data linking actual crime rates with temperature). There are a number of explanations as to why this might be.

Firstly, subjects in the laboratory-based studies can often escape by walking out of the hot room, whereas people in more natural hot conditions are often unable to escape the aversive conditions. Secondly, the way in which aggression is measured is often different in the laboratory, compared with the outside world. It would clearly be unethical for psychologists to expose their subjects to excessive heat, and then test whether they assaulted or murdered others in the room! For this reason "aggression" is traditionally measured by the strength of electric shocks that the subject believes he/she is administering to another person. It is a debatable point as to whether pressing a button on an electric shock machine is really equivalent to physically assaulting another person. This author for one believes that the external validity of some of these studies is questionable. One must also be cautious in the conclusions reached from recorded crime rates. Any research which uses recorded crime rates must bear in mind that what is recorded is only an approximation of the actual level of crime. It may be that violence is more likely to be reported, and subsequently recorded, when temperatures are high.

The fact that high temperatures are correlated with increased levels of aggression does not necessarily prove that one *causes* the other. In hot weather some people will drink more beer which in itself may lead to increased aggression. During hot weather people are also much more likely to congregate outside, where the potential for aversive interactions may be greater.

Population Density

Over the years, studies of many different animal species have shown how overcrowding can lead to a number of problems. Perhaps best known is Calhoun's work with rats and mice. Calhoun (1962) found that allowing these animals to overpopulate in a protected enclosure led to a breakdown of the social order, one consequence of which was a large increase in the number of violent attacks. Although we may not wish to make direct comparisons with human overcrowding, Calhoun's work was seen to have implications for a human population which was congregating more and more in large cities. As we saw earlier with the phenomenon of noise, living in overcrowded conditions produces increased physiological arousal and, in some cases, increased stress (see e.g. Sherrod, 1974). However, the link between density and aggression is not as straightforward as might be assumed.

One difficulty is that population density and crowding are not necessarily the same thing. Whilst density can be easily measured (e.g. the number of people per acre), crowding is a much more subjective assessment of any given situation. For example, a Saturday night disco, or a football match, may well produce high levels of density, but for those attending these functions the large number of other people may not be seen as aversive. Thus there are situational variables which mediate the effects of density, but there are also cultural and personal variables. For example, a person brought up in Tokyo may experience little discomfort when with large numbers of others, whereas the person raised in a remote rural area may well find coping difficult. There are also relevant personal variables. For example, some people seem to need larger personal space zones than others, and so will be affected more by overcrowding. (Many of the studies on crowding have found, for example, that females show less discomfort than do males in such situations.)

A further mediating variable is that of control. People are more likely to be affected by aversive conditions if they are unable to relieve the situation. This is one important area where the animal studies may differ from those involving human populations. For example in Calhoun's studies, the rats and mice were completely unable to get away from each other. However, for most humans this is not the case. People often say things like "I need some space" or "I need some air", and are then able to escape the aversive overcrowding by simply walking out. Perhaps this is one reason why the link between crowding and aggression is not a straightforward one. While some studies have shown that increased density does lead to increased aggression, others have not.

Matthews, Paulus and Baron (1979) have suggested a possible explanation for this. They believe that crowding may in fact interact with other situational variables to produce aggression. For example, if people are in a noisy, hot environment and are also victims of overcrowding, they may find the situation difficult to handle. The combination of all of the aversive factors may well result in increased aggression up to a point, but beyond that point the person may simply leave. The fact that escape provides a viable alternative to heightened aggression has interesting implications for those who are living in overcrowded prisons. For such people escape is rarely a viable option, so overcrowding may have more of an effect (see Ruback & Innes, 1990).

Crowding may also be linked with aggression in non-obvious ways. For example, the more people there are in an environment, the fewer resources there are to go around. Thus overcrowding in itself may not make people more aggressive, but competition for scarce resources might. Inmates of overcrowded prisons may suffer the indignity of living three to a small cell, but the overcrowding also means that there are fewer resources (e.g. room in workshops, seats in the television lounge) for all the inmates.

Air Pollution

A fourth aversive factor which has been identified recently is air pollution in its various forms. Pollution can affect humans physiologically, but recently it has been recognised that there may also be psychological effects, including possible increases in levels of aggression. Physiological damage (or even the fear of it) may well interact with psychological discomfort. For example, a non-smoker might dislike another's cigarette smoke, especially when eating. The smoke might make the diner cough or feel sick, but the fear that it might also cause damage to their lungs could mean that the person behaves aggressively towards the smoker. This is particularly likely if the smoker is flouting "No smoking" regulations. In some countries direct action is now taken by some non-smokers in putting out the cigarettes of smokers. The potential for violence in such situations is obviously quite high. Some studies have shown that the presence of cigarette smoke can provoke people, especially if they are already in a heightened state anyway (see Zillmann, Baron & Tamborini, 1981).

Other types of air pollution can also affect people in negative ways. For example the presence of noxious smells has been found to provoke some people to act aggressively, especially if they have been previously angered (see e.g. Rotton, Frey, Barry, Milligan & Fitzpatrick, 1979). Research has also found that the presence of other atmospheric pollutants (e.g. smog) can affect the number of family arguments (see Rotton & Frey, 1985). This latter study found that when high winds were recorded (which would presumably disperse the pollutants) the number of family disputes fell. Some recent research has suggested that even the presence of positive or negative ions in an environment can affect the levels of aggression (see Baron, Russell & Arms, 1985).

Environmental Factors in Perspective

The previous sections have identified a number of external factors which might affect the levels of aggression. As has been seen, each factor does not always operate in a straightforward way, but rather interacts with many other factors, both external and internal. It is not appropriate to assume that the presence of one of the above factors *will* produce increased levels of aggression; rather what we can say is that when certain environmental conditions exist, there is a greater chance that aggression will be fostered. By identifying a number of external factors, psychologists have shifted their focus from assuming that only personal, internal factors cause aggression, to an admission that external factors can and do mediate aggressive behaviour. An appropriate conclusion to reach is that a person's biological make-up, and their social learning experiences, may well predispose them to behave in aggressive ways. However, it will then be environmental factors which elicit the aggressive response. In other words, aggression may be only one of a number of possible reactions to a situation; whether aggression follows may be partly determined by environmental factors.

RESPONSE TO ATTACK FROM OTHERS

One factor that has not been discussed so far is that of retaliation. It could be argued that an attack from another person is one of the foremost factors in arousing aggression in others. Diamond, Scheiderman, Schwartz et al (1984) have argued that interpersonal attack is far more likely to arouse aggression than frustration does, though quite clearly there are questions of degree in both cases. An attack may be relatively minor or much more serious; similarly, frustration can be mild or intense. In the case of attacks, *intention* acts as an important intervening variable. The victim of any attack will assess whether it was deliberate and malicious. Some authors (e.g. Geen, 1990) have argued that the attacker's intention is a more important factor when considering retaliation than the intensity of the attack. As we have seen previously (in Chapters 1 and 4), the way in which people interpret events is partly a function of the event itself, but is also a function of the victim's personality and background. It is thus not easy to predict whether any given person will accept that another's attack was unintentional and does not warrant retaliation. We have seen from the work of Hans Toch (see above) that some people's perceptions of the world can be rather distorted, and such individuals are likely to perceive even the most trivial exchange as something more serious and threatening. This theme will be taken up in more detail in the next chapter.

ALCOHOL AND AGGRESSION

Police officers may hardly need reminding that a link exists between alcohol and aggression. A great deal of interpersonal violence is associated with alcohol consumption, the peak period for street violence being around pub and club closing times. Psychologists have also long since recognised that links are often found (see Wolfgang & Strohm, 1956). However, like many of the other variables discussed above, the link is not a simple one. Some studies have found that whilst large amounts of alcohol do produce higher levels of aggression, small amounts may actually reduce it (see Taylor & Gammon, 1975). Interestingly, this latter study showed that different types of alcohol may also have different effects – subjects who had drunk vodka were more likely to be aggressive than those who had consumed Bourbon.

Of course not everyone who consumes large amounts of alcohol becomes aggressive. Geen (1990) points out that there are a number of identifiable factors which may interact with alcohol consumption to produce aggression. These are:

1 Situational variables.
2 The cognitive state of the drinker.
3 Features of the drinker's personality.

An important situational variable that interacts with alcohol consumption is that of threat. We saw earlier how an attack or even the threat of one can produce aggression. When the person being threatened is intoxicated, they are more likely to react in an aggressive way than when sober.

Peer pressure facilitating aggression is also enhanced when a person has consumed alcohol. Not only will peers be more able to encourage another to aggress, the same peers will find it more difficult to restrain the other, when he/she is intoxicated.

Alcohol has been shown to affect cognitive (i.e. thought) processes. It is a debatable point as to whether alcohol consumption simply impairs complex cognitive processes, or produces completely different ways of thinking. (In other words, does the person simply have difficulty in thinking or in perceiving situations accurately, or are new thought processes produced as a result of the alcohol?) It is interesting to note that some studies have shown that people are likely to become more aggressive when they *believe* that they have consumed alcohol, although in reality they have not (see Lang, Goeckner, Adesso & Marlatt, 1975). One explanation for this finding is that people may feel less responsibility for their actions when they believe they are under the influence of alcohol. It is very common for an offender in court to claim that he/she does not normally behave in a violent way, but that on this occasion alcohol removed the normal restraints on aggression.

The link between alcohol and aggression is also mediated by the personality of the individual. Renson, Adams and Tinklenberg (1978) found that those with aggressive personalities were more likely to aggress when intoxicated than were others with less aggressive dispositions. Similarly, Pihl, Zacchia and Zeichner (1982) found that whilst most social drinkers did not become aggressive after drinking, those who had quick tempers, or were normally unfriendly and unhappy, were much more likely to do so. The link between alcohol and "difficult" behaviour will be explored further in Chapter 6.

OTHER FACTORS WHICH CAN AFFECT AGGRESSION

In addition to those causes identified above, a number of other factors have been found to mediate the likelihood of aggression. Signs of suffering in a victim will often discourage further aggression; however, this is not always the case. If someone has been severely provoked by another, then the other's signs of suffering may actually produce more aggression (see Baron, 1979). A related notion is that of empathy. It has been found that empathy (i.e. an ability to identify closely with the other) discourages aggression. Signs of pain in a victim are more likely to lead to a cessation of violence if the victim is similar to the attacker than when this is not the case. Thus cross-racial attacks may well continue after suffering has become evident, whereas the same may not occur when the victim and attacker are of the same race.

Fear of retaliation also has an effect on the likelihood of aggressive behaviour. It has long been argued that Britain and America's nuclear weapons act as a deterrent to other nations and prevent those contemplating an attack from carrying this through. Not all agree with such a supposition, but there is some evidence from psychological research that threat of retaliation does, up to a point, discourage aggression (see Baron, 1971). Although this is generally the case, if provocation is extreme the threat of retaliation has been found to have less of a constraining influence.

THE DISCOURAGEMENT OF AGGRESSION

The above heading is deliberate. It may be unrealistic to expect that aggression and violence can be completely eliminated from society, but more realistic to consider ways in which such actions can be controlled or discouraged (see Goldstein, Carr, Davidson & Wehr, 1979). As has been seen above, many different theories have been put forward to explain aggression. It would appear that aggression in most cases does not stem from one factor, but rather results from a complex interaction between dispositional and situational variables. Having identified what factors are likely to lead to aggression, we are in a better position to know how to control it. The identification of many of the factors described above has resulted in practical methods of reducing the amount of aggression. To take one example, pubs or clubs which encourage the consumption of large amounts of alcohol, and are invariably noisy, hot, and overcrowded, are much more likely to provoke aggression than other establishments. Indeed the police may well object to a club having its licence renewed because there has been a history of violent incidents. The identification of some of the causal factors in aggression means that conditions can be altered so that such behaviour becomes less likely. Police officers who understand some of the causal factors in aggression will be in a much better position to deal with aggressive people. Knowledge of triggering factors will also alert the police officer to the possibility that violence is imminent. Understanding of causal factors also allows individuals (including police officers) to anticipate situations that might provoke a violent reaction, and to handle these in a more constructive way. Some ways of dealing with violent behaviour will be outlined further in the next chapter.

SUMMARY

We have seen in this chapter that aggression is multi-causal. Whilst there may be some degree of disagreement amongst psychologists as to whether humans are "naturally" aggressive creatures, a large number of variables have now been identified. Both internal and external factors can produce aggression, and in most cases interact with each other to produce an aggressive response. By understanding some of the causative factors, work towards controlling aggression can proceed more rapidly and is more likely to be effective. Whilst in most cases there is not one single reason which determines whether or not a person will behave aggressively, it is possible to work to eliminate some of the more obvious antecedents of aggressive behaviour. Some of the ways in which police officers can better deal with aggressive individuals will be discussed in the following chapter.

FURTHER READING

Bourlet, A. (1990) *Police Intervention in Marital Violence*. Milton Keynes: Open University Press.

Breakwell, G. M. (1989) *Facing Physical Violence*. Leicester: British Psychological Society & Routledge.

Geen, R. G. (1990) *Human Aggression*. Milton Keynes: Open University Press.

CHAPTER 6

Dealing with Specific Individuals

A preliminary report from the Royal College of Psychiatrists published this week revealed that psychiatric patients had committed 34 murders in 18 months . . . The report also disclosed that only one of the 22 cases investigated involved someone who was still an in-patient at the time of the killing. (*The Guardian*, 29 August 1994)

(*The Guardian*'s reporting of these cases is worrying enough, but in the same month, the *Daily Telegraph* ran the headline "One murder a fortnight by mentally ill" (*Daily Telegraph*, 17 August 1994). Such sensationalist reporting is likely to worry a population already fearful of those labelled as mentally ill. Of course the headline could have made the point that in the 18 month period, over 700 people were killed in Britain by persons who were *not* mentally ill!

So far this book has considered the way in which police officers might deal with members of the public. We have seen how different approaches might be appropriate for different people, a theme which will be enlarged upon in this chapter. In particular, we will examine the concept of mental illness and start to consider some of the more common forms of such maladies. This will allow police officers to be able to identify different types of mental illness, and be better able to predict and deal with the mentally ill. In addition we will consider drug and alcohol abuse as police officers often have to deal with the victims of such addictions. Finally the chapter will examine some of the ways in which police officers might better handle interactions with individuals whose behaviour is unusual, bizarre or threatening.

Police officers are often seen as the first line of defence when dealing with such people as the mentally ill or drug addicts. Although society trains experts to handle such people, in the first instance it is the police officer who must make a preliminary diagnosis and decide on a course of action. This is especially the case when a society such as Britain moves towards a policy of community care. Whilst applauding the aims of such treatment, the reality of this policy means that a larger number of the mentally ill are to be found on the streets of big cities. Whilst it may not be appropriate for all police officers to be trained in counselling skills, an understanding of some features of mental illness may be helpful. Although it is the job of the courts and psychiatrists to decide on a person's mental health, an appreciation of some features of the more common forms of mental illness would be valuable to the serving police officer.

MENTAL ILLNESS

There are a large number of myths about mental illness. It is also an area which provokes very negative stereotypes. It is difficult to imagine any group for which there are more derogatory slang expressions (e.g. nutter, weirdo, out of his tree). Most members of the public are afraid of anyone with the tag "mentally ill". When someone so diagnosed commits a crime, there is an outcry and questions are asked about why the person was not locked up (see Report of Clunis Inquiry, 1994). Whilst such cases achieve notoriety, they are the exception rather than the rule. The vast majority of mentally ill people are not dangerous to themselves or others and actually pose little threat to society. In many cases the behaviour of those with severe mental illness can now be controlled by drugs, meaning that it is not necessary for them to be locked away in back wards of asylums. According to the Mental Health Foundation, one person in 10 suffers from mental illness. But many such people do not fit the stereotype that people have of this group.

So why are people afraid of those who are labelled as mentally ill? The main reason is that the behaviour of such people is said to be incomprehensible, and thus somewhat unpredictable. As we saw in Chapter 1, dealing with other people relies on well established rules and norms of behaviour. Although such rules are often unwritten they regulate social interactions, and allow people to proceed in well established ways. Waddington emphasises the importance of stereotypes and predictability in the following way:

> "In conditions of unpredictability, it is necessary for the police to have some rough-and-ready idea of who they are dealing with . . . stereotypes [are] a way of making the potentially unpredictable predictable. Stereotypes allow an officer to anticipate how people will react . . . " (Waddington, 1984, p. 7)

There are many things which people take for granted when communicating with others. For example, in traditional British cultures there is an unwritten rule which says that a person should look at another's eyes while talking to them (though this rule does not necessarily apply in other cultures). If one person insists on staring at the other's ear when they are talking, it makes them feel uncomfortable and disrupts the conversation. In fact social interactions rely on a large number of these so-called social skills. People are often unaware of the rules until one of them is broken. Because some mentally ill people have inappropriate social skills, people tend to avoid interacting with them (see Trower, Bryant & Argyle, 1978). This can of course exacerbate the problem, and lead the mentally ill person to have an even lower self-image. Suffering from mental illness may be bad enough in itself, but when the person is ignored or ridiculed by others, this can make the sufferer feel much worse.

People thus tend to assume that if a person cannot hold a conversation appropriately, then other aspects of their behaviour will be unpredictable and perhaps threatening. Any behaviour that is unusual arouses a person's suspicions and sets off alarm bells. If suddenly the world becomes an unpredictable place (because the other person is not following the rules) then people will be inclined to become worried and perhaps walk away. However, in many cases, the person is not a threat, but merely different. Some writers have gone so far as to suggest that the behaviour of such people is in fact much more comprehensible than we might assume, and that it is society that is crazy! (see Laing, 1964). There is a tendency to assume that if an individual's behaviour is not immediately explicable, then the person must be mentally ill. There is, however, a very permeable dividing line between the mentally ill and the mentally healthy. For example where does eccentricity, individuality or quirkiness end, and mental illness begin? Should a person who shows great sadness following the death of a loved one be diagnosed as suffering from clinical depression, or as just going through a normal grieving process?

It is not easy to convince members of the public that the vast majority of the mentally ill are not a threat. There is a knee jerk reaction produced when, for example, a facility for the mentally ill is proposed in a residential area. It is not uncommon for local residents to oppose such plans vehemently, pointing out perhaps that there are lots of small children who would no longer be safe from such people. Of course the vast majority of the mentally ill are not child molesters, yet their sometimes unpredictable behaviour leads to great anxiety amongst members of the community. The fact that most child abuse and molestation is carried out by a relative, friend or acquaintance of the victim is forgotten in the outcry against any such proposal. The vast majority of crime in society is committed by those who are not defined as mentally ill, and yet the public are still fearful of those who show signs of mental ill health.

There is also an interesting double standard applied when it comes to the commission of crime by those who may be mentally ill. For example if someone commits a large number of horrific murders, the perpetrator's state of mind may well be assumed to be abnormal – he/she will be described as being crazy, a psychopath, obviously severely disturbed, and so on. After all, nobody "in their right mind" could do such things. However, if the person is subsequently caught and tries to account for their behaviour in this way, society tends to question such "excuses", and demands that the person should not be allowed to get away with it by claiming that they are mentally ill. This was what happened in the case of Peter Sutcliffe, the Yorkshire Ripper. This was a man who murdered 13 women in the North of England, and was eventually caught in 1980.

His crimes were such that they could "only have been committed by a severely disturbed person", so the media claimed. However, when he was caught, Peter Sutcliffe seemed to confirm what had been said about him, claimed to have been hearing voices, and led psychiatrists to believe that he was suffering from schizophrenia. At this point members of the public protested and insisted that he should not be allowed to "get away with his crimes" by claiming that he was mentally ill. The public demanded their pound of flesh and a battle ensued in which Peter Sutcliffe's mental state was discussed at great length in court. In the end the diagnosis of schizophrenia was rejected by the court and Peter Sutcliffe was found guilty of 13 murders. (For a more detailed discussion of this case see Jones, 1992.)

The above case raises a number of interesting questions, not least of which is whether a mentally ill person really is responsible for his/her actions (see Raine, 1993). There are clear precedents in legal terms in that a person who is insane cannot be convicted of a crime. The insane are said to be incapable of having the necessary *mens rea* or guilty intent. There are also clearly established rules as to whether a person may be said to be guilty, but had "diminished responsibility" at the time. An interesting phrase that last one; it implies that a person was not insane, but was not *fully* responsible for what he or she did. Of course deciding whether or not a person is insane, or even mentally ill, is not a straightforward matter, as was seen in the Peter Sutcliffe case mentioned above. Faced with such a confusion it is not surprising that some members of the public have little faith in a system that produces important differences in diagnosis between professionals.

Problems of definition abound in the field of mental illness. It is another of those areas where people are heard to say "Well I can't define it, but I can certainly recognise it when I see it". The problem with such a statement is that it may well apply to someone who fits society's stereotype of a mentally ill person, but not to the vast majority of those who suffer the condition. The media tend to portray the mentally ill in a very negative way. They are often depicted as having grossly disturbed thinking, peculiarities of movement, and showing signs of menace and threat. Whilst such behaviours are associated with some severe forms of mental illness, they are not typical of most sufferers.

Both psychiatrists and psychologists have tried to come up with an objective definition of exactly what constitutes mental illness. Despite the production of such weighty tomes as the *Diagnostic and Statistical Manual of Mental Disorders* (American Psychiatric Association 1987; 1994) it is still not easy to classify a person as either mentally ill or not mentally ill. Perhaps this is not surprising given that there are so many different forms of mental illness. There are also new forms of mental illness being identified all the time, such as Munchausen's syndrome. The nurse Beverley Alott, who murdered a number of children in her care at an English hospital, was said to have been suffering from such a condition. It is also true that many so-called mental illnesses are simply extensions of things that most normal people experience. When does an understandable fear for one's safety become paranoia? There are also changes in the way in which certain behaviours are classified at different times or in different countries. For example, homosexuality was classed as a form of mental illness 20 years ago, but is seen differently today.

Mental illness is still seen largely in terms of a medical model. It is diagnosed in the same way as other "illnesses" and often treated medically through drugs. Opponents of the medical model have suggested that the diagnosis of mental illness is a subjective rather than an objective process. For example, Szasz (1961) has argued that there is really no such thing as mental illness. He asks how can one have an "illness" in something which is an abstract concept, in this case the mind? He accepts that there can be diseases of the brain which produce abnormal behaviour, but not diseases of the mind. He argues that a deviation in a person's behaviour should be seen as just that – a deviation. There is rarely if ever an identifiable underlying physical cause, and so Szasz claims that it is inappropriate for such behaviours to be treated medically (e.g. by drugs). The person may be exhibiting unusual behaviour but does not have a medical problem, or an illness as such.

As Szasz has suggested, one of the main problems with defining mental illness is that there is often no obvious physical abnormality which can be identified as the cause. If a person experiences great physical pain and is unable to walk, an X-ray examination may reveal that he/she has a broken leg. This can be treated and, in most cases, the person will make a full recovery. Some months later, a second X-ray examination might be used to prove that the broken leg is now "cured". Diagnosis in mental illness is not so straightforward. A physical examination of a mentally ill person's brain would in most cases show no obvious abnormalities. Given that physical evidence is lacking, a course of treatment might also be difficult to prescribe.

There is a further interesting difference between physical illness and mental illness. In many cases, a person with a physical illness can be diagnosed, treated and cured. However, those treating the mentally ill may well be less clear about whether they have actually cured the problem, or just relieved some of the symptoms. People tend to make the assumption that if a person shows signs of mental illness, the problem lies within the person him or herself. To use terminology introduced in Chapters 1 and 3, people make an internal attribution. This being the case, it is assumed that the person will always be mentally ill, but may not have severe symptoms all the time. It is interesting to note that in the Rosenhan study (see Chapter 3) the pseudo-patients were released from hospital with a label of "schizophrenia in remission". In other words, they were still schizophrenic, but the symptoms had, for the moment at least, subsided. Similar diagnoses are used in some cases (e.g. cancer) but in others this is not usual. One wonders how many people are discharged from hospitals with a label "broken leg in remission".

Szasz and others may have a point in bringing such difficulties of definition to our attention. However, their views are of little practical help to those who have to deal with abnormal behaviour as and when it occurs. If an individual's behaviour is a threat to him/herself or others, then society tends to assume that it has the right to protect itself by incarcerating such people, irrespective of the reasons behind their behaviour. Whether we choose to call it mental illness, abnormal behaviour, or a problem in coping with life, the fact remains that such people do often come to the attention of the authorities, and have to be dealt with.

The law gives police officers certain powers to deal with those who are apparently mentally ill. Most societies also have laws which allow for the compulsory detention of those suffering from mental illness. The time of such detention can vary enormously from society to society. Although treatment in the community is now much more common than 20 years ago, the most severely disturbed can still be detained against their will for a specified length of time. Such decisions are made by trained medical staff or social workers, but there are occasions when police officers will need to make a preliminary decision as to a person's mental state. For example, in the inquiry into the case of Christopher Clunis (a mentally ill person who killed an innocent bystander at a London tube station) a police officer was severely criticised for not realising that Christopher Clunis was a danger to the public and to himself.

As with many other cases, it is easy to be wise after the event, and to suggest, with the benefit of hindsight, that a different course of action should have been taken. Most police officers, at least in Britain, are given very little training in how to identify the mentally ill, let alone how to decide from which form of disorder the person is suffering. This is perhaps not surprising given that psychiatrists are only allowed to make diagnoses after many years of intensive training. A woman who is threatening to throw herself off a building will probably be identified as suffering from some form of mental illness, and would clearly be seen to be a danger to herself, if not others. Police officers would have little hesitation in intervening in such cases. However, most cases involving mental illness are not so straightforward. As was discussed above, there is a very thin dividing line between eccentricity and mental illness, and police officers should be aware of this. Some commentators have suggested that there are class and race biases in the defining process. For example, an upper-class person's unusual behaviour will tend to be defined as eccentric, whereas the same behaviour exhibited by a working-class person might well be defined as mental illness. There is also a suggestion that race can affect diagnosis. In Britain people of Afro-Caribbean origin are much more likely to be labelled as schizophrenic than are whites.

If deciding who is and who is not mentally ill is difficult, then deciding who is dangerous and who is not is even more taxing. History contains many cases in which even the medical experts got it completely wrong. There are a number of well documented cases where people have been released from psychiatric hospitals only to commit further serious crimes within days of their release. Society is entitled to question how the experts can be so wrong, and demand to be reassured that it could never happen again. The problem is that predicting dangerousness is not an easy job, nor it is an exact science (see Blackburn, 1993). Society wants to feel that the non-dangerous are not locked up unnecessarily, but it also wants to feel sure that those who are a threat are not allowed to roam freely. It is assumed that the vast majority of decisions made by psychiatrists and other experts are correct ones, but when they get it wrong, there can be serious repercussions. Perhaps the decisions made by experts in these cases are no less accurate than decisions made by bodies such as the Parole Board, or even judges in cases where a potentially dangerous suspect is given bail. It is never easy to examine a person's previous behaviour and make totally accurate predictions about their future conduct. Psychologists are only too well aware of this. It is thus inevitable that some mistakes will be made when making predictions, given that most humans are not totally predictable. Perhaps the best that can be reasonably expected is that the ratio of wrong decisions to correct ones remains at an "acceptable" level, however society defines that.

Having appreciated that is often difficult to make accurate predictions, it is still important that the reader be introduced to some of the more common and serious forms of mental disorder which are likely to be encountered. Most psychiatric disorders are classified as either *psychotic* or *neurotic* illnesses. There are a number of differences between the two, but perhaps the most important distinction to make is that psychotic illnesses tend to be typified by a clear cut break with reality, whereas neurotic illnesses are not.

Schizophrenia

Schizophrenia is the most severe example of a psychotic disorder, sufferers often having great difficulty in coping with the world. Schizophrenia is often mistakenly thought of as involving a "split personality" or a Jekyll and Hyde type of character. There is a recognised syndrome of multiple personality disorder (see Schreiber, 1973) but this is different. In fact the "splitting" in schizophrenia refers to a splitting of the thought processes from the emotions. A person may for example be describing a particularly distressing incident, and yet giggle throughout. Schizophrenia often involves highly disturbed thought processes, and the person's speech becomes incomprehensible to others. Schizophrenics are often thought to be responding to stimuli (e.g. imagined voices) in their head, rather than to things in the outside world. Their speech and behaviour is thus seen by others as totally incomprehensible, suggesting that the person really has gone "crazy".

One of the foremost identifying criteria for a diagnosis of schizophrenia is the experiencing of hallucinations. These can be auditory, where the person hears voices (inside their head), or visual, where the person claims to be able to see something that others present cannot. Sufferers often think that the hallucinated voice or image is telling them to do certain things. Sometimes these acts are illegal or dangerous, and thus the person raises concern in the minds of those around. Of course we need to be careful in suggesting that anyone who claims to hear voices is schizophrenic. An eminent Chief Constable (now retired) from North-West England often claimed that he heard a voice from God telling him how he should act! It is not uncommon for members of certain religious groups to claim that they asked God for guidance and that he answered them in a loud voice. Society would not, however, consider these to be auditory hallucinations, and would probably not define the person hearing the message as mentally ill.

We have so far described schizophrenia in its most severe form, but there are many sufferers who exhibit much milder symptoms. In fact there are now a number of quite different forms of schizophrenia recognised by the medical establishment (see Halgin & Whitbourne, 1993). For present purposes though, the more severe forms are the ones which are likely to cause concern. Sufferers who claim to be hearing voices may well act in irrational or unpredictable ways. Most normal people may well be tempted to commit certain illegal or anti-social acts, but their "inner voice" or conscience tells them that this would not be appropriate, and they resist the temptation. However, the person who hears voices telling him/her what to do may well behave in unusual ways, later admitting no liability for the acts and claiming that "the voices made me do it". It can be difficult to talk rationally to such people, as they have often become accustomed to listening to their inner voice rather than an external one. However, some idea of the person's likely actions can be gained by asking what the voices are telling them. It should also be noted that administration of the major tranquillising drugs (e.g. chlorpromazine or Largactil) can have fairly rapid and dramatic effects. Even the most disturbed patients tend to calm down within 24–48 hours, and experience a relief of most of their symptoms. This is one reason why the straitjacket and other physical restraints are largely unnecessary today.

For the police officer, perhaps the most worrying type of person would be one suffering from paranoid schizophrenia. A person with this condition tends to experience most of the symptoms described above, but in addition is deeply suspicious of other people. The paranoia can take the form of a belief that people around are planning to persecute, harm or even kill him or her. Although there is a general fear or distrust of others, the most intense suspicions can fall on those who are closest to the sufferer. This may mean that if the condition is not treated, the suspicions can intensify and eventually lead to the patient attacking one or more of those around. It should be noted that there is a separate mental illness known as paranoid personality disorder. Such patients experience similar symptoms of paranoia, but do not have the other symptoms of schizophrenia such as hallucinations.

Again we must keep a sense of proportion here. The vast majority of schizophrenics, even paranoid schizophrenics, are not dangerous. However, like anyone else, they have the capacity to become aggressive, and to attack others around them (see Chapter 5). Because their actions are apparently guided by an imagined voice, their behaviour may well appear irrational or unpredictable. Having said that, valuable insights can be gained by listening to what the person says. There is a tendency to dismiss anything said by such people as simply the product of a severely disturbed mind, and thus unworthy of attention. However, it is possible to discover who the person fears most (in the case of the paranoid) or what the voices are telling him/her to do.

Depression

Depression is an example of a neurotic, as opposed to a psychotic disorder. It is usually seen as an affective (i.e. mood) disorder. For most people suffering from depression, there is no clear cut break with reality, but rather the condition is seen as an exaggeration of something that most people feel from time to time. Almost everyone feels low or sad on occasions, though some experience such feelings much more often than others, and for some, the experience is much more severe and debilitating.

One problem with depression is that people who have never experienced it cannot really imagine how bad it can feel. Patronising comments such as "pull yourself together", or "snap out of it" are likely to have little effect on a person who has come to believe, because of their depression, that there is nothing worthwhile left in their world.

There are a number of different theories as to the origins of depression, only some of which will be covered briefly in this chapter. There are in fact two distinct types of depression recognised by mental health professionals, i.e. unipolar and bipolar (or manic) depression. In the case of the former, a person experiences just the symptoms of depression. However, in the case of the manic depressive, the person experiences violent mood swings from one day to another, at times feeling very high and elated, and at others feeling incredibly low. The two types of depression are normally treated differently. The manic depressive may well be prescribed lithium salts, which level out the violent mood swings by stopping the highs as well as the lows. By contrast the person suffering from unipolar depression will be prescribed anti-depressants which elevate the person's mood.

A number of famous artistic or creative people were thought to suffer from manic depression. Typically they would produce a massive amount of material in their manic phase, only to then deride it when they viewed it through a deep depression a few days later. The composer Robert Schumann was believed to have suffered from manic depression. His music can actually be divided into two distinctly different camps, either energetic and exciting, or slow and melancholic. It has been suggested that the two very different styles of music reflect the ups and downs of his manic depression, and were composed when in one or other extreme of mood (see DeAngelis, 1989). For most manic depressives, the mood swings are regular and predictable, meaning that those around them know that a manic phase signals the impending onset of a depressive phase. Again, we should point out that although the symptoms may appear similar to the general up and down moods of normal people, the swings for the manic depressive are much more severe and violent.

It is difficult to say which of the two forms of depression is the more serious. Obviously both can vary in severity, but each can be life-threatening. Perhaps for the police officer, the manic depressive may signal more danger. An officer who is unaware of such a condition may well assume that the manic phase has been produced by drugs rather than a form of mental illness, and may thus deal with the person inappropriately. The other danger is that a manic person may well be put into a cell and left there to calm down. The mood of such a person may then change rapidly and the ensuing depression lead to self-harm.

As was the case with aggression (see Chapter 5), there is no theory of unipolar depression to which all psychologists would subscribe. There are a number of different theories, some of which are complementary. Some theories suggest that depression can be explained by reference to chemical imbalances in the brain (see Halgin & Whitbourne, 1993) whilst others suggest that it follows from some event in a person's life which has led them to believe that they are helpless (see Seligman, 1975). However, the most popular current psychological theory is termed the Cognitive Model (Beck, 1967).

The cognitive model sees depression as stemming not from a chemical imbalance, but rather from significant errors in the logic of the depressed person's thinking. One need talk only briefly to someone who is depressed to realise that he/she thinks and speaks somewhat differently from non-depressed people. There is a great negativity about everything that they say. They believe that there is nothing that they can do to make themselves feel better. Others' attempts to help will often be rejected as the depressive convinces him/herself that they are beyond help. Their own situation is viewed as hopeless, so they believe that there is little point in trying anything positive. Depressed persons distort even very positive information about themselves so that it is seen negatively. Thus whilst the non-depressed person who does well in an examination may feel proud, the depressive may instead think that they were just lucky, and still maintain their low self-image. Given this frame of mind, it is not surprising that the most severely depressed people may attempt suicide.

Images of a police officer talking down a person about to jump from a tall building make good television viewing but such suicide attempts are rare. A previous volume by the current author has covered the area of crisis intervention so this will not be dealt with here (see Ainsworth & Pease, 1987). However, it is important for the police officer to at least be aware of some of the symptoms of depression, in order that such sufferers can be dealt with appropriately. We saw earlier in this chapter how difficult it can be to differentiate the dangerous from the non-dangerous person. It is also true that it is not always easy to tell the genuine suicide risk from the "cry for help". Mental health professionals are not infallible in this regard, so the police officer cannot realistically be expected to assess such risks totally accurately.

Statistics tell us that women are more likely to attempt suicide, but that men are more likely to be successful in their attempts. A lot of this reflects the differing methods of suicide which are typically employed. For example, men are more likely than women to use firearms as a means of committing suicide. Women are more likely than men to take drug overdoses, which means that prompt medical attention can often save a life. Statistics tell us that women are more likely than men to suffer from depression, though at least some of this difference may be accounted for by differences in the diagnostic process. Some relatively recent research suggests that there may be a genetic link in depression, but the condition is much more likely to be transmitted to a female child than a male (McGue, Pickens & Svikis, 1992). One suggestion is that although both men and women may inherit the gene which makes them vulnerable to depression, the condition is more likely to manifest itself in women. Men who inherit the same genetic vulnerability may instead become alcoholic. Perhaps one reason for this is that what is inherited is a tendency towards low serotonin levels in the brain. This in turn leads to a difficulty in handling the stresses and strains of modern life. Unable to cope, women may become depressed whilst men in the same position may turn to alcohol as a relief. This can be what psychologists call a maladaptive response – drinking does not actually help the person to deal with the problem, and in fact the alcohol (a depressive substance) may exacerbate the condition.

ALCOHOL DEPENDENCY

In the previous chapter we discussed the possible links between alcohol consumption and aggression. Alcohol dependency is now recognised as a form of mental disorder, often requiring treatment. As police officers have to deal with inebriated individuals, it would be appropriate here to consider the ways in which alcohol affects cognitive processes (i.e. the way in which people think). Taylor and Leonard (1983) suggest that the main effect of alcohol is a pharmacological one. Alcohol works on the central nervous system in such a way that normal thinking processes, especially complex ones, are impaired. This means that the inebriated person is less able to take in subtle cues in the environment, and more likely to react to the most dominant or salient cues.

If a person is provoked, they will weigh up the situation and decide whether or not retaliation is appropriate. Often the person's own internal constraints will intervene at this point, resulting in a decision not to retaliate. However, when under the influence of alcohol, the person is less able to make complex or even subtle judgements about the appropriate course of action. Geen, commenting on Taylor and Leonard's work, suggests that:

> "Ingestion of alcohol will facilitate aggression when instigational cues are strong (provocation, peer support for aggression) and inhibitory cues are weak (e.g. mild peer pressure). However when a strong inhibitory cue is introduced (clear statement of an anti-aggression norm), alcohol drinking reduces aggression." (Geen, 1990, p. 151)

Any casual observation shows that people who drink heavily often do things which they later regret. Alcohol interferes with a large number of both physical and psychological functions. After sobering up, a person may well ask in disbelief "How could I have done such a stupid thing?" For some people alcohol appears to bring about a complete change of personality. This may be temporary, but results in behaviour which is so completely different as to be unrecognisable by those around. Whilst alcohol remains a legal drug, its abuse will continue to affect a large number of people. Its use is so ingrained into most societies that any significant decline in its popularity remains a long way off. It is somewhat ironic that whilst alcohol (so often associated with violence and aggression) remains legal, other drugs such as marijuana (consumption of which does not lead to increases in aggression) remain banned. Because alcohol use has become so socially acceptable, the potentially harmful effects of its abuse are all too often ignored. Despite dealing with the harmful effects of alcohol on a daily basis, police officers themselves are not immune from abusing this legal drug. In such cases it can have a detrimental effect on the officers' work and health (see Stratton, 1984, ch. 10).

ABUSE OF OTHER DRUGS

Whilst alcohol remains the most commonly used legal drug, the number of illegal drugs on the market seems to grow daily. Drugs such as Crack and Ecstasy are widely known today, yet were virtually unheard of only 10 years ago. What are termed designer drugs appear in different forms week by week, making their banning a difficult legal problem. It would not be appropriate to describe the hundreds of illegal drugs currently available, but instead we will here examine the prevalence of drugs and their possible links with anti-social behaviour, and consider ways in which the police might deal with those who take illegal drugs.

There are two points which are usually made when discussing illegal drugs. Firstly, it is believed that people who are addicted to drugs will do anything to get their "fix". A drug user is thus seen as someone who will readily resort to crime in order to feed their habit. Although estimates vary as to the proportion of crime which is drug-related, most police officers believe that a significant amount of crime is committed by those who are on drugs. Drug dealing is also associated with increased levels of violent crime, often involving fatal altercations between rival groups involved in dealing.

Secondly, virtually all the major initiatives introduced to eliminate the trade in illegal drugs have been unsuccessful. Whilst some schemes have shown partial success in reducing the demand or supply of illegal drugs, in most Western societies a large number of illegal drugs are all too readily available. Some commentators have questioned whether the billions spent by the authorities have really been worthwhile. Whilst the problem is much more severe in the USA than in Europe, it is believed that countries such as Britain are set to become the new drug capitals.

Taking the first of these points, it must be acknowledged that for some people drugs do become a major addiction, and for such people a resort to crime is understandable if not condonable. However, it must also be acknowledged that the vast majority of people who take illegal drugs do not become addicted, and do not commit crime in order to feed their habit. Whilst the media may have us believe that the vast majority of "normal" people will have nothing to do with illegal drugs, some recent research has shown just how commonly available some drugs are. This research (Measham, Newcombe & Parker, 1994) studied some 776 14–15-year-old schoolchildren in North-West England. Some 60% of the sample reported having been offered drugs, and some 36% admitted having used such drugs. Whilst cannabis was the most widely used drug, nitrites, LSD, and amphetamines had also been tried by significant numbers of the sample. Heroin, once considered the major problem drug, had not been tried by any in the sample.

This research showed how "normalised" drugs have become for a significant number of young people. It also showed how blissfully unaware most parents and school authorities are of the ready availability of many drugs. The stereotype of a drug user may well be that of a working-class male with few prospects in life, but Measham's research challenges such assumptions. It shows that an increasing number of females are being offered, and are using, drugs, and that the number of young people in middle-class schools who have been offered such drugs is increasing significantly.

If drug availability is as common as such surveys suggest, one wonders whether the police service can realistically reduce the level of drug-taking, especially amongst young people. The survey discussed above shows that for many young people, the taking of illegal drugs is not seen as the first step towards a criminal career. In fact they often made little distinction between legal drugs such as tobacco and alcohol, and illegal drugs. Part of the normalisation process means that for young people who take illegal drugs, the threat of being caught and punished has little deterrent effect. Ultimately it is up to society to decide which drugs should be declared illegal, and how people who defy the law should be treated. We hope, however, to have made the point that the distinction drawn between legal and illegal drugs is not one that is acknowledged by many young people. There may be a certain irony in a group of police officers celebrating a successful drugs raid by retiring to the local bar and consuming large amounts of alcohol!

PERSONALITY DISORDERS

Earlier in this chapter we discussed psychotic and neurotic disorders. There is a category of mental disorder which some see as separate from these, but which in some cases overlaps. (For example a person may well have a neurotic personality disorder, which leads them to experience an affective disorder like depression.) Perhaps nowhere is the dividing line between normality and abnormality less clear than in the case of personality disorders. Each person has, by definition, his or her own personality. Whilst some of their traits will be shared by others, it is the combination of the many facets of a personality which makes each person unique. Deciding where uniqueness ends and a disorder begins is not so easy. Most psychologists would see personality disorders as having a maladaptive quality. By that they mean that the person's way of behaving has unpleasant or unwanted consequences for the individual him/herself or for others. Thus a person who shows excessive dependency, an overwhelming fear of intimacy, or excessive and uncontrollable rage will experience great personal difficulty, especially in relationships with others. These personality disorders form part of a person's whole being and as such are often the most difficult to treat. The person has probably been behaving in a certain way for many years. Whilst perhaps wanting to lead a more fulfilled and less difficult life, sufferers find it very difficult to change their habitual behaviour.

There are many different types of these disorders, ranging from obsessive compulsive, to anti-social personality disorder. The latter is an interesting one, implying that some people behave in anti-social ways because they are suffering from a disorder, and not just because they are anti-social. This could be seen as one area in which the psychologist and the police officer would disagree wildly. The stereotyped view would be that the police officer would see any wrongdoing as deliberate, and thus requiring punishment. Conversely, the psychologist might identify a recognised "medical" disorder, and thus suggest that the person needs treatment rather than punishment (see Hare, 1983).

Anti-social personality disorder is characterised by a total lack of regard for society's moral or legal standards. It encompasses the sort of person who may previously have been labelled as a psychopath or sociopath, though such terms have always proved difficult to define. Robins, Helzer, Weissman et al (1984) suggest that this disorder is surprisingly common – 5% of males and 1% of females in America are thought to exhibit such traits. Although such people may not commit serious crimes, their lives are said to be riddled with anti-social acts. Halgin and Whitbourne (1993) describe them thus:

> "their lives are characterised by a long list of disreputable or manipulative behaviors. They lie, cheat, steal, fight, abuse alcohol and drugs, act promiscuously, and ignore family and job responsibilities. They behave in an impulsive, aggressive and reckless manner, and show no remorse for the harmful effects of their behaviour."
> (Halgin & Whitbourne, 1993, p. 143)

Whilst such behaviours may well be found in the "common criminal", for those with a recognised disorder the problems are likely to be much more long-standing and enduring. Their difficulties will usually have started in childhood and persisted throughout their adult life. Having said that, more recent research (see Hare, McPherson & Forth, 1988) suggests that their anti-social behaviours start to decline from the age of 40 onwards. The behaviour of such people is thought to stem from childhood, when they will have experienced great difficulty in impulse control. This will then have led them into difficulty at home, at school, and on the streets.

Many of the factors identified as precursors for aggression (see Chapter 5) are also found in the backgrounds of people with anti-social personality disorder. Certain biological factors may have an influence, but the most important seems to be disharmony in the home (see Robins, 1966; West & Farrington, 1973). Inconsistent discipline in the home may also lead to later difficulties. Parents who switch from one extreme of harshness to the other extreme of great laxity send confusing messages to the child about what is appropriate behaviour. Buss (1966) suggests that children raised in such a climate fail to appreciate the consequences of their actions, be they good or bad. Extreme leniency and inattention to a child's demands have also been found to be associated with the development of anti-social personalities.

Having started this chapter by emphasising the point that the vast majority of mentally ill people are not dangerous or violent, we will conclude by examining some strategies which may be effective in dealing with the small number of people (both mentally ill and those not so defined) whose behaviour is threatening or violent. This approach is linked closely to the theories of aggression discussed in the previous chapter.

DEALING WITH THE UNPREDICTABLE AND THE AGGRESSIVE

Police officers are very much in the front line when it comes to dealing with unpredictable people and their potential for violence. Police training has traditionally focused upon the ways in which such people can be physically restrained. It is, however, now recognised that the way in which those dealing with a potentially violent and dangerous incident approach the scene can significantly affect the outcome. Whilst it is normal to blame an assailant for an assault, some aspects of the victim's behaviour may well be a contributory factor. For example, research by Rowett (1986) suggests that social workers who are victims of assault are thought likely to be more provocative, incompetent, authoritarian and inexperienced. Similar findings apply to other occupations, including police work.

One factor perhaps unique to police work is that simply walking away from a violent incident is rarely a viable option. Whilst many people face potentially violent encounters in their day-to-day work, it is the police officer who has to take some positive action to handle the situation. Whereas a social worker might be able to say to the client "I am not willing to talk to you until you calm down", such an option would rarely be considered realistic by the police officer. Having said that, there are some parallels to be drawn from the ways in which other groups handle potentially violent situations. A recent book by Breakwell (1989) deals with such problems. Whilst some of the advice offered therein is perhaps more relevant to social workers and probation officers, a number of the points made are pertinent to police officers.

One of the most useful aspects of Breakwell's book is what she calls a "dangerousness checklist". Whilst some of the factors identified are specific to the caring professions, many of the notions are highly relevant to the police officer. For this reason, the checklist is reproduced here in full.

The Dangerousness Checklist

When assessing the extent of the risk of violence in a situation you are about to enter you should consider the following questions. The more often you answer "yes", the greater the risk of violence:

- Is the person I am dealing with facing high levels of stress?
- Is the person likely to be drunk or on drugs?
- Does the person have a history of violence?
- Does the person have a history of criminal convictions?
- Does the person have a history of psychiatric illness?
- Does the person suffer from a medical condition which may result in loss of self-control?
- Has the person verbally abused me in the past?
- Has the person threatened me with violence in the past?
- Has the person attacked me in the past?
- Does the person perceive me as a threat to his/her children?
- Does the person think of me as a threat to his/her liberty?
- Does the person have unrealistic expectations of what I can do for him/her?
- Does the person perceive me as wilfully unhelpful?
- Have I felt anxious for my safety with this person before?
- Are other people present who will reward the person for violence?

Facing the client or patient, other cues should be examined. Again, the more times you answer "yes" in a situation, the greater the danger:

- Is the person showing signs of atypical excitement or passivity?
- Are there weapons or similar cues to violence in the room?
- Is the person showing signs of atypical high arousal?
- Is there a breakdown in the normal pattern of non-verbal communication?
- Is the person showing signs of rapid mood swings?
- Is the person oversensitive to suggestions or criticisms?

The implications of the risk are greater if you answer "yes" to several of the following questions:

- Am I alone and without back-up?
- Are colleagues unaware of my whereabouts?
- Am I without any means of raising the alarm if attacked?
- Am I likely to be trapped without an escape route if the person becomes violent?

- Am I unaware of how I react in violent situations?
- Am I unaware of the assault cycle?
- Am I unaware of the cultural norms which are likely to control this person's exhibition of violence?
- Have I ever considered what I would do if attacked?
  (From G. M. Breakwell, *Facing Physical Violence*. Leicester: BPS/Routledge, 1989. Reproduced by permission of British Psychological Society.)

It may be impractical for a police officer to run through such a large checklist before dealing with any potentially violent encounter, but an understanding of the many factors identified would be good preparation, and may contribute to a less violent outcome.

Having identified those factors which should alert the person to the violence potential, Breakwell suggests a number of strategies which can help calm the situation. These include:

- Giving the impression of being calm and confident rather than overbearing or dismissive.
- Keeping talking, ideally in a normal voice, and "mood matching"; shouting if the person shouts, or speaking with intensity if the other is doing so.
- Using diversionary tactics. This could be anything from asking for a drink to making jokes.
- If the person appears to demand dominance, a feigned submission, and then talk to redirect attention may be used.
- If it appears obvious that an attack is imminent, the person should examine escape routes, and make their way towards them. This may appear to be an inappropriate response for a police officer (who does not wish to be seen to be backing down from confrontation) but in some cases this would be an appropriate, albeit temporary strategy.
- Try to disperse onlookers who may be acting to incite the violent person. As we saw above, this is particularly relevant when the person has consumed alcohol.
- Rather than asking generally for assistance from a crowd, pinpoint one person and address them directly, telling them to phone or go for assistance.
- Use appropriate non-verbal behaviour to calm the situation (see Chapter 1). Police officers should be aware of how their body language might signal aggression or submission, calmness or confrontation.
- Be aware of the assault cycle. Breakwell suggests that a person who has been aroused to aggress, will stay in this heightened state for up to 90 minutes. During this time, the person will be particularly

sensitive to provocation. Thus the removal of a physical restraint too early, especially if accompanied by some incitement, may well produce further aggression.

Use of some of the above strategies would clearly help those dealing with the aggressive individual, whether they were disturbed or not. Whilst different strategies may be appropriate for different situations, there are common themes which run through many such encounters. Adoption of some of the procedures discussed here can result in a better understanding of the disturbed, and a reduction in the likelihood of an assault.

OTHER STRATEGIES FOR DEALING WITH AGGRESSION

Before concluding this chapter it would be appropriate to consider some of the ways in which society has traditionally dealt with aggressive behaviour. Perhaps the most obvious of such strategies is punishment. Punishment has been used throughout history both as a means of "teaching aggressors a lesson", and in deterring others who may be tempted to behave in similar ways. Psychologists have traditionally suggested that punishment may make society feel better, but is actually not very effective. There is also a view that corporal punishment may simply teach people that it is acceptable to use violence against another person. This is perhaps best exemplified by the father who beats his child saying "This will teach you not to fight at school". Sceptics suggest that the child simply learns that violence is appropriate, especially if you are more powerful than your victim. Having said that, some psychologists now believe that punishment can be effective, but only under certain conditions.

Baron and Byrne (1994) suggest that the essential ingredients are:

1 Punishment must be prompt. It must follow aggression as soon as possible.
2 It must be intense. This does not mean a severe beating, but the punishment must be seen as sufficiently aversive to evoke avoidance.
3 The punishment must be probable. There must be a high probability that each and every aggressive act will be followed by an appropriate punishment.

Unfortunately, as Baron and Byrne point out, these conditions are not found in most criminal justice systems. Punishment tends to come months after the event, may well be too lenient, and can obviously only be used on the relatively small number of people who are actually convicted of having committed criminal acts.

Another strategy which has been used to reduce aggression is catharsis. This is the process by which aggressive people are encouraged to get the anger out of their system, by engaging in some form of physical exercise (see Chapter 5). Thus the person who has been provoked or aroused will be encouraged to blow off steam in a non-harmful way. This idea stems from the work of Sigmund Freud, who believed that if tensions are allowed to build up too much, there will be an explosion. But does catharsis work? The evidence is not too clear. It would appear that engaging in vigorous physical activity does reduce arousal levels, but only temporarily (see Feshbach, 1984). Once the person again thinks of the situation that produced the arousal, the desire to harm the source of the provocation returns. It thus appears that attacking inanimate objects (e.g. kicking the door) may make people feel better in the short term, but does little to reduce aggression in the long term.

Another factor which may mediate against the desire to aggress is the role of apologies. There is strong experimental evidence to support the view that an apology can be an effective way of diffusing another's aggression (see Baron, 1990). Whilst it is difficult for most people to admit that what they did was wrong and that they are sorry, it can be an effective counter to another's intention to harm, especially if the apology also contains a request for forgiveness. Having said that, it does appear that the nature of the excuse offered with the apology affects the likelihood of its being accepted. In particular if the reason was seen to be out of the person's control (an external attribution) it is more effective than if it was thought to be within their control.

In Chapter 5 we considered the role of the media as a possible instigator of aggression. If violent models on television produce imitation, then exposure to non-violent models may actually reduce aggression. In particular the showing of a person dealing with a tense situation in a non-aggressive way may act as a good model. There is some evidence to support this viewpoint (see Baron, 1972). However, one must question how practical such an approach is, given that the vast majority of television programmes do not show people reacting to tension in non-aggressive ways.

We saw earlier that aggression can stem from a poor ability to interact with others. A great deal of everyday interaction relies on a whole series of learned social skills. People who have deficits in this area may well become frustrated by the fact that no one ever listens to them. This frustration may then turn to anger, and result in aggression. This is one area where the source of the frustration can be removed relatively easily. Through social skills training, people can be taught more appropriate ways in which they can interact with others, and this in turn can lead to a lowering of aggression (see Trower et al, 1978).

SUMMARY

This chapter has introduced the reader to some of the more common forms of mental illness. Whilst acknowledging that there is some difficulty in differentiating objectively between normality and abnormality, it is important for the police officer to be able to recognise the symptoms of the more common forms of mental illness. Schizophrenia, depression, and personality disorders have been outlined, and the behaviour associated with such conditions identified. The thorny issue of drug abuse has also been covered briefly.

Strategies for dealing with aggressive behaviour have also been outlined, and it is hoped that police officers can improve the way in which they deal with potentially violent individuals and incidents.

FURTHER READING

Blackburn, R. (1993) *The Psychology of Criminal Conduct*. Chichester: Wiley.

Goldstein, A. P., Carr, E. G., Davidson, W. S. & Wehr, P. (1981) *In Response to Aggression: Methods of Control and Prosocial Alternatives*. New York: Pergamon.

Halgin, R. P. & Whitbourne, S. K. (1993) *Abnormal Psychology*. Orlando, FL: Harcourt Brace Jovanovich.

PART II

The Police as an Organisation

CHAPTER 7

Psychological Testing and Police Selection

Stories such as the above are obviously worrying for both the police and the public. Any organisation whose members are charged with controlling the behaviour of others will inevitably come under attack from some members of that society. Headlines such as these may well appear in many countries, where bias is alleged by groups within society, including ethnic minorities. However, such headlines and reports are clearly of great concern to an organisation which is charged with serving and protecting the whole of a population. In this chapter we will start to consider what sort of person might make the best recruit to the police service, and whether recruiting the right sort of person might mean that the police are more able to police society in an even-handed way. Is it possible to recruit the sort of person who will never show bias in dealing with different members of the public, or is this an unrealistic goal? Even if such people could be recruited, might the prevailing subculture within the organisation change their noble ideals? In this chapter we will consider the extent to which psychological testing might help in selecting the most appropriate person for the organisation. Starting with the example of racism, the difficulties inherent in selection strategies will be explored and suggestions made.

The many demands of an increasingly complex society have pressured police forces to re-examine many of their selection, training and management methods. Although a number of changes in styles of management have been tried (see Butler, 1992), there has also been an increased focus on the way in which the police choose recruits to their organisation. It is something of a cliché to say that any organisation is only as good as its staff. However, it is obviously important that any organisation recruits the best qualified and most suitable people if it is to function efficiently and effectively. When complaints are made against "the police", it is invariably the actions of one single police officer which tarnish the name of the police force. As we saw in Chapter 1, because the police are seen as a homogeneous group, the bad actions of one officer may well be assumed to be representative of the whole organisation. Bad behaviour by one police officer is also more newsworthy than the good actions of all the others (see Chapter 11). It is thus vital that the police service recruits officers who are not only likely to be good at their job, but who are also unlikely to discredit the police service as a whole.

PREJUDICE, RACISM AND RECRUITMENT

There are many difficulties surrounding selection and the use of psychological testing. It is not a straightforward matter of giving applicants a quick test, and then making a selection on that basis. Let us take as an example a person who joins the police service but who possesses racist attitudes. Throughout training the person may pay lip service to the anti-racist messages put across, but still maintain an underlying belief that people of certain races are inferior, or perhaps more troublesome than members of his/her own race. When patrolling, especially if alone, the officer will inevitably treat people of different races differently, and may feel justified in using racist language towards, say, a black suspect. The suspect may resent such treatment, become hostile and be arrested. This will produce suspicion, animosity and hostility on the part of other members of the arrested person's racial group. It may thus lead to a worsening of relations, or perhaps official complaints.

One can see why getting things right at the selection stage is so important. In this example, the reputation of a whole police force may be damaged by the recruitment of just one "bad apple", especially if the actions of that officer become well publicised. Headlines such as the one at the beginning of this chapter can only serve to alienate those who already feel uncomfortable about the police role. The fact that the article referred to goes on to say that overall complaints fell by 7% is lost in the text, and the reader is left with a bad impression.

In Britain, as in many other countries, accusations of racism by public figures are never far from the surface. It is understandable that members of any minority group, angry at its perceived mistreatment by society, may express hostility towards the symbol of that society's authority – in this case the police officer. Reports such as those of Lord Scarman (1981) advocated major changes in both recruitment and training of police officers. The Scarman inquiry was set up to investigate the causes of a number of riots in Britain's cities. It identified racism within the police service as one of the causative factors, and suggested that strategies should be adopted to reduce this. The report advocated that police forces should avoid recruiting those who showed racist attitudes, and also suggested that there should be training in anti-racist strategies. Despite some improvements in this area, the recent report (Police Complaints Authority, 1993) highlighted above has shown that complaints of racial discrimination made to the British Police Complaints Authority have risen significantly – from 49 in 1991 and 73 in 1992 to 291 in 1993. As with any such statistic, it is difficult to say what proportion of this increase may be due to increased racism by police officers, and what proportion is due to differences in reporting and recording practices. The Authority's chairman Sir Leonard Peach makes the point that: "The increase in claims of assault and racial bias could be a result of a more violent society and a greater unwillingness to tolerate racially offensive behaviour" (Peach, 1993). However, the perception by members of the public, especially those from ethnic minorities, may well be that members of the police service do still show racism in some of their actions.

The issue of alleged racism raises a number of interesting points in respect of psychological testing and police recruitment. If the absence of racism were seen as the most important criterion upon which police officers should be recruited, it would be relatively straightforward to administer psychometric tests to identify applicants who show such tendencies. There is some evidence that some people do have deeply prejudiced personalities (see Adorno, Frenkel-Brunswick, Levinson & Sanford, 1950) and such people would clearly make unsuitable police officers. They would exhibit racial prejudice but also show animosity towards many other "minority groups", and would thus discriminate on gender, religious, physical disability, or other grounds. Such people could certainly not be expected to uphold the law "without fear or favour" which is part of the oath which a British police officer has to swear.

However, prejudice is not necessarily an all or nothing issue. Whilst psychological testing might identify those who are the most prejudiced, and those who are the least so, the majority of people would fall in the middle area and show neither extreme. We saw in Chapter 4 how group membership results in people tending to favour the in-group and tending to dislike the out-group to some degree. In other words everyone shows some degree of prejudice in their dealings with others. This can be as simple as a person choosing to strike up a conversation with a person of their own race, as opposed to someone of a different race. Thus it is perhaps naïve to say that the police service should simply avoid recruiting anyone who shows any form of prejudice. It was argued in Chapter 4 that some degree of prejudice is an inevitable consequence of people's group membership. But at least by bringing such tendencies to the attention of people such as police officers, they are less likely to allow such tendencies to manifest themselves in actual discrimination.

Whilst avoiding the recruitment of racists is obviously desirable and perhaps essential, there are clearly a large number of other important criteria which must be met by any potential recruit. Although impartiality is an important concern, so too are such qualities as honesty, integrity, reliability, ability to deal with all members of the public fairly. There is a danger that by singling out one criterion (in this case anyone who shows the slightest racist tendencies) the police service will not consider people who have many other good qualities that would make them excellent police officers. It is certainly *not* being suggested that people who are clearly racists should be encouraged to join the police service. Rather it is being suggested that those who, through ignorance or misinformation, express unacceptable views, might have such views challenged and changed by the use of appropriate training (see Chapter 8). If a very slight tendency to racism is perceived as being simply an inappropriate attitude, then it may be a relatively straightforward matter to change that attitude to one that is more acceptable to the organisation. We must, however, still bear in mind that those with the most deeply prejudiced personalities will be highly resistant to any attempts to change attitudes.

If an organisation is inherently racist, then previously unprejudiced recruits may well change their own attitudes so that they fall into line with the majority view. But by the same token, an individual who already has slight racist tendencies might be persuaded to change these views if the organisation shows clear disapproval of such attitudes. Whilst the making of racist behaviour a disciplinary offence may produce compliance, it may well not produce a change in the person's underlying belief system, and thus not produce an internal acceptance of non-racist views.

Psychologists have identified that there are a number of ways in which conformity can be produced. For example, Kiesler and Kiesler (1969) made a clear distinction between *compliance* and *internalisation*. In the former, the person may well comply with rules and regulations in order to avoid punishment, but will revert to previous attitudes and behaviour when such threats are no longer present. For example the racist officer might quickly learn not to express prejudice in the presence of senior officers, but may continue to espouse such views when off duty with colleagues. Thus compliance is temporary and superficial. By contrast, internalisation is much more likely to be permanent. It will be shown by a person who comes to believe in certain attitudes, and holds them because they are correct.

The informal subculture of the organisation must thus demonstrate to the recruit that such attitudes or behaviour are inappropriate, inaccurate, and unacceptable. Any organisation which is already multi-racial in its composition will also carry a different message to the recruit than will one which is almost exclusively white and male. Many British police forces recognise this, but so far have found it difficult to attract larger numbers of ethnic minorities into the service. Holdaway (1991) puts the point thus:

> "If people from ethnic minorities join the police in significant numbers, fears of criticism from peers, the white public and police colleagues is at worst manageable and at best inconsequential. When ethnic minority officers routinely patrol the streets of market towns, seaside resorts, villages, suburbs and the great cities, an important change in patterns of police recruitment will have taken place, with implications for the whole of British society." (p. 1)

This really is something of a chicken and egg situation. If the police service is perceived as being racist, it will remain an unattractive career choice for those from ethnic minorities. However, whilst this perception remains, people from ethnic minorities will also look at the absence of non-white officers in the force, and claim that it is unrepresentative, and possibly unfair.

Greater recruitment of people from ethnic minorities is unquestionably desirable, but may not be the simple panacea which some writers have suggested. Although recruitment of people from such groups is clearly an important goal, the person chosen will be expected also to possess the many other qualities needed to be a good and effective police officer. In other words being a member of a minority group will never be the sole reason for a person's appointment. Positive discrimination may attract a larger number of recruits from ethnic minorities, but is fraught with its own difficulties. Some senior police officers have in the past pointed to a possible resentment by the white majority, and a suspicion that non-whites can never be "as good" if they need to have special entry requirements. Clearly it is inappropriate to say that because the majority might object, we should do nothing. As Holdaway says in the conclusion of his report:

"All the evidence from this study indicates that without a clearly positive stance, ethnic minority recruitment rests on ambivalence, or good intentions which are not translated into principles of action to underpin policy. Without a positive stance and the special efforts associated with it, the status quo will be perpetuated." (Holdaway, 1991, p. 185)

We must acknowledge that positive discrimination is not the same as an absence of discrimination. The latter can be reflected in a genuine and effective equal opportunities policy which is perceived as fair and even-handed. One can also take positive action without this becoming positive discrimination.

Let us now take a hypothetical example to illustrate one potential difficulty. Supposing a police force wishes to recruit a larger number of officers from say Afro-Caribbean backgrounds. They may succeed in attracting suitable applicants and be proud of the fact that their force is now much more multi-racial than had previously been the case. However, does this necessarily solve all the problems which have been identified above? There may be an assumption that because the new officers are black, they will not themselves exhibit the racist tendencies which may have been found in some white recruits. It may be assumed that, having been victims of prejudice themselves, they will see the evils of racism and work towards its elimination by being completely even-handed with all members of the public. But what if one of the black officers actually does have some racist views, for example towards Asians or whites? What if one of the officers was blatantly sexist towards female officers? This would clearly pose a real dilemma for the police force. Should they ignore the racism or sexism shown by the black officer and keep up the appearance of being an integrated multi-racial force? Or should they accept that racism in whatever form is unacceptable, not employ the black officer and then risk being accused of bias in recruiting strategies?

This hypothetical example has been used not to imply that black officers will be prejudiced, but merely to make the point that some degree of prejudice may be found across almost all human populations. The organisation needs to decide whether it can tolerate any degree of in-group favouritism (and its corollary, out-group hostility) in its recruits. To deny that such preferences exist appears to be naïve in the light of evidence put forward in Chapter 4. However, the police service can establish procedures which allow genuine equal opportunities, and can teach officers that discrimination is totally unacceptable to the organisation.

CHANGES IN RECRUITMENT STRATEGIES

We can thus see that there are difficulties in terms of recruiting the most appropriate type of person for the police service. Changes in recruitment strategies can eventually produce change within the organisation and are thus commendable. However, any such changes may not show immediate benefits for two important reasons:

1 The effects will be long term. It will take a considerable number of years before the new recruits are really in a position to influence the organisation.
2 New recruits will quickly become socialised into the organisational culture and may have to abandon "new ideas" in favour of doing things the way the organisation expects them to be done (see Fielding, 1988). A new recruit who constantly says "I don't think we should be doing it this way" is unlikely to advance very far or very quickly within the organisation.

Despite these difficulties, it is important that the police service should attract and employ the "right sort of person". As we have already seen, the problem lies in deciding just how this should be defined. Clearly it is important to attract the sort of person who is able to have a positive influence on the functioning and efficiency of the organisation. However, here we hit a further problem alluded to in point 2 above. Is the sort of person who can introduce positive change to the organisation, the same person who would make an ideal new recruit? (Ideal in the eyes of the recruiting officer, that is.) For example, qualities such as *conventionality* and *conformity* may be seen as desirable in a new recruit, but would be unlikely to be found in a person who wishes to challenge preconceived ideas at top management level. By contrast, *innovativeness* may be essential for a visionary within the organisation, but would be frowned upon or feared by the staid and solid "Organisation Man" recruiting officer.

If psychologists are to be able to help improve appropriate recruitment, they need first to know exactly what qualities the police service needs in a new recruit. There are inevitably variations between British police forces, not to mention police forces in other countries (see Yuille, 1986). There is also some degree of commonality across police forces. Up until recently, height was used as one of the first filtering mechanisms; good physical health and eyesight were also considered obligatory. All police forces now have minimum age and educational requirements, and will insist that the candidate is of "good character" (however that is defined) and does not have a criminal record. Relatively recently, all British applicants have been asked to take an intelligence test. This has a Home Office specified cut-off line, with those who score below the line being rejected. There is an assumption here that a certain level of intelligence is an essential ingredient for a good police officer. This assumption may at first glance appear a reasonable one, as policing is a complex task, requiring a certain level of cognitive ability. However, many studies have found that IQ tests are good predictors of performance at the training school, but are poor indicators of future performance on the streets (see Taylor & Pease, 1988). Whilst a certain level of intelligence is clearly essential, it appears not to be the case that the most intelligent person necessarily makes the best police officer. Other qualities may be as important if not more so.

Beyond the minimum requirements mentioned above, the exact qualities specified for the good recruit become a little vague. Each force sets its own standards to some extent, and these are partially related to local needs and conditions. For example, when the Royal Canadian Mounted Police was established in 1867 the following conditions were specified:

> "Candidates must be active, able-bodied men of thorough sound constitution and exemplary character. They should be able to ride well, and to read and write either the English or French language." (Loo & Meredith, 1986, p. 3)

Such definitions may seem quaintly amusing today, but the need to find recruits with "good character" can be seen in these early days. Even then there was an image of what the good recruit would look like.

Some insight into what qualities are desirable or essential in a recruit today can be gained by asking serving officers about such qualities. It would seem a reasonable assumption that those currently doing the job can identify the essential qualities needed. A small sample of British police officers who were attending a course organised by Manchester University were asked about recruitment (see Ainsworth, 1993). The officers were asked to list what they thought were the most important qualities for a new recruit to possess. Listed below are the factors identified by this group, arranged in order of priority.

- A sense of humour
- Communication skills
- Adaptability
- Common sense
- Resilience
- Assertiveness
- Sensitivity
- Tolerance
- Integrity

- Literacy
- Honesty
- Problem-solving ability

For a psychologist, this is an interesting list. Whilst some of these traits are measurable by current standardised and validated psychological tests (see Anastasi, 1988) others are not. One that falls into the latter category is the quality which came first on most lists of priorities, i.e. possessing a sense of humour!

One problem with asking questions such as the one posed to the serving officers above, is in knowing how the question will be interpreted. When asking about "the most important qualities needed" we need to know if these are deemed the most important for a recruit about to start training school, a probationer, a community constable, a detective, a senior officer or whatever. The qualities required are clearly not identical in all these cases, indeed in some instances the qualities required for each of these may be at opposite ends of the spectrum. An officer whose ambitions go no further than wanting to be a local friendly community constable, may have different qualities from one who sees him/herself as a future Chief Constable. As long as most police forces continue to adopt a common entry format (i.e. where all recruits, despite their ultimate destiny in the service, go through an identical training procedure) it will prove difficult if not impossible to agree on one psychological test which identifies the "ideal" recruit. Whilst there are some cases where different criteria are used in selection (e.g. the Graduate Entry Scheme in Britain) in most instances common entrance requirements tend to produce a homogeneous group of recruits.

It is difficult to think of many other organisations where each recruit, irrespective of their qualifications, background or special expertise, is expected to go through identical training procedures and assessments. One consequence of this is that the police service tends to contain senior officers who have all proved themselves as good "organisation men or women" but do not necessarily have any special expertise in the position to which they are eventually appointed. Most commercial organisations succeed by bringing in people who have demonstrated their good management skills in other organisations and are then head-hunted. By comparison, the police service still tends to hold the view that only those who have risen through the ranks of the service can hold positions of authority within the organisation. Whilst there are transfers and promotions between forces, we are still a long way from a position where an "outsider" is brought in and given authority to introduce change. It is interesting to note that the current British government has recently tried to introduce a number of "free market" ideas to the police service, most of which have now been abandoned as a result of protests from the police themselves (see Chapter 9).

Whilst psychologists traditionally dismiss anecdotal evidence, it is hoped that one such anecdote will serve a useful purpose here. This concerns a police recruiting officer whom the current author met at a recent schools' careers conference. On being questioned about the things he and his organisation were looking for in potential recruits, he summed it up in one sentence: "We're looking for people with *the right personality*".

As a psychologist interested in personality testing I naïvely asked which particular personality test his force used to assess this "right personality". I received a rather blank stare. The recruiting officer went on to explain that in his opinion you could tell a person's personality during an interview – you didn't need all these fancy tests. Fascinated by this reply I again naïvely asked exactly what sort of personality he was looking for – was it extrovert, stable, conformist, authoritarian or whatever. Again came a blank stare and the reply: "No, I mean the right sort of personality, you know, you can tell when you've been in the job as long as I have."

Perhaps this anecdote merely serves to illustrate the gap between academic psychologists and some police officers! Or perhaps it shows that non-psychologists may have difficulty in defining "the right personality" but believe that they will recognise it when they see it. The danger in this rather subjective approach is that the applicant who is selected may well be someone whom the recruiting officer thinks is most like him/herself – or can be moulded into that through training. There are after all more objective ways of measuring personality using psychological tests (see Lorr & Strack, 1994).

A further source of information which is helpful in understanding what the police might look for in a recruit is provided by police recruiting advertisements. The following are some representative examples from the British press. (These adverts are from some years ago, as economic conditions in Britain have resulted in most police forces no longer having to advertise for recruits.)

The first advertisement appeared in the *Sunday Times*, 31.3.82. It showed a black and white police officer patrolling together, and was entitled "Brothers in Arms". It read as follows:

> "Ask any Policeman or Policewoman why they joined the force and you'll get the same answer. To get involved with people. To get involved with the community they patrol ... He needs to be something of a social worker on the one hand, yet on the other, he is invested with the authority of the law."

Another advert appeared in the *Sunday Times* of 8.2.81, and was headed "Could you provide the service the public demands from a Police Officer?" It contained the following information:

"It's a complicated job. For society itself has become more complicated. Whether you're a man or a woman you'll have to be responsible, decisive, occasionally courageous. You'll need plenty of common sense, and a sense of humour too . . . We'll help you develop self-confidence to deal with even the trickiest situation."

A further example is again taken from the *Sunday Times* dated 10.11.80 and went under the heading "Are good coppers born or made?" It read as follows:

"You may sometimes wonder if you've got what it takes to be a good copper. . . Some people are practically born coppers. . . Not wearing Size 12 boots and saying Ello, Ello, Ello, but born with the qualities every copper needs: like intelligence, commonsense and a real interest in people . . . , if you're not interested in people it's doubtful whether the police will be interested in you. We need people who genuinely want to help other people. It's what the job is all about.

We hope you will acquire a balanced outlook on life. That's absolutely essential for every police officer. . . You will have to learn to keep cool and always be impartial. There is no place in the police service for extremists.

Police Officers must be able to stand on their own two feet. They must be capable of making decisions . . . and taking the responsibility for those decisions . . . could you cope? Yes if you're the right kind of person (and we'll only select you if you are).

What we're looking for in fact is raw material and lots of enthusiasm . . . After all the teaching, theorising and talk about whether a copper is born or made, it eventually comes down to the qualities you possess."

These examples provide an interesting insight into what police forces (at least British ones) are looking for. The adverts do suggest that the police force needs "the right sort of person" but there is some confusion over what exactly this person looks like. The most important criterion seems to be "a sense of humour" as it appears in most advertisements. You will recall that this same quality was identified as most important by the groups of serving officers mentioned earlier. One is left to imagine just how this quality might be assessed during interview.

PSYCHOMETRIC TESTS

It is clearly important to establish the extent to which psychometric testing can help, once explicit criteria for selection have been identified.

Psychological tests have developed rapidly in recent years and many are now well refined and sophisticated instruments (see Anastasi, 1988). There are literally hundreds of different tests available, testing intelligence, personality, aptitude and other qualities. Tests can provide information and should be able to inform decision-making. In the case of recruitment, the results of a test should tell us whether someone is: (a) appointable, or (b) not appointable.

In reality there is of course a large grey area in between these two categories. But we may well wish to know more than simply whether someone is appointable or not. A force with a large number of applicants and a small number of vacancies needs to know which of the appointable applicants would make the best officers. A number of applicants may well be appointable but may not prove to be the best police officers. In America, where tests are used much more widely, screening *out* undesirable applicants is sometimes seen to take priority over selecting the best person – best that is in terms of ultimate career prospects (see Spielberger, 1979; Burbeck & Furnham, 1985). We should also note that candidates will often try to complete any test in a way that flatters them, or at least shows them in a good light (see Castello, Schneider & Schoenfeld, 1993).

Whether or not someone is considered suitable can be determined by a test score which *should* predict future performance. There may still be difficulties here though. As some previous authors have pointed out (Taylor & Pease, 1988) it is difficult to know where the criterion point should lie. In times of high recruitment, the cut-off point may need to be lowered, whereas at times of low recruitment, the organisation can literally be more selective and can raise the decision point (out of the grey area).

Psychological tests are useful in deciding whether or not a person possesses certain qualities or attributes. These can be tested and each person given a numerical score. As we have already seen, the problem is often in deciding *which* qualities should be tested for. The next task is to test usefulness considering what is called *criterion referenced validation*. This refers to whether scores on a psychological test correlate with some measurement of job performance (e.g. promotion). If this is so, then the test is said to have high validity and would be particularly useful.

Psychological testing is an attempt to be objective rather than subjective (which the traditional recruitment interview tended to be). Providing one can select and measure the attributes required, then psychological tests can be very useful. However, as we have seen earlier, the problem arises in selecting which attributes are the most important. Should the selection process look for qualities associated with the traditional "good copper" (criteria which an officer's peers might well use – a copper's copper)? Or do we use qualities defined by senior officers, the Home Office, the Police Authority, or the general public? The point is that there may well be differences in what each sees as the most important criteria, and thus what should be measured. Can we really assume that the most desirable characteristics for the raw recruit are the same as those for a senior officer?

An important notion to bear in mind in relation to testing is that of *concurrent validity*. This is a procedure in which a psychologist might subject all experienced police officers to a battery of tests and correlate their scores with some measure of their quality of performance. In other words the psychologist could identify those attributes which appear to be associated with good job performance. Those items in the test battery which were correlated with good performance could then be used to screen applicants.

The theory here is that applicants who perform well on the tests (i.e. in ways similar to good or successful police officers) would be selected, and those who do not would be rejected. The problem with this approach is that it does not necessarily have *predictive validity*.

Test items that distinguish good and bad police officers *now* may be different from those that distinguish between people *who are likely to become* good officers – i.e. those who can change and adapt most easily. In fact many of the skills of a "good police officer" may be those that have been learnt during training, rather than those which the person has always possessed. Thus the best potential recruit may be one who has natural ability, but few specific skills on entry. This person may well gain the most from training, and emerge from training school as an ideal officer. By contrast, a person who looks very good on paper may respond poorly to the training school and end up with fewer relevant skills (see Chapter 8).

A better approach would be to give a whole range of tests to all applicants to the police service. These test results could then be put away. Some years later, *all* the police officers should be assessed and divided into those who have been successful in their work and those who have not. Their test scores obtained some years earlier can then be checked and cross-referenced, to see which were predictive of future good performance. This could also prove useful in terms of identifying what factors were linked with wastage from the police service.

The advantage of this system is that it is a true *predictive test* and allows us to compare scores which people obtained *at the time of recruitment* and correlate them with future success. Of course there may be a potential problem with this in that the requirements of the police service may well change over time, and so some retesting may be required.

Predictive Tests are thus of great value, and are far more suitable than Concurrent Validity Tests. Unfortunately a great deal of the literature on psychological testing and recruit selection has looked at tests of Concurrent Validity (see Spielberger, 1979). These tests may have some use in terms of deciding whether people with certain personalities are better suited to certain roles within the police service (e.g. firearms officers). They may also be useful in terms of optimal career development. For example it may be possible to identify the sort of person who would make a good commanding officer, or a good detective, early in that person's career.

There are a large number of studies in the American literature which have looked at testing and recruit selection. Many of these have been reviewed by Burbeck and Furnham (1985). After examining a whole series of studies they conclude:

> "The varying criteria of what constitutes a successful police officer result in different studies which are not comparable. More use needs to be made of job analysis so that the essential elements for success can be identified and used in the selection process." (p. 67)

In fact these authors are quite negative about the findings of the many research studies. In addition to the problems already outlined, they make the following points:

1 Socialisation into the police role and police culture may be as important as personality variables.

Whilst this is undoubtedly true, it may reasonably be argued that this may not apply equally to all personality types. For example, the person with a particularly strong or dominant personality may be more resistant to the influence of police culture and training.

2 Comparison of studies across different forces in Britain, let alone in different countries, may not be appropriate.

Clearly, the requirements for a "good" police officer in Devon and Cornwall may be different from those in the Metropolitan Police. Similarly when we compare Cumbria (UK) with Paris or New York, should we really expect to find a strong common denominator? Different policing requirements demand different skills, and perhaps even a different type of personality. Detailed and specific *job analysis*, on a local basis, is thus needed before we can specify exactly what qualities are to be tested (see Baehr & Oppenheim, 1979).

As was pointed out earlier, the British police service chooses not to recruit specialists, nor different people for specific departments. Yet it is assumed that individuals who will make a good dog handler, detective, or senior officer should have the same qualities *at the time of selection* into the police service.

As mentioned earlier, there is far more use made of psychological testing in the USA than in Britain (almost 70% of US forces use it). In Britain, the Home Office's view is that there is not at present a suitable psychological test available. Home Office Circular 17/1984 states quite simply that: "The introduction of psychological testing into the recruit selection procedure is not recommended."

Despite this, various British forces do use some form of psychometric testing in selection, though this is never used as the sole selection method. Having said that, some forces do use such tests as part of an initial screening programme, with those applicants whose scores are considered abnormal being rejected or subjected to more detailed examination. Tests are also used in selecting officers for promotion, and in some cases, for specialist duties such as firearms officers. In the case of promotion selection, psychometric tests are often used in conjunction with other techniques. The problem with many such tests is that they are neither administered by, nor interpreted by, a qualified psychologist. Psychometric tests are not toys and they should only be administered by a person with appropriate training. In reality, it is not uncommon for police forces to buy in packages and then try to make sense of the results. The value of such testing is thus questionable or, in some cases of misuse, dangerous.

Some recent British work (Labuc, 1991) has made claims for the use of the *Labwick Personality Inventory*. Labuc claims a very high correlation between the results of the personality test and actual job performance. He asserts that any suitably qualified assessor can evaluate the present and future potential of an individual. This work is very much in its infancy, and it remains to be seen if these early claims are substantiated by more detailed research.

ASSESSMENT CENTRES

There is now increasing use made of assessment centres in Britain (see Wallace, 1994). These can be used to measure the requisite qualities in a candidate, and to allow assessment in relevant situations. Skills in areas such as decision-making, communication, maturity, can be tested more easily in this type of situation. Assessment centres are, however, expensive to run, and are often used in conjunction with other filtering mechanisms. There is also a danger that assessment centres do not simply identify all those people who are suitable for promotion, but are instead used to identify the best people in a group, and recommend for promotion a number which matches identically the number of current vacancies (see Wallace, 1994). Assessment centres can be useful in that they allow officers to role play situations which they will encounter if and when they are promoted. However, there are still difficulties with this approach, in particular the expectation that officers should know how to handle situations before having been given appropriate training.

PSYCHOLOGICAL TESTING IN PERSPECTIVE

Having reviewed some of the evidence, it would appear that psychological testing can help, providing the following points are borne in mind. Firstly, a detailed job analysis is needed in order to understand just what an officer is expected to be able to do, and exactly what skills are needed for this. The qualities that are required can then be divided into those which:

1 Are necessary components within the personality of the recruit.
2 Can be acquired during training.

In the case of the former, these can be measured objectively using standardised and validated psychometric tests. It may also be possible to tell at this early stage the particular branch of the service to which a person may be best suited. This is already done to some extent with the Graduate Entry Scheme – based largely on education. But might not this idea be extended? After all many people apply to join the police service with a firm idea about which branch of the service they would like to eventually join. Disillusionment might be reduced if recruits were told at the time of application that it was highly unlikely that they would end up in the branch of the service which first attracted them.

We may still wish to ask whether it is possible to recruit people who will have a positive impact on the organisation and produce change where this is appropriate. It would appear that it is possible, but admittedly difficult given the complexities and dominant subculture of the police organisation. As discussed earlier, someone who is genuinely innovative may well be feared and rejected – either at the recruiting stage or once within the organisation. Someone with ideas and vision may also be viewed with suspicion – and attempts be made to bring them back into line.

By using instruments which do have predictive ability, psychological tests can still inform decision-making – provided the force can be clear about exactly what it does require. When such requirements are made clear, the psychologist can provide the tools to measure and assess whether or not a given person does possess these qualities. Again we do need a very clear definition of what we mean by "a *good* police officer". We need to decide whether we use promotion, staying out of trouble, or being well liked by colleagues or senior officers as the criterion. Only when these criteria are spelled out clearly, can the psychologist truly help.

SUMMARY

This chapter has attempted to address some of the difficulties associated with the use of psychological tests in recruit selection. It has been pointed out that while the use of such tests can prove beneficial, there are a number of difficulties which need to be overcome. In particular, detailed and local job analysis is needed before psychologists can decide which qualities should be tested for in the recruit. The thorny topic of racism has also been addressed and ways suggested of reducing such prejudice within the organisation. Realistically speaking, psychological tests are unlikely ever to become the sole criterion upon which applicants are accepted or rejected. Having said that, such tests can provide useful and objective information about a candidate and can help to identify those most and least suited to the complex job of law enforcement.

FURTHER READING

Blau, T. (1994) *Psychological Service for Law Enforcement.* Chichester: Wiley.
Burbeck, E. & Furnham, A. (1985) Police Officer Selection: A Critical Review of the Literature. *Journal of Police Science & Administration,* **13**, 58–69.
Spielberger, C. D. (1979) *Police Selection and Evaluation.* Washington: Hemisphere.
Yuille, J. C. (1986) *Police Selection and Training: The Role of Psychology.* Dordrecht: Martinus Nijhoff.

CHAPTER 8

Training and the Police Culture

"Police training centre initial ten-week course, most rewarding job. I never went for good 'results'. If my class shook hands at the end and said, 'Thanks for all you've done,' I thought, 'That's given them something to go on, some good advice from the past.' I'm not bothered about the lad with the 92 per cent in the back row . . . Some still write to me and that's the success I measure . . . We've got too much round examinations and results instead of moulding a person to get out into the community." (Police training instructor quoted in Fielding, 1988, p. 77)

The above quote identifies one of the major dilemmas about police training, i.e. the conflict between learning of the law, and the more practical side of dealing with others. In the previous chapter we saw some of the difficulties associated with selecting the most suitable person for the role of police officer. In that chapter it was acknowledged that recruits might not possess all the right credentials at the time of their appointment, but that many of the skills and qualities needed in police work can be learned during appropriate training. In this chapter the training of police officers will be considered in some detail, and comparisons made between official training procedures and qualities learnt via the informal subculture. The chapter will focus on the training of British and American police recruits, and comparisons made between the different approaches.

Police work is one of the most multi-faceted occupations imaginable. The number of different duties which a police officer may be called upon to perform is almost endless. Indeed one of the attractions of a career in the police service is this very diversity – it is said that no two days' work are ever the same. There are literally hundreds of different types of incident which a police officer will be called upon to deal with, each requiring its own specialist skills. Dealing with a traffic accident, chasing a young vandal, delivering death messages, arresting a drunken reveller, dealing with lost children, settling a domestic dispute, quelling a riot, giving evidence in court, tackling mounds of paper work, are just some of the tasks which the average officer may be expected to be able to handle. Whilst many other occupations require a high level of skill, expertise and training, there are few professions in which the breadth of skills required is so great. For this reason, police training always involves a compromise in terms of what should be included and what should be left out. It is difficult to imagine any training programme which would equip the police officer with the skill to deal with every incident which he/she comes across during a day on the streets. As Dean (1976) put it:

> "After two centuries of grafting new parts onto the role of the policeman, the end product is, indeed, a complicated, often inconsistent, sometimes impossible role with high and increasing expectations." (p. 186)

The advent of personal radios, and the fact that officers are increasingly working in pairs, means that help and advice from others is never far away. Nevertheless, the young police officer still needs to be reasonably well equipped to deal with the more common incidents once he/she has left the training school.

One interesting aspect about police training is that it varies greatly from one country to another (see Yuille, 1986). The actual length of time spent in training differs significantly, as indeed does the content of such instruction. A significant proportion of an American recruit's time is spent on firearms training. Currently in Britain this is not included in initial training. Training also varies from one historical point in time to another. In the 1920s and '30s police officers received very little formal training, but over the years the average length of time spent in training has increased. Having said that, the amount of formal training is still considerably less than that of some other occupations. If one thinks of professions such as social work or probation, or even law, or medicine, the amount of time spent in initial training is considerably more. Whilst police officers may well receive more in-service training, the formal training input received before officers are allowed to interact with the public is significantly less. For this reason it is important that the training is appropriate, relevant, and concise. Stratton, an American psychologist who works with the police, makes an important point in saying:

> "It is amazing that as much knowledge is imparted in the relatively brief training period, and understandable why information related to interpersonal relationships and communication skills may be at a minimal level if even existent." (Stratton, 1984, p. 57)

One interesting study of training needs was carried out by Phillips (1984). He sent out questionnaires to over 16,000 American law enforcement agencies, asking for their training priorities for both general and specialised police services. The ten highest priorities (in rank order) were as follows:

1 Handle personal stress.
2 Conduct interviews/interrogations.
3 Drive vehicles in emergency situations.
4 Maintain an appropriate level of physical fitness.
5 Promote a positive public image.
6 Determine probable cause for arrest.
7 Write crime incident reports.
8 Handle domestic disturbances.
9 Collect, maintain, and preserve evidence.
10 Respond to crimes in progress.

This is an interesting list and gives an insight into where American trainers put their resources. No such exhaustive study has been carried out in Britain, but priorities do appear to be somewhat different. Certainly comparatively little time is spent on "handling personal stress", the item at the top of the Americans' list (see Manolias, 1988). One might suggest that an important aspect of personal stress could be the fact that officers are not adequately trained to handle many of the situations which they will encounter on the streets. It was suggested in the previous chapter that detailed job analysis was necessary before selection could become more effective. The same argument would appear to be true in respect of training programmes.

Whilst many professionals' training incorporates a large amount of communication skills teaching, the traditional police training school has tended to largely ignore such matters. Phillips's research cited above does not mention communication skills as a training priority, though such skills play an important role in many of the subjects cited. There is almost a naïve assumption that effective communication will come naturally and does not need to be taught formally. For this reason far more time is spent on such subjects as self-protection techniques and disarming and arrest of suspects. But the way in which police officers approach a situation and communicate with others can have important effects on things like the level of cooperation or aggression shown by the other person. Whilst today's violent society means that personal safety is given priority in the training school, everyday face-to-face communication should also be seen as a crucial teachable skill.

Differences in training partly reflect differences in what the public demands, but also can be related to different philosophies about training. Reisser, another American police psychologist, has noted:

"The complex demands of the police role, the structure of the police organisation, the policing goals in regard to the community, and the basic philosophy of the department all influence the kind of training that will be provided ultimately and the ways in which that training will likely impact the officer's relationships with the citizens in the community, with peers and also with superiors in the police organisation." (Reisser, 1986, p. 21)

Twenty years ago much of a British police officer's time at training school was spent on learning police powers and legislation, often parrot fashion. Today there is far less emphasis on rote learning, and much more on dealing with different types of incidents.

One common thread that does run through most police training is the belief that it is best carried out by other police officers. There is an assumption that those with their own experience of police work are in the best position to pass on the benefits of their experience. Similarly there is a view that good practitioners will automatically be good teachers. This belief partly reflects the closed occupational culture of policing described in Chapter 4 and by Fielding (1988). Whilst there is undoubtedly merit in using seasoned practitioners to train new recruits, the danger is that some poor practice is taught along with the good. The other danger is that by using predominantly people from within the organisation, insularity and suspicion of outsiders is encouraged. It is also unlikely that much change will be introduced into the organisation, but rather there will be a perpetuation of well entrenched values, stereotypes and prejudices. It has been said that if change does occur in what is essentially a conservative bureaucratic organisation it is likely to be evolutionary rather than revolutionary.

Increasingly, police training schools do now utilise people from outside the organisation, but such experts are still by no means in the majority. When outside speakers are used there also tends to be a different emphasis put on their input. For example in British training schools in the 1970s, outside speakers were invited in, but their contributions were rarely included in any written examination taken by the recruits. The recruits would inevitably pick up such signals and learn that the views of "outsiders" were of less importance than those from within the organisation. It has taken a long time to reach the point where the views of psychologists are sought and even welcomed in police training. Ray Bull's pioneering work with the Metropolitan Police in London was a turning point in this respect (see Bull & Horncastle, 1988). The introduction of "Human Awareness Training" demonstrated a major shift in thinking and a recognition that psychology did have something of value to offer in the realm of police training.

However, like all innovations this was not without its problems, with many senior officers remaining suspicious. One illustration of this was the subsequent changing of the title from Human Awareness Training to "Policing Skills" – a title which was less emotive and did not threaten the status quo. One other problem with such innovations concerns the way in which new subjects are taught. Because most training is carried out in-house, it is the generic police instructors who will be given the task of teaching new material such as psychological perspectives. However, in most cases the instructor will have no background in psychology and will thus have a very limited knowledge base. The training which the instructor him/herself receives will be considerably less than the three years plus which a psychology undergraduate would receive before being considered as a "psychologist". As with the use of psychological research in selection (see Chapter 7), a small amount of knowledge in a complex field such as psychology can be potentially dangerous. Like other social sciences, psychology does not lend itself easily to clear concise statements couched in black and white terms. As was shown in Chapter 3 of this book, there is a danger that lay people will latch on to a finding from psychological research and apply it indiscriminately and inappropriately.

Amongst the major recent changes in British police training has been a move away from teacher-centred learning towards student-centred learning (see Southgate, 1988). The old method of "chalk and talk" has to a large extent been replaced by an interactive approach between instructor and student. The skills needed for such an approach are clearly quite different from those formerly required. Traditionally, teaching could be described as didactic, with much formal instruction. However, more recently the approach has become more facilitative, with the teacher enabling and encouraging the student to learn in his/her own way. For this reason, the instructor's role has changed, from one where he/she is seen as the fount of all knowledge, to one where his/her role is in knowing how best to provide the appropriate learning experience when the recruit is most receptive. There is thus a far greater range of methods used in training today than was the case only a few years ago. Whilst classroom instruction is still used to some extent, far greater use is made of individual reading, projects, class discussion, role play, and what is termed reflective learning. This can be based on self-diagnostic questionnaires (often quasi-psychological in nature) and experiential group learning. One can imagine why such methods were treated with suspicion by those long-serving officers who had undergone a much more traditional form of training. Such doubters were concerned that a recruit emerging from training school would know how to discuss issues, but would lack the formal knowledge and discipline which many would formerly have considered essential.

The new mode of instruction has the advantage of encouraging creative learning, rather than simply ploughing through a predetermined syllabus, page by page. However, there were problems when this new approach was introduced, as neither training schools nor instructors were geared up for such a fundamental shift of emphasis. Not only instruction methods, but also assessment techniques had to be changed significantly in order to accommodate the new philosophy. Training schools could no longer rely on regular written examinations to test knowledge of definitions and legal powers. Instead, recruits were now to be assessed on their ability to handle situations encountered during role plays and other practical exercises.

Today it is perhaps surprising to realise how little time was formerly spent on such tests of an officer's ability to deal with real everyday incidents. When such episodes were staged at training schools previously, they were treated as something of a joke, the primary aim of which seemed to be to embarrass the hapless trainee. Whilst such incidents may now appear amusing, it is interesting to think about what effect they may have had on the students. If the "suspect" (played by an instructor in most cases) always runs away, or always becomes violent, this will tend to stick in the minds of the impressionable recruits. Consequently, when dealing with similar incidents on the streets, their priority may well be to physically restrain every suspect, rather than to use such restraint only when it is really necessary.

Perhaps the most fundamental shift in recent training has been the teaching of what could be called practical policing skills. Learning the letter of the law was seen as less important than learning how to enforce the law appropriately. Previously issues such as the use of discretion were largely ignored at training school, and were expected to be learnt during the officer's probationary period on a division. This was changed in the light of new thinking, and sensitive topics such as discretion and wider social issues are now covered. For the first time social studies have been incorporated into the core curriculum, rather than being seen as an afterthought. This change was more fundamental than it may appear, as it acknowledged for the first time that subjects such as psychology should be seen as an integral and integrated part of training. Psychology, sociology, or race relations were thus seen to be bound up with the many other aspects of a police officer's required knowledge base. Thus learning about powers of arrest was integrated with the effect of that arrest on the person, and even the possible effects on the community from which the person was drawn. Even the officer's non-verbal behaviour during the arrest might be covered and seen as part of the total learning experience. There was thus a much greater emphasis on practical policing, rather than simply knowing what the law was. Southgate (1988) makes the following point.

> "The message here is, in fact, twofold: first, there is the recognition that policing must be taught at a primarily practical level. Second, it is clear that there should be a reconsideration of what practical policing skills actually consist of. Thus policing is now seen as primarily a job of talking, negotiation, persuasion, mediation, etc."
> (p. 231)

In some respects the cornerstone of the new approach could be said to be that of communication. As with many other professions (e.g. medicine, social work, teaching, sales) a simple knowledge base is insufficient to guarantee effectiveness or consumer satisfaction. Rather, there must be an understanding of interaction and communication skills in order to be able to function in an appropriate way. In the same way that the most gifted researchers or surgeons may be very poor communicators, so too might the knowledgeable police officer lack the ability to interact with others effectively.

Stratton makes the point that police trainers would do well to consider what techniques other agencies have found to be successful in relating to others. Drawing on work from helping professionals, he cites the following skills as being important.

> *Respect* – Recognizing human beings as worthwhile and capable of determining their own destiny.
> *Empathic understanding* – The ability genuinely to feel and understand how people become involved in various situations.
> *Genuineness* – Being honest and sincere with others, sharing reactions, beliefs and values.
> *Self-Disclosure* – The ability to share experiences with the client which identify the helper as having similar struggles and problems.
> (Stratton, 1984, pp. 62–63)

At first glance such a list may appear much more appropriate to professionals such as social workers than to those in the supposedly tough and dangerous world of policing. However, despite its public image, the majority of police work does not involve the chasing and arrest of criminals, but rather is about interacting with ordinary members of the public (see Punch, 1979; Brown, 1981; Stephens & Becker, 1994). To a certain extent some of the above qualities may be sought in the new recruit (see Chapter 7) but they can also be encouraged during the training process. Reisser puts the point succinctly when he says:

"The modern officer cannot behave and function as an occupation trooper in a hostile village. He must operate as a crisis intervener and keeper of the peace with community support and approval." (Reisser, 1986, p. 24)

As was stressed earlier in this volume, overall impressions of the police service often originate from the way in which individual officers deal with those with whom they come into contact. For this reason more emphasis needs to be placed on the way in which officers approach citizen encounters than on rote learning of legalistic jargon.

IDENTIFYING GOALS

In the previous chapter attention was drawn to some of the difficulties associated with choosing the right sort of person for the role of police officer. Many of the difficulties stem from the fact that the exact qualities required of a recruit are not clearly established. There are similar difficulties when it comes to training. The exact requirements of a newly qualified police training school graduate are not clearly set out. Consequently it is difficult to establish the extent to which the training has been successful. The fact that over 90% of recruits pass out from the training school at the first attempt might be taken as some measure of success. However, such figures fail to take into account whether the training itself has been appropriate in terms of the skills and qualities which the successful graduates possess. Training may be effective in the short term, but may in reality lack long-term effectiveness (see Levens & Dutton, 1980).

Those involved with the development of psychometric testing (see Anastasi, 1988) have long recognised that measurement itself is relatively easy – the difficult part is in ensuring that what is being measured is appropriate and relevant. This is succinctly expressed by Southgate:

"in looking at what the goals of training should be, one is asking what the goals of the police service are and, if training does not aim to produce police officers who pursue the goals of the service, then it is failing in its basic task." (Southgate, 1988, p. 233)

In other words training needs cannot be isolated from the demands placed upon the police service by the public. Whilst there will be inevitable prioritisation of needs, an ability to deal with different members of the public in an effective way must be seen as paramount. If the police service views itself as essentially authoritarian, this message will filter through to all recruits going through the training process.

Such authoritarian attitudes may then manifest themselves as hostility towards "out-groups" and minorities (see Chapter 4). Manifestly, the distinction needs to be made between a police officer behaving in an authoritarian way, and one who is using his or her authority appropriately.

To some extent the British police service has tried to bridge the gap between training school and the real world of street policing by the use of integrated training for two years, and by the use of tutor constables. This has been partially successful, but there still remains a suspicion that recruits emerge from the training school ill-equipped to deal with the many demands that will face them. This is perhaps surprising given that most trainers themselves have been drawn from operational police duties, and are merely seconded to police training schools for a set period, usually two or three years. There is clearly a debate about whether this is the most appropriate way of training. On the positive side, trainers will have had recent experience of practical police work, but on the negative side the relatively short period of secondment gives them little time to learn to be effective teachers, and to develop the expertise needed for such a specialised role. As with many other professions it is certainly the case that the best practitioners are not necessarily the best teachers.

The other problem relates to recent changes in the backgrounds and educational qualifications possessed by today's applicants. Whereas previously the number of applicants with degrees was relatively small, today the ratio of graduate to non-graduate recruits is much higher. This raises potential difficulties in terms of the expertise of the trainers and the level of any instruction (see Stratton, 1984). Training needs to be pitched at such a level that it is understood by all, yet needs to be challenging enough to arouse interest in the brightest and most highly qualified new recruit. The police service has not always responded quickly to such changes and is in danger of failing to recognise increases in the educational level of its average recruits. An intake which is largely composed of graduates will clearly require a different level of tuition than will one composed mainly of less qualified recruits. Stratton (1984) has suggested that there are a number of ways in which today's American applicants differ from yesterday's, and such changes necessarily have consequences for the content and level of training programmes.

The police organisation itself appears ambivalent about officers who choose to become trainers. To some extent such secondment is seen as a positive career move, yet time spent at training school is seen as wasted in terms of acquiring the range of practical experience deemed necessary for promotion. Given that the instructor becomes the first role model whom most recruits encounter, it is essential that they are chosen with care. As was discussed in Chapter 1, first impressions are powerful, and can have long-lasting effects on the values and judgements which new recruits internalise. It might be argued that an officer's first instructor at training school is the person who will have the most effect on that officer's subsequent values and attitudes. As such, instructors should embody all that is best in terms of good practice within the organisation, and their contribution should be recognised as important by the police service itself. It must, however, also be recognised that, after leaving training school, the recruit will meet many new role models on whom to base his/her world view. Researchers refer to the "canteen culture" which describes how the "real" way to do the job is learned during conversations with older colleagues in the police canteen.

Much of the discussion so far has been concerned with changes in British police training, but there have been similar changes of emphasis in the USA. Following World War II, many police officers were recruited from the military, and training was similar to that used in military establishments. Stratton describes this militaristic approach as a stress approach which includes:

> "Strict military procedures and atmosphere; a superior–inferior relationship between cadets and trainers, with minimal interaction or support; doubts openly expressed about cadets' abilities with frequent recognition of their inferior status; isolation and/or extra work for failure to comply with accepted standards; loud public verbal abuse and public discipline; punitive physical training for mistakes; and requirements that cadets speak in a loud, commanding voice and at times command and control the training class marches, drills and in the classroom." (Stratton, 1984, p 51)

One can see why officers trained in this way are unlikely to be the most tactful in dealing with members of the public. They are likely to imitate the role model of their trainer, and treat others with an air of disdain and superiority. As we saw in Chapter 5, social learning can have a powerful long-lasting effect on interactions with others. Earle (1973) found that officers trained using the high-stress approach tended to be more aggressive, less flexible, had difficulty with decision-making in crisis situations, and were less able to consider appropriate options in situations requiring the use of force.

Training of this kind is unlikely to produce an officer who has sympathy with a victim, an area which is now of increasing concern (see Salasin, 1981). An officer who exhibits little sympathy, or even empathy, and who interviews the victim in an insensitive way will undoubtedly antagonise or offend the person. By contrast, an officer who appears non-judgemental, supportive, caring and concerned may well reduce the chances that the victim will suffer from post traumatic stress disorder, and will also promote a favourable impression of the police service.

Supporters of this militaristic, high-stress approach believe that it has three main advantages: it builds up the recruits' tolerance for stress; it strengthens their ability to work as a unit when needed, and it teaches officers to follow commands and orders without question. Such an approach does, however, fail to recognise the fact that most of the time the officers will be working independently and will exercise their powers using their own judgement and discretion.

By contrast with the 1950s, most of today's applicants to American police departments do not have a military background and are much more likely to have college degrees. (Indeed some police departments such as that in Glendale, Arizona, have now opted for an all-graduate recruitment policy.) Consequently the stress approach would be much less appropriate. Increasingly police academies in America now use a non-stress approach and provide a much more relaxed and supportive environment. Relationships between trainers and cadets will tend not to be based on rank and power, but rather on counselling and support. One can see how such an approach will produce an officer with different values and attitudes from those found in the military-type training schools.

Officers who were themselves trained in the more militaristic style tend to view the new non-stress approach with a mixture of suspicion and contempt. They fear that the lack of discipline will mean that officers thus trained may not be relied upon to do what they are told, and there will be a breakdown in the effective functioning of the police department. As with many other aspects of police work, change does not come easily or swiftly. An organisation which feels itself to be almost permanently under attack is more reluctant to admit its past failings and to make drastic changes. Rather there will be a tendency to believe that things should continue to be done in a certain way because that is the way that they have always been done. Change when it does occur tends to come about when forced upon the organisation, for example as a result of new legislation, or in response to a public inquiry or, in Britain, in response to a Royal Commission (see Chapter 9).

As was pointed out earlier in respect of British police training, the type of regime favoured tends to be dependent upon the current view of the role of the police in society (see Reiner, 1992). One of the core questions is whether police officers should emerge from training school prepared to think through a range of possible courses of action, or simply to react in an automatic and predetermined way. Should they be told what to do in a step-by-step manner in each situation, or should they be given a range of options which they should consider? Quite clearly the vast gamut of different situations with which the officer will have to deal means that it is virtually impossible to cover all eventualities in the relatively brief period of time spent at training school. Given that, it is perhaps more appropriate that general guiding principles are taught, along with an ability correctly to identify the type of incident being encountered. There are, however, some situations (e.g. the use of firearms) where an officer's best interests are served by a strict adherence to rules and department policy (see Waddington, 1984). There are, regrettably, a number of incidents where inappropriate use of firearms has had disastrous consequences (e.g. in the shooting of Stephen Waldorf). If training is inappropriate then this can lead to disillusionment and a high level of wastage from the police organisation. As with selection, getting it wrong at the training stage can prove costly in terms of wasted resources, or, in the case of firearms, lives lost.

SOCIALISATION AND THE POLICE CULTURE

In Chapter 1 we discussed the way in which the police service has come to be regarded as having a closed occupational subculture. It has been generally assumed that once officers leave training school they fall into line with more seasoned practitioners and adopt an almost siege-like mentality when dealing with members of the public. However, some aspects of this insularity can be introduced as early as the first few weeks at training school. This can be illustrated by the following two passages cited by Stratton. The first is by an American officer himself.

> "here we are trained that once we get in that black-and-white car everyone who isn't in a black-and-white is our enemy."

The second is the comment of the wife of a recent male recruit:

> "Those cadets sure change a lot when they go through the academy. He's only been there six weeks and I'm trying to find a way to let him know that the kids and I are not 'assholes' or 'pieces of shit'!" (Stratton, 1984, p. 66)

Whilst such anecdotal evidence may not be wholly representative, it does seem to make the point that there is a great deal of informal as well as formal learning taking place during training. Associating with other recruits and experienced practitioners lays the groundwork for understanding the essential tenets of the police occupational culture. As Fielding (1988) points out, this can be communicated during the formal teaching, but is more likely to manifest itself in the expression of ideas, the types of examples used, and the style of formal and informal conversations. In other words, recruits do not pass through training simply picking up the formal knowledge which has been put before them. As with anyone joining a new organisation, recruits will look for all the subtle interpersonal cues given off by their instructors and role models, in learning what are the expected attitudes, beliefs and views of the world.

With the telling of "war stories" and descriptions of more violent incidents, new recruits learn to fear or distrust others and come to believe that only colleagues can be trusted or relied upon. This again takes the officer away from the notion of a citizen drawn from the community and being an integral part of it. Yet the more fear that is inculcated in recruits, the less willing they will be to participate in the overall functioning of the community which they are serving. Similarly a training programme which spends a large amount of time dealing with law enforcement and very little dealing with the social service aspects of policing (see Stephens & Becker, 1994) will leave recruits ill-equipped to deal with the reality of police work. It will also mean that they are unlikely to seek out the cooperation of other agencies in the community in trying to solve community problems (see Chapter 12).

As can be seen, socialisation is as much about conforming to subcultural norms as it is about learning what police officers need to know. There are often real attempts to play down any differences in the backgrounds of recruits and to emphasise similarities and commonalities of police officers (see Manning, 1981). Or as Van Maanen put it:

> "Organisational socialisation. . . provides. . . the new member with a set of rules, perspectives, prescriptions, techniques, and/or tools necessary for him to continue as a participant in the organisation."
> (Van Maanen, 1974, p. 81)

Fielding (1988) has described socialisation as a process of identity transformation. Both during and after training, officers start to acknowledge changes in their sense of identity. They are more likely to define themselves with reference to their colleagues than to others outside the organisation. Their circle of friends starts to become smaller, and is much more likely to include fellow officers. Successful completion of training school may be seen as a demonstration of competence, but there will be other hurdles which the recruit will need to overcome before being fully accepted into the organisational subculture. As with many hierarchical and militaristic organisations there will be informal (or at least unofficial) "initiation ceremonies" to be negotiated before status is conferred on the new recruit. Those who seek to legitimise such practices claim they are essential in order to weed out the oversensitive recruit, and to prepare him/her for just some of the stresses and strains which will be encountered later in their career. It is perhaps interesting to note that female officers may well be expected to survive more testing initiation ceremonies than their male colleagues, before being accepted into the subculture (see Jones, 1986). This is because the male-dominated subculture espouses values and attitudes (e.g. toughness, lack of feeling) which are supposedly more likely to be found in male than female recruits.

Many writers have referred to what has been termed the "reality shock" felt when officers leave the training school and are faced with life on the street (see Harris, 1973: van Maanen, 1975; Niederhoffer, 1967). Expectations produced whilst attending training school are often severely dented once the recruit starts to carry out policing on the streets. Bennett (1984) suggests that this is partly caused by the recruit internalising the formal organisational rules and conforming to these whilst in training, but coming to realise that there is a different set of "informal" rules (or at least a difference of interpretation) which governs the way in which the job is actually done. One nice illustration of this is the new officer's introduction to the so-called "Ways and Means Act". This is a piece of legislation which does not exist, but is referred to by experienced officers to justify any act which results in a job getting done in one way or another, despite the lack of formal powers to do it. (This has been referred to as the Crime Control Model by Skolnick, 1975, and contrasts with the Due Process Model in which everything is done by the book.)

In reality, a number of pieces of recent legislation (e.g. PACE) have sought to restrict severely the actions of individual officers, and to some extent have succeeded in ensuring that correct procedures are followed. The same is true in America where failure to comply with the exact letter of the law can lead to cases being thrown out of court before much of the evidence has been heard (e.g. in cases where there has been an illegal search carried out, despite the fact that incriminating evidence was found, this cannot be admitted in evidence).

Bull (1986) has described some of the resistance which experienced officers show towards the "new ideas" put over during training. To some extent this antipathy manifests itself in hostility towards the probationer whose head is full of the new way of thinking. The danger is that the probationer comes to believe that the only way to gain acceptance into the subculture is to reject the sound ideas put forward during training and embrace the more pragmatic approach of the old-time officer. This is perhaps too simplistic an approach, as the experiences of probationers will vary greatly from one to another. Whilst some may have pressure applied on them to "forget all that rubbish you learnt at training school" others will have their first practical experience with officers who do things by the book and whose views are similar to those put forward at training school. For this reason, the selection of tutor constables may be as important as the content of the training school syllabus (see Stradling & Harper, 1988).

The training school thus has a crucial role to play in forming ideas, values and attitudes in the new recruit. Its syllabus must, however, ensure that it is not seriously at odds with what the probationer encounters when faced with the realities of life on a division.

BEYOND INITIAL TRAINING

So far this chapter has focused mainly on the initial training course and its effects on those who choose to join the police service. This heavy emphasis is appropriate as initial training is likely to have the most dramatic and long-lasting impact upon the officer. Of course, as with many other organisations, training takes place throughout a person's career, and is evolving constantly. It is thus important that we also consider some of the ways in which training proceeds later in an officer's service, and the possible effects that such training has on police officers.

Because police work covers such a vast range of different duties, and is often being updated, it is not surprising that a great deal of time needs to be spent in the learning of new material. Whilst this is important, it can be a constant source of irritation to management in that at any one time up to 20% of officers may be on training courses of one kind or another. Some of the main types of courses are as follows:

- Specialist courses for those entering specialist departments (e.g. dog handling, detective work).
- Courses designed to teach or update skills which may be called upon at some point (e.g. riot training).
- Courses which aim to bring officers up to date with new legislation which affects their working (e.g. following the introduction of PACE in Britain).
- Courses which are designed to change officers' attitudes where a clear need has been established (e.g. race relations training following the Scarman Report, 1981).
- Courses which follow promotion within the organisation and which equip the officer with the new skills needed for the supervisory role (e.g. the newly promoted sergeants' course, or the Senior Command Course at Bramshill).

It would be more appropriate to have a psychological input in some types of courses than in others. As with initial training, the vast majority of courses tend to be taught by serving police officers, often of senior rank, and with years of experience (and in some cases great expertise) in the field. There is a long tradition of using those who have proved themselves in the field, to teach those who have something to learn. This is understandable, and in some cases valuable, but it does mean that police procedures will change only slowly, if at all. The police service has traditionally had great respect for the experienced detective whose main claim to fame may well be the solving of one or two famous cases. The words of such experts are revered and those in training will obviously be greatly influenced by them. When put onto such a pedestal, ageing detectives may well be "economical with the truth" when it comes to admitting how much help they received from others in solving cases.

In this way, the mystique of the detective with stunning deductive powers is maintained, and the help which people such as psychologists can offer is minimised (see Chapter 10). This can have disastrous consequences. For example in the search for the Yorkshire Ripper in the 1970s, the detective in charge ignored a psychological offender profile which had been drawn up, and also refused other offers of help from the FBI. It was said that the senior detective was suspicious of such new ideas, and preferred to rely on more traditional detective methods. It has been suggested that this was one of the reasons why the investigation was unsuccessful for so long, and why Peter Sutcliffe evaded capture for so many years (see Ressler & Shachtman, 1992).

As in the case of probationer training, when psychology is introduced it is either rarely fully integrated or it is introduced by police officers with minimal knowledge of the subject matter. To take one example, there has recently been criticism of some British police officers for using what are considered to be oppressive interrogation techniques (see Chapter 3). Responding to this, many forces have now introduced training courses designed to make officers change their interviewing style and adopt a more ethical interviewing approach (see Shepherd, 1991). However, in many cases, forces have given their own trainers a brief course in ethical interviewing techniques, and these people then become the "experts" who train others. There are clearly dangers in such an approach, as the "experts" putting forward the theory have little knowledge of underlying principles and no knowledge of how theories have been developed. There is a similar problem with training courses in which the interviewing of witnesses is tackled. Techniques such as the Cognitive Interview (see Chapter 2) have taken many years to develop and are still undergoing refinement. It is thus perhaps inappropriate that those with relatively little experience of the technique, or knowledge of the theory upon which it is based, should be training others in its use.

Training evolves partly to meet new demands which are placed on the police service. As long as there are a substantial number of "generalist" officers it is inevitable that there will be a large number of courses which officers will be required to attend. For example, riot training is now considered an essential component and, increasingly in Britain, firearms training for selected officers. The latter highlights one of the dilemmas associated with training, i.e. is it better to intensively train a small number of officers to a very high level, and to then call upon them when required? Or is it better to train a larger number of officers who will draw weapons as and when required? Initially many British forces opted for the latter approach, but following some infamous cases where things went badly wrong, most now favour the former more specialised firearms unit (see Waddington, 1984).

This book has already identified a large number of important areas in which psychologists can make valuable inputs. There is scope for numerous new or revised training courses in most of the areas we have covered, but especially those discussed in Part I. Having said that, psychologists will still need to convince more traditional senior officers of the value of their input, especially at a time when training budgets are being squeezed. Traditionally psychology has been more accepted by American police departments than by those in Britain, though there are now clear signs of change in the latter. As was pointed out in the Introduction, a number of British forces do now employ occupational psychologists who are slowly having an impact on the organisation. Such individuals are also having a growing impact on the training of officers, despite an initial reluctance on the part of the organisation. A number of British forces have now followed the American example, and employ psychologists to assist with recruit selection, hostage negotiation, and in many other subjects. It is also now much more common for forces to bring in psychologists to help with individual training needs (see Blau, 1994). However, this is not without its problems, as the following quote suggests:

> "The attitude on the part of some consultants in approaching police administrators is that of omniscient saviour condescending to educate ignorant and insensitive police types. As might be expected this approach rarely makes friends or influences people." (Reisser, 1986, p. 22)

It would be naïve and churlish to suggest that all the police's training needs could be met by the employment of more psychologists. There are obviously a large number of other subjects which need coverage but which are outside the realm of psychologists' expertise.

In an interesting paper, Denkers (1986), himself a psychologist, argues for the retention of much of the legal and theoretical basis of police training. Whilst agreeing that psychology does have value, he believes that the teaching of such subjects should not be at the expense of more traditional subjects. This is illustrated in the following quote:

> "Social skills are of help when the normal duty of the officer brings him into a problematic encounter with the public, but these skills are of no avail when these encounters are made problematic because the officer in question does not know what the law requires him to do." (Denkers, 1986, p. 59)

As Denkers points out, an officer who is unsure of his/her powers, or unsure about exactly what the law is, will lose self-confidence very quickly, and may create a situation which all the social skills in the world will be unable to resolve. Denkers thus suggests that while training is important it should not be seen as the panacea of all ills within the organisation. Training should be seen alongside the overall structure and culture of the organisation and should be realistic about what can be achieved. The role that the police officer plays in society can only be partly affected by training. Denkers argues that part of this training should allow individual officers to handle their emotions in a mature way, and to be able to express those emotions within the organisation. However, he ends on a pessimistic note by pointing out that the police organisation has a very poor record when it comes to encouraging its members to express their true feelings. For this reason police officers will continue to have great difficulty in effectively handling the emotional problems of others.

Perhaps one final area in which psychology's value should be borne in mind is in its use of a scientific methodology needed to actually evaluate training programmes, and to provide a cost–benefit analysis. Evaluation of any training course needs to go beyond simply asking each participant how much they enjoyed the course and how interesting they found different speakers. As Reisser (1986) notes there have been relatively few scientific research projects carried out to evaluate the effectiveness of training and the influence of the police environment. The one exception to this has been the work of Bull and Horncastle with the Metropolitan Police in London (see Bull & Horncastle, 1988). Their report goes some way towards understanding the difficulties of evaluation, but offers a good model for understanding the complexities of such a process.

SUMMARY

In this chapter it has been argued that training, especially in the early days of a police officer's career, can have a fundamental effect on that officer's values, attitudes, and perceptions of the world. Officers trained in a militaristic training school will tend to emerge with different value systems from those trained at a more modern non-stress establishment. Not only do the formal aspects of training have long-lasting effects, so too do the many informal socialising processes which the officer encounters.

It has been suggested that more emphasis needs to be placed on training in communication skills, as these are central to much of the day-to-day work of police officers. Many of the subjects covered in previous chapters of this book could and perhaps should be included in training programmes, but it is important that where psychological principles are taught, this should be done by those with an in-depth knowledge of the subject matter.

FURTHER READING

Southgate, P. (1988) *New Directions in Police Training*. London: HMSO.

Stephens, M. & Becker, S. (1994) *Police Force, Police Service: Care and Control in Britain*. Basingstoke: Macmillan.

Yuille, J. C. (1986) *Police Selection and Training*. Dordrecht: Martinus Nijhoff.

CHAPTER 9

Efficiency, Effectiveness, Quality and Change

"Police forces must strive to be seen in the eyes of the community as operationally effective, efficient users of resources and deliver services to a quality that meets their expectations. These are all dimensions of the judgements the public will make in determining their satisfaction with, and confidence in, the police service they receive." (Butler, 1992, p. 3)

We have seen in a number of chapters of this volume that there have been some fundamental changes taking place in policing in the last 10 years. Not least of these changes has been a focus on what might be called "quality" issues. In this chapter we will start to consider issues of quality, efficiency and effectiveness, and assess how feasible it is to measure a complex task such as policing in terms of quality and service. Given the focus of this book, we will not be considering police accountability in the political sense, but the interested reader may wish to consult other recent thorough reviews of this topic (see e.g. Jefferson & Grimshaw, 1984; Lambert, 1986; Reiner, 1992).

THE PUBLIC'S SATISFACTION WITH THE POLICE

Looking back today it is surprising to think how relatively straightforward things were for the British police in the 1960s and '70s. The Royal Commission on the Police (1962) had presented an image of police forces doing a good job and having the support of the vast majority of the population. Indeed the commission itself said that its report was "an overwhelming vote of confidence in the police". Over 80% of the population were said to have "great respect" for the police, although there were slight differences between different groups within society. By the early 1980s, there was still a high degree of support generally.

Hough and Mayhew (1985) report that over 80% of people who approached the police (other than as victims) found them to be helpful and pleasant. However, significant differences emerged between different sections within society. Older people were happier with the police than were the young; women were more supportive than men; non-manual workers were more content than manual workers. There were also geographical differences, with the police in rural areas generally seen more favourably than those in the cities. McConville and Shepherd (1992) even found that there were differences between rural and city dwellers' perceptions when both were policed by the same police force.

Despite the generally favourable view of the police which these surveys found, perhaps most worrying was the fact that in Hough and Mayhew's research some 52% of young men reported some form of impolite treatment in police-initiated contacts. These findings were supported by other research including that of Bennett (1990) who found a similar pattern in two areas of London, but noted additionally that there were differences in levels of satisfaction according to race; whites were generally more satisfied than non-whites with the police.

These differences in perception of the police were also supported in research by the Policy Studies Institute (1983). This report talked of a disturbing lack of confidence in the police among young whites, and what was called a "disastrous lack of confidence" amongst young West Indians. Having said that, the report concluded that this did not amount to a complete rejection of policing methods. In fact Afro-Caribbeans were as likely as whites to report crimes, and were to some extent willing to cooperate with the police. The Islington Crime Surveys (see Crawford, Jones, Woodhouse & Young, 1990) reported considerable dissatisfaction with policing tactics. Most importantly there was a large and increasing majority of people who saw the police as unsuccessful in dealing with crime. The British Crime Surveys (1982, 1984 and 1988) also showed a decline in public confidence in the police, and this decline was found amongst those people who had traditionally been strong supporters of the police (e.g. women, the elderly, and residents of rural areas). To be fair, it is not all bad news. The latest British Crime Survey (1992) shows that there has actually been a slight increase in the public's satisfaction with the police (see Mayhew, Maung & Mirrlees-Black, 1993; Mayhew, Mirrlees-Black & Maung, 1994).

Against such a background a number of writers suggested that there was a worrying crisis of confidence in British policing. Some of the reasons for this crisis will be discussed in more detail in Chapter 11. However, for present purposes we should note that there was an important change taking place in the way in which sections of the public saw the police. Amongst the concerns many appear to revolve around issues of accountability, efficiency and effectiveness. Such terms have come to dominate the thinking of many police managers. However, as we will see later, measuring such terms is not easy in an organisation like the police service.

The results of recent research discussed above are clearly disturbing, but we must recognise that such surveys are actually quite difficult to interpret. Policing is such a complex and diverse task that simply asking members of the public if they are satisfied "with the police" can be misleading. As McConville and Shepherd (1992) point out, it is not easy for people to provide a Yes/No answer to a question about such a wide range of activities. These authors note that in their own research it was quite common for people to say that they were satisfied with the police, and then go on to criticise the actions of some police officers. McConville and Shepherd explain this difficulty:

> "The position adopted here by respondents is a result partly of the psychological difficulty of being objective about an institution that is supposed to be viewed in a favourable light, and partly of the problems in assessing an institution with multiple and often contradictory functions." (McConville & Shepherd, 1992, p. 18)

The other difficulty people have in answering such questions of satisfaction is that many members of the public actually have very little day-to-day contact with the police, and therefore form an impression by anecdote or images portrayed in the media (see Chapter 11). McConville and Shepherd report that it was quite common for people to say that they were very satisfied with the police, and then to admit that they had actually had no contact with any police officer for many years. As we will see in Chapter 11, image can be very important. McConville and Shepherd's research also found a significant number of people who said that they were dissatisfied with the police, but who also had had very little recent contact with them. Amongst the reasons for this dissatisfaction were the low visibility of the police, the poor communication skills of individual officers, and a failure to keep up with community needs and wishes. Amongst those who said that they had had recent contact with the police, some were content and some were not.

The results of such surveys indicate that there are two distinct problems facing the police in respect of their image. Firstly, the actions of individual officers can significantly affect the image that people have of an entire organisation. Secondly, people invariably have a favourable or unfavourable attitude to the police despite having had very little contact with members of that organisation. The first problem can to some extent be tackled by better selection and training procedures (see

Chapters 7 and 8). However, the second problem is much more difficult to tackle given the media's ability to affect and change public opinion.

As we can see, an increased contact with the police can have both positive and negative outcomes. However, there is a further conundrum here. If the police have been very effective in preventing crime, there will be little need for them to have a large number of patrols in any given area. Yet as we saw above, the absence of police patrols may in itself be a cause of dissatisfaction.

MEASURING POLICE EFFECTIVENESS

There are a number of difficulties in trying to measure police effectiveness objectively. One of these difficulties concerns crime prevention. Whilst it is relatively easy to measure the number of crimes recorded and detected, it is all but impossible to measure the number of crimes that have been prevented by any given police action. One can measure the crime rate, introduce an initiative, and then measure it again. In most cases there is an assumption that merely having police officers visible on the streets has a deterrent effect and prevents crime. The research evidence, however, appears to show that having more police officers visible on the streets makes the public feel more secure, but actually has little effect on the local crime rate. A community constable may take the credit for maintaining a relatively crime-free area, but his/her superior may demand that the officer "feels some collars" to justify his/her existence, and in order to do something which is quantifiable. The police service tends to reward with promotion those officers who make a large number of arrests. However, we must bear in mind that as the crime rate rises, so do the number of arrests. Conversely if the police become very good at preventing crime, the number of arrests will decline.

Thus, whether or not the police are judged to be successful in one of their primary functions (i.e. the prevention of crime) is very difficult to measure objectively. If crime rates continue to rise (as is the case in many countries in most years) then one could argue that the police are being neither efficient nor effective. Yet we can never know how high the crime rate would have been if the police had not been active.

Whilst some aspects of police performance can be measured relatively easily, others are much more difficult to quantify. Let us take one example. In Chapter 12 we point out that, despite the image presented in the media, a great deal of everyday policing is not concerned with crime-fighting. Rather, a significant amount of police time is actually spent on what are called "service calls". These can be anything from giving directions to a lost tourist, to resolving minor disputes between neighbours or partners. In most of these cases, no official action is needed on the part of the officer, and so little account is taken of what part his/her actions play in the general orderliness of a community. In the case of, say, a domestic dispute, the activity log may simply record "Parties advised: no further police action needed". But this may actually cover a wide variety of actions by an individual officer, some of which may be effective, and some of which may not. One officer might actually resolve a dispute to the satisfaction of both parties, while another might serve only to stop the immediate confrontation, but do nothing to calm the underlying antagonism.

In this example, both officers' actions have dealt with a call from the public, both have attended promptly and both have dealt with the matter swiftly and "efficiently". But clearly the actions of one officer are considerably better than the actions of the other. One officer may have improved the image of the police by his/her actions, whilst the other may have diminished it. One officer's actions are likely to result in fewer repeat calls to the police, whilst the other's may actually increase the number of recalls. It is possible that the different actions will be recognised if the police conduct follow-up calls, but in most cases the actions of these two officers will be assumed to have been equally effective. Both arrived at the scene within the stipulated time limit; both dealt with the matter within a few minutes; neither officer had an official complaint lodged against him/her. Thus in terms of traditional ways of measuring performance, both officers' actions would be rated similarly. We can thus see that measuring performance is more difficult in respect of some police duties than others.

It is often the case that the types of police duty which are the most important prove to be the most difficult to measure and assess. Conversely, those that are less important prove to be the easiest to measure. One obvious example of this is police response times. Most forces now have standards in terms of the average time it should take to deal with 999 calls. It is very easy to check on these, provided the time of the original call is logged along with the officer's time of arrival. The Chief Constable's annual report may then proudly announce that "95% of emergency calls were responded to within the target time". Whilst this could conceivably be called a measure of efficiency, it is hardly a measure of effectiveness and certainly not a good measure of quality. In some cases (e.g. where a crime is actually taking place) a fast response time is important. However, in many other cases this is not so important. To members of the public, *how* the police deal with the call is often more important than *when* they arrive. Similarly, a member of the public telephoning a police station on a non-emergency call may appreciate that the phone is answered relatively quickly. Yet if the person answering the phone then appears arrogant, impatient, or unhelpful, this is unlikely to lead to "customer satisfaction".

Responding quickly to an emergency call gives the officer a legitimate reason for driving quickly with sirens wailing. Yet this has a cost in terms of the danger which the officer puts him/herself into, not to mention the danger faced by other motorists. There are also other costs; the more the public see police officers hurrying to what are assumed to be emergency calls, the more they may come to believe that there is a lot more crime today than a few years ago (see Chapter 11). There is also a "cost" in terms of the physiological arousal of the officer dealing with the call. An officer who arrives having just driven at high speed to the scene will be more physiologically aroused and stressed than if he/she had driven at normal speed (see Brown & Campbell, 1993). Consequently the actions of the officer might well be different in each case, and could lead to different levels of satisfaction on the householder's part. Many of these considerations are lost in the crude measurement of response times.

MOVES TO MONITOR EFFICIENCY

Attempts to introduce some measures of effectiveness and efficiency are important in any organisation which draws heavily on public funds. For perhaps far too long the police were content to do things the way they had always been done, without any real consideration of whether they were making the most efficient use of their resources. The insular nature of many police forces meant that any attempt by "outsiders" to improve things was met with suspicion if not outright hostility. When the ever increasing crime rate was brought to the attention of senior police officers, there was a tendency always to blame the lack of resources for the increase, rather than to seriously examine current police methods and strategies.

The first important change in terms of financial accountability for the British police came in 1983 in the form of Home Office Circular 114. This sought to apply the Conservative government's Financial Management Initiative to the police service for the first time. In this circular the watchwords of economy, efficiency and effectiveness (later joined by excellence and enterprise) were introduced to police thinking. For virtually the first time Chief Constables and police authorities were asked to formulate clear objectives and priorities for their force, and to base these partly on the needs and wishes of the public. Forces were also asked to introduce systems which would allow them to assess whether the stated objectives had actually been achieved. The need to do this was further reinforced by a Home Office Circular in 1988 which stipulated that any increase in force establishments would be contingent upon forces being able to show (through quantified measures) that objectives were being met. Such a strategy has been adopted in the case of many other public sector organisations, including higher education.

Since the 1983 circular's publication there has been a gradual tightening of financial and managerial effectiveness. The main change following from the circular was a vast increase in the powers of HM Inspectorate of Constabulary, particularly in respect of measuring each force's efficiency. Prior to this, the Inspectorate carried out annual inspections, but Horton and Smith (1988) describe these as little more than ceremonial parades when the force had to be on its best behaviour. However, the new Inspectorate became much more professional and now demanded detailed documentation and statistics. In particular the Inspectorate established a Matrix of Performance Indicators (comprising some 700 items) by which "efficiency" could be measured. Through these the Inspectorate could now report (for virtually the first time) on the actual *performance* of each force. Thus the Home Office was able to monitor and evaluate the management of each force in Britain, and in particular to evaluate their senior officers. The guidance to the Inspectorate is modified each year and in 1993 comprised more than 40 policy statements and more than 300 questions. Seven key areas were specifically identified: personnel and organisation, use of technology, operational performance, quality of service, community relations, complaints and discipline, and counter-terrorism and war-emergency planning. Each force had to supply three different forms of information, i.e. a description of what was happening; the way in which the force was monitoring and assessing what was happening; and information on whether policies were working successfully and how performance had improved. In theory this sounds like a good and effective system whereby each force's performance can be measured by the Inspectorate. However, Weatheritt notes that in reality the system is rather more difficult to use. She says:

"The inspectorate is given no guidance, nor has it developed any for itself, on how to go about answering these questions, so that the process of inspection remains largely one of gaining the kind of professional feel for the force that is born of considerable police experience." (Weatheritt, 1993, p. 31)

It does seem somewhat ironic that all the moves to increase accountability and objective assessments of performance may come down to "a feeling" about whether things are going well. Having said that, Weatheritt does admit that at least this feeling is backed up by a large amount of quantifiable data. Such data allow the Inspectorate to make comparisons between forces or even between different sections of the same force. The numbers may also give the Inspectorate information from which they can probe further into the workings of each force.

Some of the changes to the duties of the Inspectorate were seen to be an example of government interference – the government could now assess the extent to which each force was achieving objectives which central (rather than local) government was setting. The ultimate sanction for non-compliance was the withholding of a certificate of efficiency which could have dire financial consequences. Critics of such changes (see e.g. Reiner, 1992) saw these as yet more examples of accountability shifting from local to central government control.

The other major change was that the Inspectorate's reports would from 1990 onwards become publicly available. It was thus possible for anyone to scrutinise and comment on the performance of each force, which meant that Chief Constables were more likely to come under pressure to improve any areas that appeared to be deficient. Whether or not the Inspectorate do a good job is a subject beyond the scope of this chapter. However, it must be borne in mind that all members of the Inspectorate are themselves ex-police officers who formerly held very high rank. Thus despite the many dramatic changes which have taken place in the last few years, there may still be a perception in some quarters that evaluation is not truly objective, but rests on a shared police view of the world. In fairness, this is not the impression that might be gained from reading the Inspectorate's reports on individual forces. Many of these are critical of a number of aspects of performance. Weatheritt suggests that the wording and content of many of the reports is, however, highly unlikely to stimulate greater local debate of important policing issues. Furthermore, it is suggested that the reports actually underutilise the vast amount of information which is now publicly available through the matrix of performance indicators. Perhaps as with many organisations, the collection of data may in itself prove to be somewhat difficult, but knowing how to use the information effectively can prove to be a much more demanding and involved exercise.

VISIONS AND MISSION STATEMENTS

The impact of Home Office circular 114/1983 should not be under-estimated. It represented the start of a campaign towards greater efficiency and effectiveness which has been pursued rigorously to this day. One of the main effects of the change in thinking was that each force now produced what were essentially "mission statements". These set out exactly what each force was trying to achieve by its daily activities. Some of these documents were weighty and impressive-looking tomes, whilst others were more succinct in identifying the aims of the force. In addition to these statements of purpose, management systems were introduced to monitor the extent to which the force was succeeding in its stated aims.

The idea of the mission statements was that there should be a shared understanding by all staff as to the real purpose and intention of their work. Thus a picture was painted of an organisation whose members were all working together to achieve a common purpose. One has to say with hindsight that in some cases the way in which this was carried out appeared to be somewhat naïve. As many commercial organisations have discovered, producing mission statements is relatively easy; ensuring that all members of the organisation are united in trying to achieve the mission is considerably more difficult. Good leadership is part of the answer, but equally important are good management systems which allow changes and initiatives to be monitored and evaluated.

Inherent in the new approach was a recognition that the police have to be aware of, and respond to, the expectations of their "customers" in order to be effective. In other words each force must be aware of, and respond to the community's expectations. As Butler notes:

> "This is a fundamental issue for policing in the last decade of the twentieth century. The evidence of public perceptions of the police shows that it would be dangerous to assume that police forces have some intuitive understanding of what the public expects without the need to engage in conscious efforts to document this information." (Butler, 1992, p. 28)

FINANCIAL ACCOUNTABILITY AND THE AUDIT COMMISSION

It was perhaps inevitable that the police would join the growing list of public bodies (e.g. the National Health Service, Local Authorities, the Probation Service) whose efficiency and accountability was to be questioned and monitored (see e.g. Humphrey, Pease & Carter, 1993). The Audit Commission Report (1990) served further notice that changes were needed in the way in which the police operated. The Audit Commission's two main functions are to appoint auditors to local authorities and to promote economy, efficiency and effectiveness through the best use of available resources. By early 1994, the Audit Commission had published 11 reports on the police, many of them critical of some aspects of the service. The reports came as something of a nasty shock to police forces who were more accustomed to internal or peer monitoring of their own performance. As with many other reports on the police, the Audit Commission's findings were criticised by the police themselves, mainly on the grounds that no outsider could ever fully understand the inner workings of a complex organisation such as a police force.

Over time the Audit Commission has probed deeper and deeper into the workings of the police service, even recently striking at one of the core police "flagships", i.e. the workings of the CID. Reports compiled by the Audit Commission differ from those of the Inspectorate in that they have a more explicit empirical knowledge base (see Weatheritt, 1993). These reports then become the basis for argument about changes in practice, which should lead to greater efficiency. Many of the recommendations concern internal management issues, although there have been attempts to address wider questions such as the role of police authorities in improving performance. The Commission has recommended that police authorities develop "output-based quantifiable performance indicators based on specified standards of service delivery". In this respect the Commission casts police authorities in the role of "consumers' champion", identifying local needs through such things as public surveys. Under the Local Government Act (1992) the Audit Commission has also been mandated to specify lists of performance indicators on which local authorities must report annually. The Commission has identified some 20 indicators for the police covering five key operational areas.

The Audit Commission's reports were followed by a White Paper on the police (Home Office, 1993) and the publication of the Sheehy Report (1993). All of these documents had implications for the way in which the police approached their work, not least of which was the questioning of many long-held assumptions about police performance. Some of these aspects will be discussed later.

As we can see from the above discussion, performance measurement is never easy or straightforward, but proves to have its own special difficulties when applied to policing. As Weatheritt (1993) notes:

> "the technical problems involved in measuring performance are daunting. The relationships between inputs, outputs and outcomes – between the assignment of resources, what gets done and what effects that activity has – are not infrequently complex, tenuous, unknown and difficult to know." (p. 24)

This somewhat pessimistic view stands in stark contrast to that expressed by Butler (1992). Butler, who holds a PhD in psychology and is also a senior police officer, puts forward a much more upbeat message in saying:

"The police service has made significant progress in the past ten years in the area of operational effectiveness and the control of costs, through improvements to management systems and structures. The service is now more finely tuned and therefore better prepared to meet the continuing challenges of social change and the public's expectation of higher service standards." (p. ix)

Because performance measurement is so difficult, there is a danger that the police might improve some easily quantifiable measures of their efficiency, whilst neglecting other more important but less quantifiable areas. In addition, the police might feel pressurised to take short cuts in order to be seen to be achieving some of their objectives. For example, pressures on the police to improve their clear-up or detection rate may mean that suspects are treated inappropriately and that attempts are made to coerce a suspect into making a confession. As we saw in Chapter 3, the end result of this is that the police may elicit a confession from an innocent person.

THE SHEEHY REPORT AND ATTEMPTS TO QUANTIFY GOOD PERFORMANCE

The Sheehy Report (1993) was a further attempt to incorporate a business ethos into the police. That this report was instigated by a Conservative government, long seen as the British police officer's friend, came as something of a shock. As was noted earlier, the British police had become used to being given pay rises and improved conditions of service without being asked to justify such increases in terms of performance. However, the Sheehy Report contained proposals to introduce performance-related pay, fixed-term contracts, and to abolish some of the tiers of management which were felt to be unnecessary. Not surprisingly, many of the proposals met with strong opposition, to the point where police chiefs were threatening to resign, and the Home Secretary was forced to back down on some of the more radical proposals. A debate has ensued about whether one really can introduce reliable performance measures to an area such as police work. Of course the same arguments arose when such changes were introduced to other public bodies, and are still debated fiercely today (see Humphrey et al, 1993).

Quantitative or Qualitative Measures?

At the heart of the debate is the issue of whether performance can be realistically assessed by quantitative as opposed to qualitative measures.

Most reports such as those discussed above advocate a combination of the two types of measures. However, in reality more emphasis will tend to be given to the more easily compiled quantitative measures. The danger of this approach is that a great deal of what now makes up everyday policing will go unrecorded, unrecognised and unrewarded. The British government has argued that the police must make the fight against crime their most important priority. It is proposed that key objectives will be set and the police will be expected to meet these. On the face of it this is a laudable move, but the ramifications have yet to be realised. As Stephens and Becker (1994) point out, there is a danger that many other important police functions will be neglected in the diversion of resources to crime fighting initiatives. As they note:

> "It would appear that one of the best routes towards achieving performance-related pay would be by feeling sufficient collars and by successfully pursuing other crime-related activities. We may speculate once again that non-crime-related issues in the caring and service areas of policing may carry less of an operational imperative."
> (p. 228)

Thus it is important that the police have a very clear view of exactly what they are trying to achieve, before discussing how it will be achieved and how success and failure will be measured. Mission statements are all well and good, but they must be translated into specific local objectives which officers on the street can recognise and work towards. At the heart of the approach described above is what has become known as rational management or "policing by objectives" (PBO) (see Butler, 1992). Weatheritt notes that PBO has been embraced enthusiastically by most forces, and that it is not untypical for each police subdivision to produce 20–30 local objectives per year, i.e. one on average every two weeks. Local beat officers do, to some extent, work towards the achievement of at least some of these objectives. However Weatheritt adds that:

> "the way in which objectives are formulated and reviewed leaves much to be desired, both managerially and in terms of the requirements of public accountability . . . Objectives are often formulated on the basis of poor, irrelevant or incomplete information; in other words on the basis of an inadequate definition of what the problem is." (Weatheritt, 1993, p. 27)

Butler (1992) sets out a number of conditions that need to be recognised before any initiative will be effective. These are listed in full below:

1 A vision of what the police force is attempting to achieve in its response to community expectations.
2 A recognition by the Chief Constable of the problems to be solved to achieve the vision.
3 A commitment by the Chief Constable to implement the process to achieve the vision.
4 A sense of mission shared by all members of the force.
5 A structure which allows people closest to the problem to make the decisions to solve it.
6 Systems and procedures which enhance the opportunities for staff to achieve their full potential.
7 A commitment to excellence.
8 A system of management which allows results to be measured and the lessons of the past used to guide actions in the future.

(Butler, 1992, p. 1)

This blueprint for success is impressive, and represents a considerable shift in thinking from previous views of police management. However, as we have seen already, putting such laudable aims into practice can be rather more difficult. We will return to some of Butler's points shortly.

Weatheritt suggests one common problem is that the objectives which the police set are often unrealistic, especially when they seek to achieve large reductions in crime. There is at times a simplistic belief that changes in police practice will have a dramatic effect on the local crime rate. However, as we have seen elsewhere in this volume, crime is multi-causal and cannot be totally eliminated by a simple redeployment of police resources.

With so many objectives being produced at regular intervals, there is also a feeling that inadequate time is given to any single initiative before moving on to new priorities. Perhaps most worrying, however, is the suggestion made by some writers that the evaluation of new initiatives is invariably rather poor. This is because information is inadequate or, when it is available, is misused. PBO has often not been used to identify how good performances were achieved and might be repeated, nor has it been used effectively to identify why things might have gone wrong.

There has been some improvement in relations between the police and the local community especially in regard to identifying local concerns and putting in place initiatives to deal with these. However, Weatheritt suggests that feedback to local groups on the effects of such initiatives tends to be poor and is often little more than going through the motions of genuine consultation. If management systems do not allow adequate or effective internal monitoring of changes, then it is not surprising that information to external groups is poor. Consultation with, and feedback from local groups is important if the police are to be seen to be addressing community concerns. However, as the following quote demonstrates, this can be difficult:

> "I am trying to please everybody. I am very busy. I am on twenty-three main committees, some of them maybe seventy people . . . In the borough there are forty-seven different languages spoken. There are also in excess of 750 voluntary organisations . . . They are obviously part of the community but in the past we have been guilty of not bothering about them . . . If every police officer could be a Community Liaison Officer for at least six months then the problem would be solved." (Chief Inspector Community Liaison Officer, quoted in Graef, 1990, p. 94.)

This quote shows that working "with the community" is in reality more complex than might be supposed. One is reminded of the adage of "not being able to please all of the people all of the time" and it must be recognised that some aspects of police work will invariably be criticised by some members in each community.

Although the original Home Office Circular saw objective setting as a joint exercise between Chief Constables and the police authority, in reality the police authorities have had relatively little influence. The Association of Metropolitan Authorities complained that they had little say in policing matters and were often relegated to the role of approving initiatives which had already been introduced. This would seem to confirm the views expressed by some authors (e.g. Reiner, 1992) that accountability is becoming much less of a local issue, and more of a national one.

RESPONSES FROM THE POLICE SERVICE

So far we have concentrated on pressures from outside the police organisation for change to take place. Perhaps partly as a result of such pressures, police forces have now produced their own statements of corporate values which commit forces to improve the quality of their services. The reasons for this unprecedented move are discussed in some detail in Chapter 11. However, for present purposes we must recognise that such a dramatic change came partly as a result of a growing lack of confidence in the police. Senior police officers had always been reluctant to admit that this was the case, but the evidence was becoming somewhat irrefutable. For instance, the *Daily Telegraph* (30.8.93) reported the results of a Gallup survey which showed that "Confidence in the ability of the police, courts and Government to tackle rising crime has fallen so dramatically that the vast majority of the public now supports taking the law into its own hands" (p. 1). There was a feeling among a number of Chief Constables that if the police themselves did not take the initiative, wholesale changes might be forced upon them. In introducing changes, there was a recognition that a gulf existed between what the police called "quality service" and "good performance", and what the public understood by such terms. The "drive for quality" has continued with a working party now reconstituted as a subcommittee of the Association of Chief Police Officers (ACPO). Interestingly, its membership now includes local authority associations, whose influence had previously been in steady decline.

The working group established five key areas of policing and within this framework ACPO, the Audit Commission, the Inspectorate, and the Home Office have endeavoured to develop the core indicators of police performance (see Reiner & Spencer, 1993). These key areas are the way that forces handle calls from the public, crime management, traffic management, public reassurance and order maintenance, and community policing. These are to be measured by some 36 indicators through which, it is hoped, the public can assess the performance of their local police force, and through which the quality of the service delivered by the police can be readily monitored.

The police service thus appears to be listening more attentively to what the consumer wants, and to be committing itself to a higher level of quality of service. To some extent the accepted performance indicators provide a picture of how well the police are achieving their stated objectives. Yet, as we saw earlier, there will be many aspects of day-to-day policing which will not be covered by such measures. Weatheritt is quite pessimistic about the real value of the performance measures discussed here. She says:

> "no set of performance indicators, however apparently comprehensive, can offer a final judgement on the service to which they relate. Performance information . . . is primarily a way of formulating and asking further questions and promoting a dialogue with service providers about the prospects for service improvement." (Weatheritt, 1993, p. 41)

Such a view is perhaps disturbing, bearing in mind the massive investment which the police service has already made in improving the measurement of its performance, and in attempts to improve the quality of its service. However, such an assessment is perhaps inevitable given the complex and diverse nature of policing duties. Unlike many commercial organisations, police services have numerous different types of "consumers", many of whom will have different agendas and priorities. It is thus not surprising that no matter how well the police are able to measure their performance, there will be heated debates about what the core functions of the police should be. The maintenance of order on industrial picket lines may be achieved effectively, yet such police action may be criticised severely by local trade unionists. Given that different factions within society will invariably disagree about what the police should be doing, it is not surprising if there is little agreement about what constitutes quality, efficiency and effectiveness.

It would perhaps be appropriate to conclude this chapter with a thought for the lowly police constable who has lived through the massive and frequent innovations discussed above. The many changes of emphasis and switching of priorities must at times appear bewildering. Whilst forces have attempted to make sure that everyone is on board the new ship of quality service, there may remain an underlying feeling among the junior officers that the job will continue to be done in the way it has always been done. Earlier we outlined Butler's eight points for the successful introduction of new initiatives. Points 4–6 on the list recognise the value of the workers on the ground, and yet many management initiatives have failed to recognise adequately the importance of the constable on patrol.

In psychological terms, individual officers' perceived lack of control over the many changes proposed can only increase stress levels and decrease morale. Whilst officers may still use individual discretion in the exercise of their powers (see Saunders, 1993) there will inevitably be a growing feeling that their own priorities have been superseded by directives from above, or even from outside the organisation. Amongst the ever growing list of performance indicators and quality initiatives, there have been relatively few attempts to measure feelings within the forces themselves. As Moos (1976) has shown, the social climate of any organisation has a dramatic effect on its functioning. As with any organisation, one-way communication (from top to bottom) is not the best way to make people feel that their views are of any significance (see Beaumont, 1994). Faced with a perceived lack of control, and a feeling of helplessness to influence the organisation, it would not be surprising if constables adopted a negative attitude towards the organisation, its initiatives, and its clients. Before yet more changes are advocated, it will be important to re-establish and restate the value of the police constable within the organisation. Butler notes that:

"Police management strategy should seek two goals: first, to provide a better, more challenging and fulfilling job for all members of the force, and second, to improve the effectiveness and efficiency of the force, thereby improving the quality of the service provided to the community." (Butler, 1992, p. 2)

From what we have seen in this chapter, it would appear that many police forces have been so busy addressing the second of these goals that the first has been neglected. In the future, as the police embrace further the issues of efficiency and effectiveness, management will need to recognise more fully the effects of the many changes on the individual officer, and take more effective steps to ensure that he/she feels an integral part of any grand plan. Managers should also be aware that their directives have a habit of being "reinterpreted" by junior officers (see Holdaway, 1994) so that the way in which policies are implemented on the streets often bears little relation to what was intended. To some extent this can be monitored by using good management information systems, but as we saw in Chapter 1, the idiosyncratic decisions of officers patrolling alone are not always easily regulated.

SUMMARY

This chapter has chronicled many of the recent changes that have occurred in the areas of police effectiveness and efficiency. It has been noted that, despite the numerous recent innovations, effective measurement of police performance is not a straightforward matter. There is a danger that performance measures will concentrate on those areas which are the easiest to quantify, and will neglect more important but less tangible aspects of policing. Whilst most police forces recognise that they must be seen to be doing something to improve both their performance and their image, organisational shifts must carry the grass roots workers along with them if the change is to be effective.

FURTHER READING

Butler, A. J. P. (1992) *Police Management* (2nd edn). Aldershot: Dartmouth.
Reiner, R. & Spencer, S. (1993) *Accountable Policing: Effectiveness, Empowerment and Equity*. London: IPPR.

CHAPTER 10

Police Science and Forensic Psychology

"In the interests of a good plot, fictional police officers are often more amenable to new ideas and approaches to detection than are their real life counterparts. The change in style of detection required by psychological input has not been adopted unreservedly by any police force. Perhaps the recent challenges to detectives have made them more open, but in my early discussions with police officers about the potential contribution of psychology to detection one detective sergeant, who had been in the force for many years, summarized the views of many of his colleagues when he said, 'Why do we need all this new-fangled stuff Professor? After all we've got 150 years of police experience to draw upon'." (Canter, 1994, p. 12)

In the introduction to this book we saw that many aspects of police work are subjects of fascination to members of the public. Perhaps nowhere is this interest more apparent than in the area of crime detection and the identification of perpetrators. Despite the fact that such activities make up only a small proportion of the average police officer's day-to-day activity, it is the one aspect of police work which is perceived as glamorous, and can earn police officers great respect and admiration. There is a mystique which surrounds the way in which crimes are solved, but a mystique which is at times a myth. More offences are cleared up by sheer hard work than by a flash of inspiration. In addition, many more crimes are solved as a result of information received from the public than through the deductive reasoning of an Hercule Poirot or a Sherlock Holmes type of figure. That is why good police public relations are so important. In this chapter we will start to look at some recent advances in forensic psychology, in particular offence and offender profiling.

The large number of detective novels, fictional television series, and now "murder mystery dinner parties", bear witness to the public's apparently insatiable appetite for such material. This interest reached a peak with the release of films such as *Silence of the Lambs*, and, in Britain, the television series *Cracker*. In the former, Hannibal Lecter, supposedly a psychiatrist and mass murderer, assists the police to identify a serial killer through his insight and experience. Perhaps this film proved popular as much for the chilling portrayal of the sinister Hannibal Lecter by Anthony Hopkins as for the way in which serial murders can be solved. The fact remains, however, that the solving of crimes such as serial rapes and murders does arouse great public interest; this despite the fact that such offences make up a minute proportion of the total amount of crime recorded.

In their search for crime fighting aids, police officers are understandably keen to use any assistance from science. Advances such as fingerprint identification, and more recently DNA profiling, have added greatly to the resources used by the police in identifying criminals. More recently, psychological profiling has attracted a great deal of interest, and is an area in which psychology and police work can be brought together productively. However, there is some debate in psychological circles as to whether psychological profiling should be seen as scientific or merely as a subjective deduction. Garberth (1983) sees offender profiling as a combination of brainstorming, intuition, and educated guesswork.

Psychology traditionally thinks of itself as a science, and tries to use a scientific methodology in its attempts to understand human behaviour. For this reason, a great deal of psychological research is carried out in the laboratory where conditions can be controlled. The problem with some such experiments is that they may lack what is called external validity – i.e. it is not clear whether the results apply outside as well as inside the laboratory. When it comes to an area such as profiling, it is very difficult to use a laboratory experiment in order to test a hypothesis. Rather, theories will be developed as a result of visits to crime scenes and, as in the case of *Silence of the Lambs*, interviews with a number of serial offenders. The latter may provide valuable insights but such a method of gathering information could hardly be said to be scientific. The views of one person may be unrepresentative of the population as a whole, and it is for this reason that most psychological research uses a large number of subjects, ideally selected randomly.

There are then difficulties associated with methods such as those portrayed in fictional films. But that is not to say that such methods should not be considered. We wish merely to caution the reader about the likely success of such an approach, and to acknowledge that systematic controlled research is preferable to anecdotal or fictional stories.

Although there were isolated attempts at psychological profiling many years ago, more systematic offender profiling has its origins in America where the FBI's Behavioral Science Unit has now built up considerable expertise (see Hazelwood, 1983). There is much debate about what exactly offender profiling is, but underlying most definitions is a belief that *offender* characteristics can be deduced from a detailed knowledge of *offence* characteristics. Thus detailed examination of a crime scene is an essential first element. Whilst a physical examination is already carried out by forensic scientists searching for fingerprints, clothing fibres, semen samples and other traces, the scene can also reveal further clues to the trained forensic psychologist. In particular, it is believed that a detailed examination of the crime scene will provide hints as to the underlying personality of the likely offender. For instance, some psychologists have made a clear distinction between "organised" and "disorganised" offences and offenders. They believe that some offences are carried out spontaneously with little forethought or planning, whereas others are committed after detailed and lengthy planning. In the former case, a victim may be selected at random, whereas in the latter, a victim may have been targeted and observed for some time in advance of the offence. The point is that although two offences may appear on the surface to be similar (e.g. two vicious rapes), they may actually have been committed by two completely different "types" of offender. Thus in searching for the offender(s) the psychologist may well draw up two very different profiles of the likely perpetrators and advise the police that they are looking for more than one suspect.

Psychological profiling cannot in most cases tell the police who actually committed the offence. What it can do is advise on certain attributes which the offender is *likely* to possess. The emphasis there is important. Although there have been some celebrated cases where psychologists have been able to offer very detailed and accurate profiles (see Canter, 1994) there are other cases where they have been less successful. In most cases, drawing up a profile will allow the police to narrow down their pool of suspects. In some cases the profile may well fit someone whom the police already suspect, and will thus allow detectives to concentrate their investigations on the most likely offender. Let us take one case study to provide an example of how a profile can be beneficial. This is taken from Ault and Reese (1980).

A woman living in an east coast town in America was raped. She subsequently reported the offence to the local police. The investigating officer realised that the circumstances of the rape were similar to six previous rapes in the area, and that they might well have been carried out by the same man. Unfortunately the six previous rapes had yielded few good clues, and the police had no suspect in mind. The case files were then sent to the FBI's Behavioral Science Unit and a psychological profile was constructed. This suggested that all seven crimes had been committed by the same person. The suspect was predicted to be a white male, in his late 20s or early 30s. He was most likely to be divorced or separated, and to have a job as a casual labourer or similar. He probably had a high school education and lived in the immediate area of the offences. He was also thought to have a poor self-image, and to have had previous convictions for minor sexual offences (e.g. as a Peeping Tom). The Unit also predicted that the person might well have been stopped previously by the police as he might have been out on the streets in the early hours of the morning.

On receiving this profile, the police narrowed down their list of suspects to some 40 local males who met the age profile. Using other information from the profile, they then focused on one particular individual and arrested him a few days later. He was subsequently convicted of the offences.

This is a good illustration of what can be achieved, but of course profiling does not always have such dramatic and swift results. When a psychologist gets it right and an offender is caught, it becomes a newsworthy story; but the success rate is never going to be 100%. Because psychological profiling is still in its infancy, there have been few scientific and systematic studies to test exactly how useful it is. We are still unable to say in how many cases the information is better than that which the detectives working on the case could have deduced. It is important to stress that profiling cannot tell the police exactly who committed a crime; what it can do is help the police to direct their investigations more meaningfully and thus avoid wasting too much time pursuing unlikely leads or suspects. We must also be aware of the danger of the self-fulfilling prophecy. In Chapter 3 we saw the potentially disastrous result of making an assumption about a suspect's guilt once he/she is in the police station. Investigating officers must bear in mind that psychological profiles often fit a number of people, and are not always totally accurate. Just because the suspect currently being interviewed fits the profile does not prove that he/she actually committed the offence. There will invariably be a large number of people who fit the bill, and the police will need to be cautious before making an assumption of guilt. It must be borne in mind that while a psychologist works on probabilities, the police are likely to operate in more absolute terms of guilt or innocence.

Profiling is also more appropriate to certain types of crime than others. Currently the most common crimes for which it is used are those more serious sexual offences especially where it appears that there is a series of connected crimes. As the quote at the beginning of this chapter suggests, some long-serving police officers see profiling as a possible threat to their expertise and reputation. The old-time detective may believe that through his many years of experience he already has an intimate knowledge of the workings of the criminal mind, and he has a good knowledge of the local area. The difference is that the psychologist will attempt to put together pieces of information in a systematic and objective way, and prefer not to rely so heavily on gut feeling and intuition.

There are two main approaches to profiling, that used by the FBI in America and the more recent work of David Canter in Britain. Canter's work follows chronologically from that based in America, although much of it stands in opposition to the original American approach. As Canter's work has attracted a great deal of media interest in Britain, his research will be covered first.

CANTER'S PROFILING TECHNIQUES

In Britain profiling has been developed by David Canter (see Canter, 1989, 1994). Canter and his colleagues have identified five important characteristics which can help in investigations. These are:

- Residential location
- Criminal biography
- Domestic/social characteristics
- Personal characteristics
- Occupational/educational history

Whilst all of these are of some value, it has been found that residential location and criminal biography are likely to be of most benefit (see Boon & Davies, 1993).

Canter and Heritage (1990) have analysed details of reported sexual assaults in an effort to identify particular styles and patterns within these offences. They have been able to identify those characteristics which are common in most assaults of this type, and those which are rarer and thus more distinctive. By carrying out such analyses it is hoped that common factors in similar types of sex crimes can be specified, and the more individually distinctive features identified.

Canter's approach is based on the assumption that although there are similarities in many sexual assault cases, there are also identifiable differences in the way in which offences are carried out. Most importantly Canter believes that during the commission of a crime, vital clues are left behind and the distinctive personality of the offender shows through in some way. Thus the way in which the crime is committed is in part a reflection of the everyday traits and behaviour of the individual. The interaction between the offender and the victim can be studied closely and categorised along a number of dimensions, e.g. sexuality, violence and aggression, impersonal sexual gratification, interpersonal intimacy, and criminality. By careful study of offence behaviour, a pattern can be established, and structured variations between offenders identified.

Canter and Heritage (1990) developed their views by studying 66 sexual assault cases. These had been committed by some 27 different offenders. By examining victims' statements and other information in the case file, they identified 33 offence characteristics which occurred with some frequency. Whilst other characteristics were identified, these were much less common (and thus distinctive) but unhelpful in terms of general principles. The common characteristics were identified as follows:

- Style of approach
- Surprise attack
- Sudden/immediate use of violence
- Blindfolding
- Gagging
- Reaction/lack of reaction to resistance
- Compliments victim
- Inquires about victim
- Impersonal towards victim
- Demeaning towards victim
- Disturbing of victim's clothing
- Ripping/cutting of clothing
- Use of weapon
- Demanded items
- Verbal victim participation
- Physical victim participation
- Use of disguise
- Knowledge of victim implied
- Threatened if attack reported
- Stealing property
- Identification of victim
- Violence to produce control
- Violence not controlling
- Verbal violence/aggression
- Vaginal penetration
- Fellatio
- Fellatio in sequence
- Cunnilingus
- Anal penetration
- Anal penetration in sequence
- Apologetic

This is an exhaustive list, but by compiling such a collection of factors, and then carrying out a sophisticated statistical analysis, Canter was able to establish the relationship between various factors. In particular the analysis showed which factors tended to be associated with each other, and which were apparently unconnected. It was also possible to identify those actions which occurred in most of the cases, and those which were less frequent. A picture could thus be built up of the factors which were most central to the offence of rape. Perhaps surprisingly, Canter believed that overtly aggressive behaviour was not the core ingredient in all rape cases. Sexual intercourse was often one of the primary aims of the attacker, but there was not the large variety of sexual activity which might have been predicted. There was in some cases little evidence of a desire for interpersonal intimacy with the victim. It would be inappropriate to say that there was such a thing as a "typical" rape, but many were characterised by a sudden impersonal attack in which the victim's response made little difference. This is an important point which police officers who are interviewing victims should bear in mind. It is crucial that such a victim is reassured that the rape would probably still have occurred irrespective of whatever she had done. In the attacks, the victim was seen partly as a sex object, although the rapist's power over the woman was undoubtedly also an important component.

Quite clearly, Canter's work suggests that it is vital that any investigating officer spends a great deal of time interviewing victims. This needs to be done in a sympathetic but nonetheless rigorous way (see Chapter 2). The way in which rape victims are interviewed by the police has been the source of some criticism at least in Britain (see Graef, 1990). The police have been accused of being unsympathetic and uncaring on occasions. Things have improved over recent years, but there is still a public perception that a victim who goes to the police may not be treated in the most tactful or sympathetic way. Interviewing techniques need to elicit details about the exact way in which the offender behaved during the attack, and not just result in a listing of what occurred, written in legalistic jargon. Having said that, it is important that the victim understand the reasons for such probing and potentially embarrassing questions.

Canter and Heritage (1990) have been able to use their data to assess certain previous assumptions about rapes. For example earlier research by Marshall (1989) suggested that an inability to form intimate relationships with women may be an important motivating factor for rapists. If this were true, then we would expect that many rapes would be characterised by an apparent desire by the offender to relate to the woman as a person, rather than as a mere sex object. Canter and Heritage found that some rapes did show evidence of this, with offenders exhibiting seven patterns of behaviour which together were clear attempts at intimacy. Rapists who did show such signs were hypothesised to have had previous difficulty in forming intimate relationships with women, with one or more failed attempts in the person's background. For example, such a person might well have married a much younger woman and then the relationship had grown distant.

Quite clearly the primary goal of most rapes is the sexual activity itself. There is, however, a question as to whether different types of sexual behaviour are related, and form a distinct pattern, or whether the types of sexual behaviour are diffuse, and related to other aspects of the offender's behaviour. Canter and Heritage found that their work agrees with that of Scully and Marolla (1983) in that the desire for certain types of sexual experience is a significant aspect of rape. Thus when a variety of sexual activities takes place, this indicates either an offender who has a high level of previous sexual experience, or one who shows an interest in certain activities through the possession of pornographic magazines or similar material.

The fact that rapes are invariably violent and aggressive is another aspect detailed in the literature. Indeed Groth (1979) has argued that aggression is perhaps the primary motivation in many sexual assaults. Canter and Heritage confirmed this to some extent by identifying four aggressive factors which were clearly linked in some rapes, and formed a distinct aspect of the offence. As previous literature has also suggested, there is a closeness between these aggressive variables and the sexual variables, with some degree of interaction. Two examples of this are where violence is used other than for control purposes, and where anal intercourse took place.

Although some rapes are characterised by an apparent desire for intimacy (see above) many others are quite the opposite, with a cold impersonal aspect to the assault. The woman is treated with no apparent consideration for her as a person, but merely as an object of desire for the rapist. Canter and Heritage's work suggests that there are six characteristics which typify this type of attack. These include the use of impersonal language, and a disregard for the victim's reaction. This can be typified as an offender's callous lack of interest in his victim as a person. Many assaults showed some aspect of this behaviour, but the researchers still believed that it was possible to identify a number of cases where this type of action was dominant in an offender's behavioural repertoire. Interestingly, this type of behaviour is also associated with cases where the offender implies that he has previous knowledge of the victim, and has identified her as a "desirable object" which he wishes to have. The point about this work is again the fact that attacks of this nature will be more likely to be carried out by offenders whose lives in general reflect this impersonal attitude towards women. For such a perpetrator, women would be perceived as unequal to himself in all aspects of life, and would be put down (in the castigation sense) at every opportunity.

A final important variable in rape cases identified by Canter and Heritage concerns the association with other types of criminal activity. Although rape is seen as a distinct offence, with its own motives and idiosyncrasies, many rapists do have previous convictions for other types of offences, including non-sexual crimes. This fact means that perpetrators may well use techniques which would be equally appropriate for other offences, the use of disguises or blindfolding of the victim for example. This suggests that such offenders might well have previous convictions and thus be known to the police for other reasons. Some types of behaviour used in rape cases, such as binding and gagging or blindfolding a victim, may have more to do with a previous criminal career than a sexual perversion. Canter and Heritage even add such factors as warning the victim not to tell, or telling her he knows where she lives as indicative of a previous criminal lifestyle. Such research thus allows Canter to make fairly confident predictions about whether an offender is likely to have a previous criminal record. The more factors in the nine identified in this section that are present, the more likely it is that the person will have an extensive history of other types of crime.

This contribution to our understanding of rapes is an important one. Canter and Heritage's research has confirmed a number of previous theories and typologies, and in particular, has demonstrated that there are a number of different types of rape behaviour, and thus a number of different "types" of offender. One can see how this detailed study of offence behaviour allows predictions to be made about the likely motivations and characteristics of an offender. As such the contribution is welcome and helpful. Having said that, the reader should bear in mind the fact that Canter's work is still relatively in its infancy, and his theories are in need of further refinement. There is a danger that investigating detectives will latch onto some aspect of his theory and be blinded to the fact that Canter's work is based on probabilities and likelihoods rather than absolutes and certainties. The fact that an assailant wears a disguise, binds his victim and also steals from her means that it is *more likely* that he will have convictions for offences other than rape. However, it does not mean that only such suspects should be even considered. It may be that a perpetrator uses a disguise because in the past it has been a successful tool in avoiding detection. In other words, the person may have committed other crimes but never been arrested and convicted. As with many other aspects of psychology, a little knowledge can be a dangerous thing, and could allow the non-psychologist to go off believing erroneously that they have found the Holy Grail!

CRIME LOCATIONS

Another aspect of Canter's work which is worthy of consideration concerns the issue of the residence of an offender and the location of his/her offences. Drawing on research from environmental psychology, Canter introduces the idea of mental maps as a way of understanding the geographical pattern of offending. The notion stems from the idea that although a number of people might live in the same location, they might all have different representations or mental maps of the city or neighbourhood. These mental maps are internal representations of an external world, and are in many ways unique to the individual. It is possible to tap a person's mental map by asking them to draw a picture of their city, town, or neighbourhood. Whilst each of these will be unique, some consistencies are usually found. For example, people tend to draw the area around where they live first, and often leave out what others would consider central features of a town. People also tend to draw a map from their own perspective, rather than as it would appear to a cartographer. A good example of this is provided by Milgram (1976) who reports that most Paris residents who were asked to draw a map of their city showed the River Seine as being straight, when in fact it meanders and turns through the various departments of the city. The reason why people made this mistake was that from their perspective, the river appeared to be straight. If they regularly took helicopter trips across the city, their perspective would be different, and the map would be drawn more accurately.

The research on mental maps is relevant to the present discussion, as each criminal will have a mental map of his/her own residential location. When selecting areas in which to commit crime, he/she will draw on this mental map and often stick within a given boundary, albeit unintentionally. In the past, police forces would plot crimes by placing different coloured pins into a map on the wall. This was crude and often ineffectual, but did at least acknowledge that there might be distinguishable patterns to offending. The main problem with such crude methods is that they tended to consider only location, with little consideration of the time or day of offences, or of the many other factors which would affect crime patterns. Now computer programs can provide a much more sophisticated way of plotting crime patterns and analysing crime data.

Geographical mapping and crime pattern analysis are very much emerging fields which should in the future allow the police to target resources more effectively (see Chapter 9). However, the analysis of data to establish distinguishable patterns of offending relies heavily on the accurate recording of information in the first place. Unfortunately in the case of many police forces, this has proved very difficult to achieve (see Ackroyd, Harper, Hughes, Shapiro & Soothill, 1992; Ekblom, 1988).

Thinking back to Canter's work on rapes, it is perhaps surprising just how many offences were carried out within a couple of miles of the offender's home. This is further reinforced by Spivey (1994) who found that in the vast majority of cases, the offender lived less than two miles from the place of attack.

One of the points to emphasise about mental maps is that they are not a literal or necessarily accurate portrayal of the world outside. Because they are internally generated, they are subject to a great deal of subjective interpretation and personal distortion. For this reason, the simple plotting of crime locations onto a map may show little clear pattern. However, once things like footpaths, one-way streets, bus routes or location of a police station, for example are taken into account, then a pattern is more likely to reveal itself. When planning an attack most criminals do not open up a map and choose a location. Rather they make reference to their own internal map in selecting likely targets. Their mental maps may well contain knowledge of possible escape routes, dimly lit areas, or locations which have a number of available and relatively easy targets (see Bennett & Wright, 1984). The choice of target location may be affected by whether or not the criminal has a vehicle or has access to one. The rapist may well choose an area in which he will not feel conspicuous, and one in which he feels secure and comfortable. All this can make the job of the police easier, as in most cases they will examine the local area for suspects, and need not consider the entire population. Indeed some of the crimes which prove the hardest to solve are those where the offender chooses an area a long way from their home, or where the offences are scattered over a very large geographical area. In Britain in 1994, Robert Black was finally convicted of a number of child murders after some 12 years of police investigation at a cost of more than £5 million. Black, a 47-year-old van driver, had committed a number of crimes, but these were spread over a very wide geographical area, and covered several different police forces. It was only by plotting his movements (by the use of petrol receipts) that the police were eventually able to prove his guilt. One can only speculate, but had Black committed all his crimes in his immediate neighbourhood, he might well have been caught much earlier.

Canter believes that there are meaningful and identifiable patterns of space use which are typical of different criminals, and that these relate to their place of residence at the time of their offence. In particular his work has confirmed that of previous authors in showing that criminals tend to operate within recognisable distances of their home and work from this "fixed base". One interesting aspect of this work was that

Canter could draw a circle which encompassed all of a criminal's offences; in over 85% of cases the offender lived within that circle. This research concerned some 45 sex offenders and showed that a general "marauder" theory was much more applicable than the "commuter" theory, where offenders are believed to travel some distance from their home in order to commit crimes. Canter concludes that whatever a rapist's motives, his choice of location can be modelled from well established environmental psychological principles (see McAndrew, 1993, for an overview of this subject). The practical point of this work is that it can help the police to narrow down the number of suspects by concentrating on those who live within the circle of the crimes committed. For this reason it is important that detectives can establish with some certainty whether a number of offences have been carried out by the same person, or are unconnected. The circle which can be constructed might of course be rather large (and not necessarily a true "circle") and could contain a large number of people. However, by introducing other variables it might be possible to narrow the field even more. For example crimes committed by impulsive offenders are generally carried out closer to the person's place of residence than those committed by the less impulsive.

OTHER BRITISH WORK

Whilst Canter and his colleagues have done much work developing offender profiling in Britain there have been other initiatives. For example Davies (1992) has worked with the Metropolitan Police examining the content and pattern of the speech of rapists. Whilst still under development, the project has produced a coding procedure which examines semantic and syntactic speech characteristics as well as the personal, affectionate and interactive aspects of the speech.

Clinical psychologists, in some cases working with psychiatrists, have also used their professional expertise to assist in investigations. Both clinical psychologists and psychiatrists have extensive knowledge and experience of the mentally ill and can bring this expertise to bear. For example a person suffering from a particular personality disorder (see Chapter 6) may be likely to commit a certain type of crime, or to use a certain modus operandi. Professionals working in this field are also likely to have interviewed a number of such people, and can thus bring expert knowledge as to their attitudes, cognitive processes, and even their likely behaviour when interviewed.

An initiative developed by Derbyshire Constabulary has had some success, though this is more correctly described as statistical, rather than offender profiling. It goes under the totally unwieldy title of Central Analytical Homicide and Expertise Management, which for obvious reasons is usually abbreviated to CATCHEM. The project was set up in 1986 by a team investigating the murders of three young girls. It started by collecting data from all similar crimes which had occurred since 1960. When these data were analysed, they suggested that it was possible to draw inferences from the similarities between crimes and between some types of offenders. Although originally based on some 2000 cases, there is now a core of 400 cases on which extensive details are held. Whenever a new unsolved case appears, the details are compared with previous cases and from this the team can generate a statistical profile (see Copson, 1993). This will consist of a probable age band for the offender, the likely previous criminal record, the distance travelled to the scene and even the probable location of the body, where this has not already been found. This information is provided not as exact answers, but as statistical probabilities. One can see that this has some similarities with Canter's work, in that it involves drawing on knowledge of previous crimes to make predictions about current ones.

These British approaches are usually described as "bottom-up" data processing. In these cases analysis of existing evidence allows investigators to identify specific associations between crimes and offender characteristics. By contrast the American FBI approach is described as being "top-down" in that assessments are made more on subjective intuition, albeit based on the investigation of previous similar crimes and offenders. As with the British initiatives, there is a large database of information about certain crimes and criminals. This is drawn partly from previous investigations, but also from detailed interviews with over 100 serial rapists and murderers. These interviews have tended to focus on exactly what offenders did and when, but have been slightly less concerned with questions as to why they committed their offences.

HAZELWOOD AND THE FBI'S APPROACH

One distinction that is made by American writers is whether the offence can be described as organised or disorganised (see Hazelwood, 1987). Organised offenders tend to commit crimes which have clearly been planned, where there is an attempt to control, and where the victim is a targeted stranger. By contrast, the disorganised offender would be more likely to use a sudden unrehearsed style with a minimum use of restraint and little attempt to hide evidence. Knowledge is built up by studying the crime scene and the exact nature of the attack. As a result of this, the likely offender would then be classified and reference made to the probable characteristics which the offender possessed. There is, however, some degree of subjective interpretation by the individual profiler. Although all rely on the same information, each profiler decides what emphasis should be placed on the various characteristics, and thus what type of person the suspect is likely to be. It is this fact that has led some academics to question whether this really is a scientific approach, or merely personal intuition.

Hazelwood and Burgess (1987) emphasise how a very careful study of the exact behaviour of an offender leads to a better understanding of the underlying motive for the attack. This in turn provides insight into the type of person the offender is most likely to be. Although this cannot be done in exact terms, Hazelwood believes that descriptions of an offender can be built-up to a point where he will be recognisable to his friends and family. The profiler is helped in doing this by looking for a systematic behaviour pattern which allows the use of an easily understood typology. One important example of this is whether the assault can be categorised as essentially *selfish* or *unselfish*.

This typology may come as something of a surprise as crimes such as rape might be seen as the ultimate in selfish behaviour – personal gratification with no consideration of the other person. However, as with Canter's research, a careful consideration of offender behaviour allows the investigator to draw some conclusions about the offence. Although all rapes are selfish in the sense that the victim's rights are totally ignored, some rapists exhibit behaviour which Hazelwood has termed pseudo-unselfish. In this case the offender's verbal utterances are:

- Reassuring
- Complimentary
- Self-demeaning
- Ego-building
- Concerned
- Personal
- Non-profane
- Inquisitive
- Apologetic

This type of rapist tries to involve the victim in the act. To an extent he will do what the victim allows him to. He desires a form of intimacy by, for example, asking the victim to kiss or fondle him, and he will fondle parts of the victim's body before intercourse. There is no desire to harm the person physically (other than the rape itself) or to force her into acts when she obviously resists. Minimal force will typically be used, and even then only to intimidate rather than harm. Threats or the presence of a weapon are usually used to produce compliance on the victim's part.

This offender's style of behaviour may stem from a lack of confidence on his part. If the victim does resist physically the assailant might well cease the attack or even attempt some kind of compromise or negotiation. A victim's resistance might also destroy the rapist's fantasy that she is actually a willing participant.

By contrast, the selfish rapist is concerned only with his own self-gratification and shows no regard for his victim's welfare or feelings. His verbal behaviour can be described as follows:

- Offensive
- Threatening
- Profane
- Abusive
- Demeaning
- Humiliating
- Demanding
- Impersonal
- Sexually orientated

Unlike the unselfish rapist, this type of assailant will do whatever he wants, regardless of the victim's suffering or feelings. Passive, verbal or even physical resistance will have little deterrent effect as sexual domination appears to be the primary motivation. The rapist's whole attack will be characterised as aggressive, with little or no attempt at intimacy. Anal penetration followed by fellatio is a not untypical behavioural sequence. Such offenders are capable of using large amounts of force and are immune to a victim's pain and suffering. The actual level of violence used depends on the underlying motivation for the attack.

Once the rapist's behaviour has been classified as broadly selfish or unselfish, further categorisation is attempted. This is done on the basis of the apparent motivation for the assault. Hazelwood draws on the classification system first used by Groth, Burgess and Holmstrom (1977). This typology works on the assumption that power, anger and sexuality are fundamental components of all rapes. The most common type of rapist is said to be of the *power-reassurance* type.

For such offenders the primary motivation is an attempt to remove doubts or fears about their own sexual inadequacy and masculinity. Such rapists show pseudo-unselfish behaviour and do not use large amounts of force. Their attacks are usually pre-planned following surveillance of possible victims. If one attempt is unsuccessful, he may well have a second target in mind, and move on to commit a further offence on the same day. Late evening or early morning are the preferred time of attack, usually when the victim is alone or with small children. Victims might well be threatened with a weapon, though this is rarely used. The victims selected are usually within the same age range as the offender, and are often asked to remove their own clothing. The interaction is generally over fairly quickly, though if a victim is particularly passive, the offender may take the opportunity to act out sexual fantasies after the initial attack. Following the attack the rapist might well apologise or ask to be forgiven, and even recontact the victim later on.

The behaviour of such offenders goes some way to reassuring them about their sexual insecurity. However, this effect is short-lived, meaning that the offender may well strike again in the near future, and probably in the same general area. Such attackers often take an item from each victim as a bizarre kind of souvenir, and might also keep records of their conquests. They are unlikely to grow out of their offending and will continue until caught.

By contrast the *power-assertive* rapist does not harbour self-doubts about his sexuality. In fact he is very confident of his masculinity and might well see his own acts of rape as merely expressions of such masculinity, virility and dominance. He will typically use quite high levels of force, though not in the early stage of the interaction. In fact he might at first appear convivial and harmless, and put his intended victim at her ease. Only then will his demeanour change, and his true intentions become clear. Thus a typical pattern would be to pick up an unsuspecting victim at a disco, offer her a lift home, and then spring his attack. His rapes might be more scattered geographically, but reflect locations in which he feels safe. These are the types of offences which juries often have difficulty with, believing that to some extent the victim put herself in danger by agreeing to accompany the assailant voluntarily. What jurors may not realise is that this type of offender has perfected the art of appearing completely innocent and harmless on first meeting an intended victim. After a vicious rape he will revert to his former image, and appear affable and respectable when in the dock. Because he does not fit society's stereotype of a rapist, he may well be acquitted on more than one occasion.

Such assailants will often tear a victim's clothing and discard it. There will also tend to be repeated sexual assaults rather than just one, this adding to the rapist's feelings of virility and dominance. If the man has driven the victim to the location of the rape, she will often be left there, perhaps without her clothing. This means that the victim is less able to report the assault swiftly. This type of rapist is less common than the power-reassurance offender, and his crimes will tend to be less frequent or regular.

A third type of rapist has been labelled as *anger-retaliatory*. As the name suggests, this type of offender commits rape as a way of expressing his own rage and hostility. He has a great deal of anger and animosity towards women and uses rape as a way of expressing this anger and his desire to degrade his victims. His typical pattern will be one of selfishness and will show excessive amounts of violence. The attack is an emotional and impulsive outburst and as such is usually unplanned. This type of attack has been labelled as a blitz approach, with an immediate use of very direct and very heavy force. The assault tends to be over fairly quickly, once the assailant feels he has released his pent-up anger both physically and sexually. His victims will tend to be in the same age range as himself, but could be selected because they symbolise another person whom the person has a grudge against. For example, if the man has been rejected by an upper-class professional woman, he might choose a victim who appears to have similar characteristics. This type of rapist will attack again when the anger and resentment build up to levels which he cannot tolerate.

A fourth type of rapist has been labelled as *anger-excitement*. In his case pleasure and sexual excitement are produced by the viewing of his victim's suffering and fear. He will thus inflict pain in order to achieve fear and submission. Contrary to popular fiction, these are actually the least common types of rape. The assailants of this type will usually plan their attacks in a very clear and methodical way. They might even rehearse the assault, and make sure that they have planned for and covered all possibilities. They will have decided what weapons to use, what mode of transport, and will have in their possession such items as gags or rope. However, the actual victim may well not have been chosen in advance. She will typically be a stranger who fits the bill in terms of the attacker's sexual fantasies and desires, but with whom he has not previously come into contact. His sexual and verbal behaviour will be essentially selfish and he will tend to use a brutal level of force, often resulting in the victim's death. For this type of attacker physical restraint of the victim is the norm, followed by long periods of restraint and sexual assault. Torture is not uncommon, leading to intense fear and pain on the victim's part. The helplessness of his victim appears to be stimulating to this type of offender, together with degradation and humiliation.

This type of rapist is also likely to keep records of his conquests, and in some cases may take photographs or even make video recordings. Unlike some other types of assailants, the anger-excitement rapist is unlikely to attack at regular intervals, preferring to initiate an assault only when the planning is complete. It is thus more difficult to predict when this type of offender will strike again.

One can see from the above that it is naïve to believe that there is only one type of rapist, driven by an overwhelming sexual desire. This stereotype may be media-generated, but is essentially flawed. To return to the point made earlier in the chapter, a careful examination of the actual offence can reveal a great deal about the type of offender who committed a certain crime. By careful study, valuable clues can be gleaned as to the motive for the attack, and from this, the likely type of offender. Such careful consideration will also allow investigating officers to determine whether a series of offences have been carried out by the same offender; if the person is likely to strike again, and if so when; whether the assailant's next attack might be more violent, and be likely to lead to the victim being killed.

The FBI have conducted extensive interviews with serial rapists, and some of the knowledge thus gained has been of assistance in rape investigations. Such interviews also reveal a great deal about the background of offenders, and their motivations and beliefs. Clark and Morley (1988) offer an interesting insight into such offenders, based on interviews with 41 rapists who had in total committed some 837 sexual assaults. Perhaps the most important point of their study is that serial rapists do not necessarily fit the stereotype that many people have of this type of offender. Indeed serial rapists may well appear perfectly normal to those around them. Far from being isolated, disadvantaged pathetic characters, serial rapists typically come from an average or above average home background. They might be intelligent, well presented, in regular employment and living in a family context. Perhaps surprisingly, Hazelwood and Warren (1989) suggest that serial rapists are more likely to have previous convictions for theft than for minor sexual offences.

Information obtained from interviews with such offenders is of considerable value to those conducting investigations. Knowledge about such offenders will enable police officers to put pertinent questions to relatives of a suspect, for example about their sexual experiences. It also enables the police to search for relevant materials in the homes of suspects.

Offender profiling is currently attracting a great deal of media interest. It is used extensively in the United States and is gradually being utilised by a number of forces in Britain. At the present time British forces confine its use to the investigation of crimes such as murder and rape. This is hardly surprising given that these are the most serious types of crime, and are the ones on which most psychological profiling research has been based. The use of profiling in Britain is still at an experimental stage and not all forces rely on it equally. At the time of writing, no British force has its own profiling unit, although some serving officers have attended an MSc course in Investigative Psychology run by David Canter. Many forces have stated that they are awaiting the findings of a Home Office Police Research Group study before embracing profiling fully. As was noted earlier, profiling has achieved some well publicised successes, but it is not and never will be an exact science (see Copson, 1993).

As was made clear at the start of this chapter, profiling has its advocates, many of whom have a vested interest in seeing it work. On the other hand, profiling also has its critics, most of whom attack the lack of scientific rigour which the research appears to show. One of the foremost attacks has come from Campbell (1976). He believes that profiles are often too vague, or rely on little more than common sense. He also believes that police officers might be more seduced by the academic standing and status of the profiler than by the actual usefulness of the material.

There remains little systematic or scientifically rigorous research to which one can turn in trying to answer the question "How successful is psychological profiling?" Absolute success or failure are not so easily measured or defined when one is dealing with material such as that used in psychological profiling. If a profiler provides information, 50% of which is accurate and 50% inaccurate, should this be counted as a success or a failure? Can a profiler provide information which others, including senior police officers, could not reasonably have deduced themselves? Until such questions can be answered with some confidence, there will remain a slight feeling of unease among some psychologists when asked to comment on profiling. That said, a number of psychologists have made, and will continue to make, valuable contributions to criminal investigations. As their research grows, it seems likely that they will have more of an impact on the investigation of serious crimes.

SUMMARY

Psychological profiling is a potentially useful investigative tool. It is one important area in which psychologists and police officers may work together productively. Psychological profiling relies largely on a careful study of offence characteristics in order to ascertain information about an offender's likely characteristics. Specifically it allows investigators to categorise the type of offender being sought and to target those people who fit the profile. However, like any investigation in its relative infancy, much more research is needed before profiling should be grasped as the great hope for the solving of the majority of crimes.

FURTHER READING

Canter, D. (1993) *Criminal Shadows: Inside the Mind of the Serial Killer.* London: HarperCollins.

Hazelwood, R. R. & Burgess, A. W. (1987) *Practical Aspects of Rape Investigation: A Multi-disciplinary Approach*. New York: Elsevier.

PART III

The Police and Society

CHAPTER 11

The Police and the Media

In July 1994 a four-hour-old baby was stolen from a hospital in Nottingham, England. The case attracted massive public interest, and the police appealed to the media for help in solving the case. Scores of journalists attended daily police news conferences, anxious for any scrap of information that could be used in a newspaper feature. Every appeal from the police was carried in national papers, and on television and radio news bulletins. The public offered what information they could, and waited anxiously for any developments in the case. Any politician or advertiser would have paid millions of pounds for the media exposure which the police received in this case. But during the course of the investigation, the same journalists who had wanted to help only days earlier began to question the efficiency of the police in their attempts to solve the crime. Questions began to be asked when no progress in the case could be reported. As there were no new developments in the case for days on end, the media slowly lost interest. There was an additional problem for the police in that the massive publicity generated a large number of hoax calls. These not only gave false hope, but also meant that the police spent a great deal of time investigating false leads. (One such hoaxer was eventually charged with wasting police time.) When eventually the baby was found (as the result largely of a tip-off) there was great public relief and joy. However stories of the solving of the case were quickly tainted by reports that police officers had twice visited the house where the baby was eventually found, and had apparently not recognised the missing baby.

The media can be the police officer's friend but, once a case has had high exposure, those same media can all too quickly turn against the police and damage their public image. Journalists have a job to do, and if the police can say nothing new about a case, then those same journalists will look for other angles. In the case highlighted above, this new angle became stories about the police themselves rather than about the investigation. The public may well wish to believe that the police are good at their job, but it is all too easy for the public's perception of the police to be tarnished by one or two high-profile cases. We have seen throughout this book that many members of society have an apparently insatiable appetite for stories about some aspects of police work. Crime is big business both for the press and for television producers, and therefore the police often have little difficulty in gaining publicity when they need the public's help. The more horrific or unusual the case, the more coverage it will tend to receive from the media. But as the above example shows, help from the press is something of a double-edged sword. The same reporters who are all too eager to help the police one day can quickly become critics of the police the next. In this chapter we will begin to consider relationships between the police and the media and examine ways in which the police may be able to project a better public image by appropriate use of the media. We will start by considering the relationship between the media, the police, and fear of crime.

FEAR OF CRIME

One major danger which the police face when asking for the public's help is of alarming that public unnecessarily. There is something of a vicious circle here. The public expect the police to solve the most serious and high-profile cases; the police ask the public for their help in solving these crimes; the public come to believe that such cases are commonplace and become more fearful; society comes to believe that the streets have become unsafe; the public change their behaviour so as to feel less vulnerable; the same public then demands that the police should do more to make them feel safer; society also demands that more drastic measures should be taken against those people who are so terrorising society.

As has been pointed out previously, it is the most unusual (and consequently most infrequent) crimes which are newsworthy and thus receive the most publicity. Despite assurances that such cases are extremely uncommon, the public's perception is affected, and more fear is generated.

The James Bulger murder case (highlighted in Chapter 5) provides a case in point. This was a highly unusual case where a toddler was abducted and killed by two very young boys. The case attracted an unprecedented amount of publicity and subsequent fear in the local community. The police were not able to solve the case quickly and eventually made the decision to seek help through the television programme *Crimewatch UK*. For the first time, a security camera video recording was shown of two boys apparently leading James away. Partly as a result of this publicity, two boys were arrested and eventually convicted.

Clearly in this case using the media was helpful, in that the perpetrators were caught, but was there a cost? It might be argued that the amount of fear generated in both the local and the national community was an unacceptably high price to pay. Knowing that the incident had happened was worrying enough, but seeing the little boy being led away just hours before his death was a chilling and frightening sight. It was reported that millions of parents changed their habits as a result of increased fear about the safety of their children. Television programmes showed interviews with mothers who vowed never to take their children shopping again, or who now kept their children on reins. Some fathers started to escort their partners and children on shopping trips "to make sure they were alright". Shopping centre managers vowed to instal new security cameras as soon as possible. Police officers appeared on television giving advice to worried parents. At times of crisis, the public turn to some figure of authority for guidance about what they should do. At such times police officers appearing in the media will have a particularly strong influence on the audience, and can be responsible for forming and changing attitudes. This is a topic to which we will return later.

Reactions such as those described above are perfectly understandable, and might well be commended as sensible crime prevention measures. These types of actions also allow people to think that they are doing something to make sure that this awful thing can never happen again. It is reassuring to feel that one can exert some degree of control over a situation which has challenged previously held assumptions about such control (e.g. the cognition "If I am careful and take sensible precautions it is highly unlikely that my child will be abducted"). The feeling that things are beyond one's control and that one is helpless to prevent them can be particularly distressing. Indeed psychologists now recognise that learning that one is actually helpless to control things can lead to depression (see Seligman, 1975). Following all these reactions, the point may be lost that this case became very high-profile precisely because it was so unusual and unpredictable. Abduction of toddlers from shopping centres is extremely serious and sickening but it is also a highly unusual crime and is unlikely to happen with any frequency. Once it does occur, however, the consequences can be horrendous – one can only begin to imagine the horror which the parents felt in this case – but as with other crimes, the fear generated may well be out of proportion to the actual risk.

So here we have a situation where the death of a child achieves massive publicity because of its uniqueness. During the year that James Bulger was killed, many other children lost their lives in road traffic accidents. Their deaths are just as tragic, but because such cases are more commonplace (and are seen as "accidents" rather than deliberate acts) they receive far less publicity (see Douglas, 1986). Consequently, parents do not react in the same way, and tend not to make changes to their lifestyle which might lessen the risk of traffic accident injuries. We seem to be back into another vicious circle here, albeit approaching it from a slightly different angle. If the police see the saving of human life as their first priority, this could well be achieved by concentrating many of their resources on reducing the number of road traffic accidents. After all, far more people are killed or injured by "law-abiding" motorists than at the hands of "criminals". Nevertheless, the motorist stopped for speeding on the same road where a child was killed earlier, may well resent such actions and ask the police officer why he/she is not out catching "real" criminals. Yet if each child's death in a road accident attracted half the publicity which the James Bulger case did, the public would better understand why the police were taking the action they were, and might change both their attitude and their behaviour. Large signs telling the public how many people have been killed on local roads might have some effect, but there could still be resentment over vehement police enforcement of speeding laws.

There are thus very difficult decisions to be made before the police go to the media and ask for help. Obviously the police do not make public a great deal of their work, and are very selective in deciding what they will release, and what remains secret. There remains an interesting piece of research to be carried out on just what the police do release and why. It is somewhat ironic that an organisation whose work is largely private and undisclosed expects the media to be helpful in those cases on which the police choose to go public. Conversely the police complain bitterly when the media publish details of a story which has aroused great public interest, but which the police would prefer to keep under wraps. Pressure to solve serious crimes means that asking for the public's help tends to be given priority over the possible consequences of publicising what are actually very rare cases. More and more recent reports tend to show the extent to which fear of crime affects whole lifestyles. People come to believe that it is not safe to go out, especially after dark, and become prisoners in their own homes. To some extent such fears can be allayed by the police, though it will never be easy, given the media's tendency to sensationalise reports on crime. Consider the following example:

"GROWING MENACE OF THE YOUNG SAVAGES
Violent crimes have escalated during the first six months of this year to a point where police say no one is safe from the muggers. [We] investigate the alarming threat to our society by the bully-boys.
With harried crime experts forecasting the breakdown of society

under the boots of thugs [this magazine] found widespread alarm among police and public at the infectious growth of casual and vicious violence throughout the country during the past year."

It would hardly be surprising if anyone reading this report became more fearful and changed their habits. Pictures are added to reinforce the terrifying headlines. Things have obviously got pretty bad in the last few years, as this story shows. The source of the story has not until now been mentioned. The reader might reasonably assume that it was written in the mid 1990s. In actual fact it was published in 1980 by *NOW!* magazine (ironically a publication which shortly afterwards went out of circulation). The story about crime is not actually untrue, yet the emotive way in which the piece is written and presented can only add to the public's fears. Phrases like "police say no one is safe from the muggers" seek to give an air of authority to a piece of sensational journalism. "The police say" is an interesting phrase, assuming that all police officers speak with one voice. The story might have been more truthful if it had said that *some* police officers are giving such warnings, but the reader will not necessarily make such differentiations. (By the same token it is not easy to discover who these "harried crime experts" who are "forecasting the breakdown of society" actually are, or whether their views are supported by the majority of colleagues.)

This example is used partly to illustrate the danger of police officers expressing such views which can then be taken out of context. The case also suggests that the media's preoccupation with crime is not as recent as one might imagine (see also Pearson, 1983). What has changed is the ease with which people have access to stories about crime and the police. There are now a much larger number of television stations, radio networks, and free local newspapers. All of these are competing for attention and have to find enough material to interest their audience. As Sparks (1992) notes:

"The massive development of television and its associated industries has historically coincided with a period of chronic, and sporadically acute anxiety about crime and policing. Such anxieties . . . are in no sense new or unique to our own period. However, their recent scale, form and distribution none the less call for a particular and contemporary effort of interpretation. The massive preoccupation demonstrated by television and other media with crime speaks to these anxieties in certain definite ways." (p. 16)

Crime reporting thus provides a ready source of "news". A public already fearful of crime is easily seduced by another story about how much worse things are. No matter that the story is not totally accurate, so long as it gets the public's attention. Crime reporting takes up a large proportion of many local newspapers, and a significant amount of space in the national tabloids. This is not peculiar to the British press but applies equally to many other countries. Dominick (1978) found that most local American newspapers devote between 5 and 10% of their space to crime news. Graber (1980) used a broader definition of what constituted crime-related stories, and put the figure at between 22 and 28%. As Reiner (1992) points out, there is a tendency to report on specific crimes as opposed to crime trends. In addition, he notes that the amount of coverage given to crime stories bears no relationship to actual increases or decreases in recorded crime.

Douglas (1986) makes an interesting point about the public's attention to crime stories. She suggests that those members of the public who already have a high fear of crime might be the very people who will search for information which justifies their world view. In other words, such people will pay closer attention to stories, rumours, or a police spokesperson as a way of confirming that their fearfulness is "appropriate". (This can be partly explained by reference to the Cognitive Dissonance Theory discussed in Chapter 3.) For this reason, it can become even more difficult to say whether any given level of fear of crime is appropriate or exaggerated.

Some people will feel more vulnerable than others, and the most fearful will be able to produce "evidence" to support their view. No matter that this may be anecdotal, inaccurate, or the result of sensationalist media stories. Everyone knows someone who has been a crime victim, and can use such anecdotal evidence to justify whatever fear they have. Media stories can also be cited to explain what may appear to others to be paranoid behaviour. Whilst it has been demonstrated that it is often those with the least to fear who are actually the most fearful, there is a second confounding variable; those who are most afraid of crime also tend to be particularly concerned about the supposed breakdown in the entire social order of society. Such people then focus on television programmes and demand increased censorship and regulation. As we saw in Chapter 5, the media, particularly television, can be seen as a scapegoat on which to blame the increase in crime. Following the James Bulger case, there were renewed calls to "ban video nasties" and to "clean up television" as society looked for a convenient way of explaining away an incomprehensible act.

The other problem with reporting any topic is that the audience constantly needs to be given something new in order to maintain a degree of attention. To some extent people become desensitised to any given level of crime, and so something yet more horrific (or at least something portrayed as such) is needed. This was seen in news reports from Northern Ireland before the cease-fire. Those who did not live in

Northern Ireland became so used to the troubles that "yet another" murder or terrorist bomb outrage attracted surprisingly little interest. News reporters tried to find some way of making the story have more impact, and so there was often some embellishment or some personal angle put over. During one report of the killing of a heavily pregnant woman the television journalist started his report by saying "Even by the standards of Northern Ireland this was a horrific crime" (BBC Evening News, 7 August 1994). Pictures of children's toys were shown in an attempt to bring home a message that five young children had lost their mother. The police were shown searching for clues and then the newsreader moved on to another story. It is hardly surprising that terrorist organisations switch to new targets in order to maintain their level of publicity.

Throughout recent history, many people who have been asked about crime believed that the problem was worse than only a few years earlier (see Mayhew et al, 1994; Crawford et al, 1990). There is some evidence that concerns are not increasing exponentially (see Mayhew et al, 1994) but there is still considerable worry. Fear is hardly surprising given that the level of recorded crime tends to show some increase in most years. This is despite the fact that the rise is usually relatively small and the figures indicate that, in the case of, say, personal attacks, one is still very *unlikely* to be a victim. But is this the image that the public have? From what we know, the answer is a firm "no". A rich mixture of crime stories, fictional police series, and now the advent of programmes such as *Crimewatch UK* keep crime and police matters very much at the forefront of the public's mind. It is not difficult to understand why there is a great deal of anxiety. Having said that, programmes like *Crimewatch UK* do serve a useful purpose. By April 1994, some 354 of the 1235 cases covered had been cleared up – a detection rate of almost 30%. It is unclear whether this figure should be applauded or criticised. On the one hand, the police only take onto the programme those serious cases which they have been unable to solve conventionally. On the other hand, some of the featured crimes are eventually solved by means unconnected with the broadcast.

We need to ask whether it is correct to assume that the police are powerless to do anything about the public's perception? If the police never again gave any news conferences about crimes, the media would find other sources of information or new ways to put across their stories. What if the police were to make a point of emphasising the actual risk of crime victimisation at every opportunity? By all means ask for the public's help, give out some details, but in all cases stress that the reality is that most members of the public are highly unlikely to suffer the kind of crime which is currently arousing interest. Such tactics may do a great deal to calm an anxious community and to alter perceptions. It may, however, be naïve to expect that the police will do this. After all those who control the police budget are unlikely to reward the police with additional resources if the perception is that the crime rate is actually not very high (see Chapter 9). We must thus be aware that there are hidden agendas here which mean that it may not be just the media who seek to profit from a supposedly high crime rate (see e.g. Reiner, 1992, p. 172).

It is recognised that the police may not be able to totally eliminate the disproportionate fear of crime which many members of the public possess. However, they do have opportunities to go some way towards reassuring the community and actually improving the quality of life for individuals who are terrified of becoming victims. The police must recognise that they are perceived as authority figures who are in a powerful position to influence the thinking and attitudes of many members of the public. Despite the declining public image of the police discussed earlier, senior police officers are still perceived as experts in their field, and will be listened to intently. Television news producers invariably use interviews with "the police officer leading the inquiry" as a way of giving the story impact and credibility. The interview is most likely to be screened if the officer says something controversial or dwells on the horrific nature of a case. Quotes such as "this is the worst crime I have seen in my 25 years as a police officer" are almost guaranteed to make the public sit up and listen, and so will be used by the television producer. As we saw earlier, the effect of such comments will be to increase levels of anxiety and confirm that "things really are getting worse these days". Many senior police officers are now trained in media presentation skills and can learn appropriate techniques for looking good in front of the cameras. However, such training tends to focus almost exclusively on the presentation rather than the content of the message. Whilst this might be appropriate for leading politicians, it is less so for police officers whose words will be attended to closely by a public increasingly concerned about crime.

So far, we have considered the issue of crime fear, and the role that the police might play in such perceptions. There is an assumption that fear is irrational or disproportionate to the actual level of crime. Yet as some authors have pointed out (see Young, 1987) it is very difficult to say when a certain level of fear is irrational and when it is in fact rational and appropriate. As we saw earlier, different groups will have differing perceptions of crime risk, and for different reasons. But clearly any community whose overall fear of crime is out of proportion to the risk is suffering unnecessarily.

Attitudes and Source Credibility

There is a massive amount of psychological literature on the subject of attitude formation and attitude change (see e.g. Eagley & Chaiken, 1993). The reason why attitudes have been studied so extensively is that they are assumed to direct behaviour. In reality the link between attitudes and behaviour is not quite so straightforward as was originally assumed, but nevertheless attitudes do generally have some directive effect on behaviour. One aspect of attitude change which is relevant to the current discussion is that around the area of *source credibility*. Hovland and Weiss (1951) established that people are more likely to change their attitude if the person giving them information is perceived to be an expert in the field and has high trustworthiness.

Hovland and Weiss's findings have received much empirical support since their early publication (see e.g. Wood & Kallgren, 1988). Many television advertisements use this method, for example showing an intelligent looking man in a white coat advocating the use of a certain brand of washing powder. One of the more memorable (and successful) examples of this technique was when Sir Robert Mark, the ex-commissioner of the Metropolitan Police, appeared in adverts for a certain brand of car tyre and used the words "I believe that these tyres are a major contribution to road safety". This was a powerful message spoken by a figure with very high authority. After all Britain's ex-top cop must know about these things. The company chose Sir Robert Mark precisely because his speaking of the words would carry a great deal of authority to many British motorists. He would of course not have been allowed to appear in the advert while he was still a serving police officer, but he was still well enough known to be a valuable and high-prestige communicator just after his retirement.

The additional factor of trustworthiness must, however, be borne in mind. If the public learned that the high-prestige source was in fact receiving a large sum of money for saying what he did, then they might be less likely to take his comments at face value. The audience will thus need to weigh up why the person is saying what he/she is saying, i.e. they will make an attribution about the reasons for the behaviour (see Chapter 3 for a discussion of attribution theory). Taking the example of the tyre advert, the audience would be more convinced if they believed that no money was involved. In this case they would feel that Sir Robert really must mean what he is saying. However, if the audience learned that Sir Robert was paid money for appearing in the advert (even if he subsequently donated the money to charity) then his real motives might be more difficult to establish, and viewers less convinced by his arguments.

The above discussion is relevant in terms of police officers appearing in the media. To most members of the public, a police officer remains a high-prestige source when it comes to statements about crime. After all the police are the main agency charged with dealing with crime, and so their voice should be heard. For this reason, police officers should be aware that their words will be heeded in many cases. If they say that crime is really bad and that certain areas of a city are dangerous, then the public will take this world view on board, change their attitude and modify their behaviour.

Whilst acknowledging that police officers can have a powerful influence on the public's behaviour, it must be recognised that this will only be the case as long as they remain high-prestige sources. If, as a result of a number of high-profile cases, the public's perception is that police officers are not to be trusted, then their ability to influence will diminish rapidly.

The Dangers of Overreaction

We have so far seen that the police may be able to play a part in reducing a community's fear of crime, by gentle reassurance and by drawing attention to the actual level of risk whenever they are given the opportunity. However, if the public can overestimate the actual level of crime and the inherent dangers that criminals pose, might not the same be true of the police? One might assume this is not the case, given that the police themselves are dealing with crime each day and are compiling the figures which then become the official statistics. But targeting of certain crimes and areas does not always come from clearly established crime pattern analysis. In the same way that the public may overreact to the perceived threat so too might the police.

This was the view taken by Hall, Clarke, Jefferson, Critcher and Roberts (1978). In what many now regard as a classic study, Hall charted the way in which the media reported what they perceived as a crisis in law and order. The focus was on the rise in muggings in Britain. This form of robbery was quite common in America, and in the mid 1970s began to be seen more in Britain. Hall reports that the alleged large increase in such crimes coincided with a more general sense of social and political crisis. "The mugger" thus became the focus of attention for an anxious society looking for someone or something on which to concentrate their unease and anger. Once again, the actual risk from such attacks was tiny, yet the media and society in general took up the baton and berated such crimes as though they were about to engulf the entire population. (See the story from *Now!* magazine above.)

The media gave the impression of a society virtually under siege, and widespread condemnation of muggings ensued. Criminal justice agencies took up the challenge and, according to Hall, completely overreacted to the situation. Courts passed extremely long sentences on those convicted of such crimes, partly it was said as a deterrent, but also to calm (media-generated) public fears and to reassure society that something was being done. The police, as agents of law enforcement, were also expected to "do something" and target such serious crimes. Some police forces set up special squads whose primary objective was to target and bring to trial these muggers who were so threatening society. However, because the actual number of such offences was comparatively low, some of the specialist police units found it difficult to achieve their main objective and, as a result, resorted to some dubious tactics to justify their existence and demonstrate their effectiveness.

Hall's analysis goes beyond considering just the police's role in this "moral panic". However, for present purposes it is interesting to note how the police did decide to deploy their resources in response to a perceived public outcry. Obviously muggings are offences which cause alarm to members of society, but so too are the much more common crimes of burglary and vandalism. If a large number of resources were being deployed to address a "crisis" which was in fact a very rare occurrence, then other more common offences were being ignored. The police have a very large number of demands upon their time, and certainly need to think carefully about just how they should deploy their resources and prioritise their duties. As we can see from this example, the media actually have a large part to play in such decisions about what the priorities should be. If the media do genuinely reflect public opinion, then it might be appropriate that the police take on board the views of the media, and respond appropriately. However, there is a danger that if sections of the media which do not reflect society but actually inform it become the loudest voice, then an overreaction such as that described by Hall may ensue (see Chapter 9 for a more detailed discussion of priority setting and effectiveness).

PROJECTING A MORE POSITIVE IMAGE

To some extent, the police have made attempts to "give the public what they want", though this has been essentially a reactive move, designed to allay some fears about their role, and to respond to criticism (see Chapter 9). In Britain, the Police Federation, the Superintendents' Association, and ACPO all came together to produce the *Operational Policing Review* (Joint Consultative Committee, 1990). Among many sections, this document included a survey of the perceptions and expectations of members of the public. There was thus an acknowledgement that such surveys were likely to be more accurate and representative than a reliance on what the media said the public wanted. One important finding from the survey was the fall in levels of confidence in the police, especially among members of black and ethnic minority groups. Interestingly, this was a problem highlighted by Scarman (1981) some nine years earlier, but which had not been addressed satisfactorily since then. It is perhaps surprising to consider just how far the public's image of the police had changed. The Royal Commission on the Police (1962) had found that the public gave the police "an overwhelming vote of confidence". However, the two more recent reports showed a much gloomier picture of the public's perception of the police. The *Operational Policing Review* also made the point that youngsters (especially those from ethnic minorities) are likely to have the greatest contact with street patrol officers, and it is these same people who are most unhappy about the police service. In other words satisfaction with the police is highest in those who do not have many dealings with them, and lowest in those who do.

However, perhaps the most important and interesting finding from the *Operational Policing Review* was the apparent mismatch between the public's perception and that of the police, in terms of what the police role should be. Specifically, the police placed a high value on law enforcement and crime control, with its concomitant reliance on aspects such as technology and fast response times. On the other hand, the public generally were much less enthusiastic about these tactics and methods, wanting instead a community policing style of approach – policing with a human face as it were. The report concluded that what was needed was a return to traditional policing methods (dare one call this a "back to basics" approach?) which it was hoped would halt the worrying decline in confidence and begin to meet the public's expectations.

It is interesting to speculate about how the British police service, traditionally well liked and in touch with the needs of the community, had become so isolated and removed from their public. Whatever the exact reasons, there is no doubt that the media played a part in informing public opinion and questioning a great deal of what the police were doing. Take the following as an example:

> "THE WRONG SIDE OF THE LAW
> The people of Stoke Newington, in the London Borough of Hackney – the poorest in England – have lost faith in their police. Allegations of fabricating evidence, gratuitous violence and drug-dealing have blurred the line between law-enforcers and law-breakers." (Cal McCrystal, *Independent on Sunday*, 21.11.93)

This sort of story (interestingly written three years after the *Operational*

Policing Review) can have a devastating effect on the police image, and indeed on public confidence. The police are given little right to reply to the allegations contained within such reports, but even if they were, are unlikely to address the issues, claiming that as the matters are currently under investigation, no comment can be made. In fact a number of officers at Stoke Newington were suspended following the large volume of allegations. It is not just the media who have become more critical of the police. A number of politicians and academics have recently questioned various policing methods and attacked some elements of the police service. Keith (1993) has produced a text which seems to add a degree of academic respectability to the sort of story quoted above.

It may not be apparent from the sort of story highlighted above, but for a variety of reasons much of the press is largely supportive of the police. Reiner (1992) identifies three possible explanations for this.

1 *Organisational reasons.* The fact that reporters attend criminal courts to get their crime stories means that they exaggerate the level of police success in detection. In addition, concern over personal safety means that, for example, camera crews covering a riot will take up the perspective of the police under attack and their filming will show the police as defenders against a mob. Reiner suggests that for this and other reasons, the media tend to unconsciously adopt a pro-police stand.
2 *The professional ideology of reporters.* Many reporters believe that they know intrinsically what makes a good story, and thus focus on "immediacy, dramatisation, personalisation, titillation and novelty". For this reason stories (e.g. in the policing of industrial disputes) are more likely to focus on an injured police officer than on wider political issues.
3 *A predominantly conservative political ideology.* One consequence of this is that crime, industrial disputes, and political conflicts tend to be portrayed as indicators of social pathology, with only the police available to protect the public from such "evils".

Thus the police are in a relatively favourable position when it comes to the day-to-day reporting of their activities. However, it might well not feel that way to the average police officer. As many researchers have reported, there is a tendency for police officers to feel that they are constantly under attack, and that they daily have to justify their actions to a suspicious press and public. This view is epitomised by such commonly heard statements as "In this job you're always in the shit – the only thing that varies is the depth".

An organisation such as the police which feels threatened and under attack is likely to "put up the shutters" when it comes to being asked to explain their actions (see Chapter 8). The problem here is that the media, ever hungry for a story, will then consider other angles and may well become hostile to what they perceive as an unhelpful or secretive organisation. It is not uncommon for police officers to lash out at sections of the media for harming their image (see Reiner, 1992, for some particularly apt examples of this). The police service is not renowned for its ability to handle criticism in a constructive way, and tends instead to attack the source of the criticism, rather than addressing the issues. Reiner (1992) encapsulates the interrelationship between the police and media in the following way:

> "Whilst the media have played their part in the development of the crisis of confidence in policing in the 1990s, they have reflected rather than created this conjuncture. There are deeper sources of loss of faith in the police . . . not least the convenience of the police as a scapegoat for more fundamental failures of the criminal justice system and law and order policy. However the police contributed to their own problems by the way their own 'law and order' campaigns of the late 1970s and early 1980s used the media to create unrealistic expectations of what more police powers and resources could achieve." (p. 182)

The police want to be seen as a highly professional organisation, its officers trained to a high degree of expertise and skill. Given that, the public will come to expect a professional level of service. The recent surveys of the public's opinion of the police seem to suggest that this is not being achieved.

Following the *Operational Policing Review* came the *Strategic Policy Document* (ACPO, 1990). One of the cornerstones of this document was a "Statement of Common Purpose and Values" which was soon adopted by all forces in England and Wales. One interesting feature of this was the commitment to help and reassure the public, and not just to enforce the law. In particular, police forces committed themselves to dealing with vulnerable minorities in a sensitive way.

The cynical may view this as simply a public relations exercise, but it was at least an acknowledgement that some change was necessary. However, following bad publicity, the police would need to work hard to convince the public that they were trying to change, and that there was a commitment to a new style and philosophy. Yet interestingly the new image could only really be accepted if the police could get the media on their side. The same media who had become quite critical of the police and who had grown weary of a lack of official response to their allegations now needed to be won over in the battle for the hearts and minds of the public. This was particularly important in the light of evidence such as that of

Southgate and Crisp (1992) which showed that the majority of the British population do not have a great deal of face-to-face interaction with police officers. Consequently if there were to be a sea change in the attitude and behaviour of most police officers, most members of the public would not even notice. Southgate and Crisp's work showed that only about 40% of the population have any contact with a police officer in a 12-month period. Even this figure can be misleading though, as the 40% are not evenly distributed amongst the population, but tend to come from working-class and minority groups. In other words, for the middle and upper classes, significantly less than 40% will have an interaction with a police officer over the course of a year. How then will they form an impression of the police service? The answer yet again will be through media representations of the police, both factually and in fictional television series, in books, films and on the radio.

There have been many different fictional television series about the police over time (see Reiner, 1994). At present the most popular British series is *The Bill*, each episode of which is watched by over 12 million viewers (see Mason, 1992). This series shows the everyday workings of typical officers, and in general portrays a reasonably positive image of the British police. However, other series have not tended to show officers in such a good light, and it is inevitable that public opinion will be affected to some extent by these programmes. Whilst the public is aware that programmes such as *Between the Lines* (which concentrates on the work of those investigating complaints against the police) are fictional, there is a feeling that there must be some element of truth to the stories. Any series which highlights the wrongdoing of police officers will be seen as ammunition by those already hostile to the organisation. Against the backdrop of such programmes, the police will have difficulty in persuading the public that they are now a much more sensitive, reliable and caring organisation. As Stephens and Becker (1994) note:

"The creation of a positive public image of the police is vital to the tenor in which officers can carry out their role. It also has an important impact on the public's level of trust and confidence in the police, the level of which affects the extent and quality of information flow to the police from the public and which, in turn, influences police effectiveness. Image and substance are interconnected, and if the aims of the *Strategic Policy Document* are to be fulfilled then the public must become more fully aware that the police are simultaneously attempting to alter aspects of their operations and to present a new image to the public . . . And it is here, in relation to this issue of recognition and of targeting the police message, that the role of the media and the way in which the police approach the media may prove to be vital." (p. 226)

We must acknowledge that there are differences between media presentations of crime and the criminal, and the reality of such matters (as represented by crime statistics and victim surveys). These differences have been summarised by Reiner (1992) thus:

1 The media tend to overreport the more serious types of crimes, e.g. murders, serious assaults and sex attacks.
2 The media give greater emphasis to crimes that have been solved, which again overemphasises the number of the more serious types of crime (which happen to have a higher clear-up rate).
3 When the media highlight offenders they tend to focus on older adults and those from a higher social class than is the norm in officially recorded crime.

Thus it is hardly surprising if the public have an inaccurate picture of the most common types of crime, the typical offender, and the likelihood of detection. The householder who suffers a burglary might reasonably assume that he/she is extremely fortunate not to have been attacked or even murdered by the intruder. They may also be surprised and disappointed that the police see this as just another crime, and are unsuccessful in tracing the culprit.

The police must be able to work with the media in order to get across a message about any change in policy or image. However, this may not be as straightforward as might be assumed. As was pointed out earlier, the media that have been previously alienated by a secretive police service cannot automatically be relied upon to put across a new message. There may well be suspicion about the "real" reason for any change, and a belief that there is some kind of hidden agenda. The other problem is that, unlike many other aspects of police work, an attempted change in image does not have quite the same media appeal. It will still tend to be the sensational or unusual stories which will grab the headlines, and a comparatively subtle change in policing philosophy may go unnoticed. This author can but endorse the views of Stephens and Becker who say quite categorically that: "Police rhetoric and the construction of their image, as well as the manner in which they communicate their policies, need to change" (1994, p. 227).

The police would be naïve to think that they can change the public's attitude towards them overnight by the publication of such documents as the Statement of Common Purpose and Values. As politicians and advertisers are only too well aware, persuading the public towards one's own viewpoint can be a difficult and expensive business. Whilst many aspects of police work remain subjects of great interest to the media, a change of emphasis in the delivery of service is not exactly headline news. It will therefore be a long and painful process for the police to recover ground which was lost by the inappropriate actions of a number of its officers in the 1970s and 1980s. It is essential that the police win over the media if they are to make a start in reassuring the public that they really are trying to provide society with what is needed, and in a way that is professional, caring, and sympathetic. As we have seen earlier it is essential that the police have the confidence of the public because they rely on them so heavily for help with their investigations. Demands for more censorship of the media are not the answer, and may serve only to arouse further animosity.

SUMMARY

This chapter has sought to explore the relationship between the police and the media. The role of the media in generating crime fear has been examined, and ways in which the police might diminish such fears have been considered. Media portrayals of the police have also been studied as a way of understanding how the public come to form an impression of the police service. It has been emphasised that the police will find it very difficult to win over public support without the help of the media. The police must therefore consider carefully how they interact with the media, and how they can use the media to portray a more positive image.

FURTHER READING

Reiner, R. (1992) *The Politics of the Police* (2nd edn). (Chapter 5.) Hemel Hempstead: Harvester Wheatsheaf.

Sparks, R. (1992) *Television and the Drama of Crime: Moral Tales and the Place of Crime in Public Life*. Milton Keynes: Open University Press.

White, S., Evans, P., Mihill, C. & Tysoe, M. (1992) *Hitting the Headlines: A Practical Guide to the Media*. Leicester: British Psychological Society.

CHAPTER 12

The Police and other Agencies

"Inter-disciplinary and inter-agency work is an essential process in the professional task of attempting to protect children from abuse . . . The experience gained by professionals in working and training together, has succeeded in bringing about a greater mutual understanding of the role of the various professions and agencies and a greater ability to combine their skills in the interests of abused children and their families . . . It is recommended that agencies should establish joint annual training programmes on child abuse issues with access for all professional groups in direct contact with children and families." (Home Office, 1991, p. 53)

Throughout this book there has been an intense focus on the police as an independent organisation. However, like most other organisations, the police must regularly interact with other agencies in order to be effective. It is something of a truism to say that the police alone can never eradicate crime, or totally maintain order, and yet the police often experience strained relationships with other agencies. Some of the possible reasons for this (e.g. the closed occupational culture, and a suspicion of outsiders) have been spelt out in Chapters 4 and 8 of this volume. In this chapter we will examine interprofessional collaboration in more detail and examine ways in which such interactions might be improved. Whilst there are many areas in which collaboration would be beneficial, we will focus on two specific areas in which interagency action might be more effective, i.e. in the prevention of crime and in cases involving interaction with social workers. As the above quote suggests, successful interagency cooperation is a crucial element in the area of child sexual abuse, and, it will be argued, is essential in other fields.

The primary aim of most police forces is the prevention and detection of crime, and the maintenance of order. However, the police acknowledge that crime is a community problem, and to some extent expect members of the whole community to accept some responsibility for its control. There are of course a large number of crime prevention initiatives which do involve other organisations. However, it will be suggested here that collaboration remains a piecemeal and often ineffectual affair. Whilst crime prevention and community liaison officers play a role, the vast majority of policing does not involve interaction between the police and other agencies.

It would be unfair to blame the police totally for this relative lack of cooperation as other agencies often adopt a closed and restricted outlook when it comes to interactions with the police. Suspicion, and the reliance on stereotypes of the police, means that interaction is not sought and, where it does occur, can be stilted and unproductive. Attempts to break down barriers have shown some success, but the overriding feeling is one of different agencies, with different agendas, priorities, and values, all ploughing their own furrows and avoiding crossing each others' paths.

It is perhaps naïve for police officers to *expect* that others in the community will help them whenever they are asked. The days when such things happened automatically seem to have long since passed. After all it is very difficult to persuade large numbers of people to donate blood freely, or to become organ donors; two very worthy causes but ones which involve a certain degree of coercion. If, through the actions of its officers, a police force has presented an isolated, unfriendly and unapproachable image, it should not be surprised when calls for help from the public go unanswered. Senior police officers may well be critical about the lack of help they receive from others, but they must recognise that some of the responsibility for this state of affairs rests with them. Smith and Gray's (1983) fascinating study of relationships between the police and public in London showed just how isolated the police had become, at least in some sections of the community. Once trust and respect break down, it is not easy to mend fences or to build new bridges (see Chapter 11).

If the public feel they can trust and respect the police service, they will generally be willing to help. If the public feel that they are uniting with the police to defeat a common enemy (e.g. rising crime) then cooperation may follow. (An integral part of Neighbourhood Watch schemes is that police officers keep such schemes informed about crime in the area.) However, in a society in which individualism is encouraged, the public are less likely to get involved and will instead leave it up to the professionals – in this case the police. Before police officers complain about a lack of help from the public, or from other agencies, they should ask themselves the question "Why *should* they help?" In other words, before assuming that everyone should want to help the police automatically they should consider the motivation of others. Some people are altruistic and will do things for the common good, whilst others are less public spirited. The pioneering work of Latané and Darley (1968) showed that people choose not to get involved in emergency situations mainly because they are inhibited by the presence of others. Such inaction is not due to apathy or callousness, but stems from ambiguity about what should be done (and by whom) and from an inappropriate defining of the situation. Latané and Darley draw particular attention to the costs and rewards of helping. Whilst their work focuses mainly on intervention in emergencies, the notion of costs and benefits may be appropriate for understanding other aspects of police–citizen interaction.

If the reader is asked the question "Would you try to rescue someone who was drowning?" there may be a simple yes or no answer; but for many people it is more likely that the answer would be "Well, it depends". Quite clearly there would be a number of considerations which might impinge on such a decision. Is the person worth saving? Might someone else try if I don't? Will I get a reward if I am successful? Will I be thought of badly if I fail? What danger am I putting myself in? Clearly these and many other questions would be considered before a decision was made to help or not to help. What is taking place here is a weighing of the costs and benefits of any action. If there is a very great danger to oneself, then the decision may well be not to intervene. Ironically, as Brown (1986) points out, by doing nothing to save a drowning person, an individual commits no crime and could not even be sued (p. 43).

It is with this in mind that the psychological theory of social exchange will now be briefly considered. Exchange theory (and the related equity theory) see human interaction in terms of costs and rewards. The theory suggests that relationships between individuals survive only as long as they are profitable to all members. In other words once the costs start to exceed the rewards, a person will be motivated to end the interaction. Here we are not talking of rewards and costs in purely financial terms, but rather in terms of anything which humans find rewarding – love, affection, esteem, praise – or costly – taking up time, losing status, being insulted. To some extent, this describes humans in economic terms and tends to portray them as basically selfish. However, the theory can still account for apparently selfless acts which appear to be altruistic. The fundamentals of exchange theory are eloquently described by Brown (1986) thus:

> "parties to a relationship must derive from that relationship *subjectively equivalent profits* if the relationship is to be experienced as fair. A second principle is that profits must be greater in the ongoing relationship than in alternative relationships if the relationship is to endure. A corollary principle, believed to be a universal social norm, is that benefits received must be reciprocated, not necessarily at once, but over the more or less long run." (p. 86)

It is therefore inappropriate for the police to expect that others will give them something, if there is not a reasonable prospect of something of equivalent value in return. This applies equally to individuals (for instance, police informants) or to other agencies (such as when probation officers learn that a number of their clients are using illegal drugs). One of the major problems with social exchange relates to the difficulty of finding exchanges which are genuinely of equivalent value. In economic transactions the common currency is money, and therefore costs, rewards and profits are calculated easily. However, in most social exchanges different "currencies" are in use, and so the calculations become much more difficult. The theory does recognise that the acceptance of equivalence is a subjective judgement; different rewards will inevitably have different values for different people. An inexpensive but thoughtful gift may be perceived as more valuable than a more expensive but less appropriate item. If the police expect help and cooperation from the public and other agencies, then they must be prepared to offer something *of equivalent value* in return. In some cases a financial incentive can be offered to those who supply information, but in many other cases a less tangible reward will need to be considered. Any agency which is approached for information will expect, and at some point demand, something in return. The police will then need to negotiate in terms of some common currency, or at least some truly equivalent exchange. Bearing this in mind, we will next examine some examples of interagency collaboration.

PREVENTING CRIME IN THE COMMUNITY

Many recent surveys have pointed to the fact that fear of crime is one of the most disturbing aspects of life in the 1990s. In general, fear of crime is not in direct proportion to the actual level of crime (see Crawford et al, 1990), but there is still an overall perception that the streets and indeed one's home are much less safe than 20 years ago. Partly in response to this, initiatives such as Neighbourhood Watch schemes have been established in an attempt to involve citizens in mutual protection (see Bennett, 1990). Governments have recognised growing concerns over crime and have tried to introduce initiatives which will reduce crime. However, in most cases these prove to be ineffective. Given that there is so much concern, it is perhaps surprising that communities and different agencies do so rarely come together to develop cohesive and collaborative strategies to make their environments safer. Instead, there is a tendency for people to withdraw behind their locked and alarmed doors and to become critical of the police for not doing more to make their environment safe. But as Newman (1972) pointed out, once people start to defend themselves as individuals rather than as a community the fight against crime is effectively lost.

The police would doubtless claim that a lack of resources means that they are unable to provide the level of service which the public demands. Consequently more and more people are now paying private security firms to protect their property. It is a sobering thought that private security firms have far more employees than does the police service in Britain. Yet, as we saw in Chapter 9, greater efficiency in the use of resources may be one answer. It will be argued that if more resources were put into developing interagency links, this could prove more productive than simply adding a couple of extra patrols in a high-crime area. To some extent this can be seen as community policing (see Alderson, 1979; Friedman, 1992), a concept which continues to attract attention but which has never been fully embraced by most police forces. There is a tendency to pay lip service to the concept of community policing while at the same time remaining cocooned in the relative security of the organisation (see Skolnik & Bayley, 1987). Community liaison panels may be set up, and regular meetings held, but there is still a tendency to see these as just an extra burden, which in reality has little to do with "real" police work.

One of the problems identified in Chapter 9 of the current volume was that it is impossible to prove how many crimes any given police action has prevented. It is far easier to count how many people have been arrested and use this as a measure of police success. For this reason, real community-based crime prevention strategies are rarely developed or are ineffectual because of a lack of commitment on the part of those involved. If the police did experience difficulty in relating to specific other agencies, then (at least in Britain) they would have felt that they could always rely on general members of the public for support. However, as we saw in Chapter 11, there was something of a change in the public perception of the police during the 1980s and 1990s, especially as regards their efficiency. As Stephens and Becker (1994) note, this has led to difficulties:

> "As police struggled to improve their clear-up rates so their image as effective controllers of crime began to suffer. Herein lies a vicious downward spiral for when public trust and confidence in the police fall so do the levels of cooperation and information, which, in turn, makes it harder for the police to detect and solve crime." (p. 223)

One problem that the police face is that crime prevention may be an important priority for any community, but it is not the only one. In any given situation there are competing priorities and agendas. Let us consider a couple of examples. In Britain there is an increasing problem with ram-raids. In such crimes, a stolen car is driven into a shop or other premises, goods are stolen from the shop, and then an escape is made in the stolen vehicle. One way of preventing such crimes is to have sturdy posts erected in front of shops so that vehicles are unable to reach the premises. This is a strategy which most crime prevention officers would advocate if advised. However, it is not uncommon for local councils to refuse shopowners permission to erect such barriers, as they would be considered unsightly or might pose a danger to pedestrians. This seems to be an example of two sets of people with different priorities pulling in different directions.

A further example demonstrates a similar problem. In Britain, as in many other countries, school break-ins are a very common occurrence. Following a large number of such burglaries one school in the Wythenshawe area of Manchester decided to act, and erected a large metal fence around the school perimeter. This proved to be a highly successful strategy, as the number of burglaries and acts of vandalism dropped significantly in the year following the erection of the fence. However, the school authorities had not sought planning permission for the fence, and the council ordered that it be removed. This appears to be another example of different "agencies" with different priorities. Perhaps if the education committee had got together with the planning committee and discussed the cost of vandalism, the outcome would have been different.

It could be argued that only when the crime problem becomes so bad, perhaps to the point where it is by far the highest community priority, will other considerations assume less importance. However, at the present time, a balance needs to be struck between crime prevention needs and other considerations. In the planning of new buildings, premises could be made much more secure by the elimination of, for example, rear entrances and fire doors. But other considerations such as building and fire regulations need to be satisfied, meaning that a compromise has to be struck. However, it should not be assumed from this that the police are powerless; rather that the more the police are recognised as an integral part of the community, the more likely it is that their voice will be heard and their ideas embraced by others. If good working relations have already been established, it is much easier for one party to make constructive suggestions to others.

A CASE STUDY – THE KIRKHOLT BURGLARY PREVENTION PROJECT

Let us consider in some detail one way in which interprofessional collaboration can lead to success. This was a crime prevention initiative established on the Kirkholt estate in Rochdale, in the North-West of England (see Forrester, Chatterton & Pease, 1988; Forrester, Frenz, O'Connell & Pease, 1990). Kirkholt is a local authority housing estate with some 2280 dwellings. Prior to the initiative the rate of burglary was extremely high with 25% of all residences being burgled in 1985. The project team consulted first with local groups, then held a half-day seminar (chaired by the Chief Probation Officer) at which all relevant agencies were invited to contribute ideas for crime prevention. It should be noted that from the beginning there was a genuine attempt to involve all relevant people, rather than the project being seen as predominantly a police or probation initiative. Interviews were conducted with burglary victims, the neighbours of the victims, and, interestingly, with a sample of convicted burglars. Data from these interviews proved to be particularly useful and the project team were able to draw up an action plan.

Rather than trying to protect every home on the estate, the researchers decided to target those homes which had already suffered a previous burglary. This strategy was adopted because research had shown that homes that had been previously burgled were four times more likely to be attacked again than were homes that had not been burgled previously. To illustrate that point further, almost half of the homes burgled in December 1986 had been burgled at least once previously in 1986. In fact, the researchers could be even more specific about the timing of repeat victimisations, showing that in most cases the repeat crime occurred within six weeks of the first. Targeting of such homes was thus seen as an efficient use of resources, and was likely to prove to be more effective than a more general strategy which tried to spread resources more thinly (see Forrester et al, 1990, p. 3).

Having identified which homes were the most vulnerable, the researchers set about identifying the profiles of typical burglaries. One factor that emerged was that in almost half the burglaries, money was taken from gas and electricity pre-payment meters, and in over a quarter of the crimes, such money was the only thing stolen. This will not come as a surprise to many police officers, and yet in the past the police might well have simply wrung their hands and said that the gas and electricity companies should do something. What the researchers were able to do was to persuade the power companies that it would be in their interests (not to mention the householders') to replace pre-payment meters with other systems which did not rely on cash. Thus the homes were made less attractive to a potential burglar as there was no guarantee of a ready source of money.

Studies of burglary techniques on the estate showed that most of the homes were easy targets in that entry was gained swiftly and easily, usually through the first point of entry that was tried. Thus more was needed than simply a few extra locks and bolts. Instead, action was needed to reduce or eliminate the many vulnerable points of the dwellings. This involved persuading the local council to carry out an overall security upgrading of homes on the estate, in particular concentrating on the weakest points. For example the doors and door frames were previously made of such a construction that a relatively weak push on the door opened it up. Similarly, some window frames were so rotten that they could be prised open with a minimum of force. The local council were consequently persuaded to carry out work on the vulnerable homes (admittedly with help from a grant) and came to believe that there would be long-term benefits. Burglary techniques were also monitored so that any changes in tactics would be picked up quickly and responded to appropriately. Householders were also persuaded to security mark all their vulnerable property with their own post code. This had the effect of deterrence, but also meant that recovered stolen property could be reunited with its owner more quickly.

A further measure which was introduced was called Cocoon Neighbourhood Watch. Rather than setting up traditional Neighbourhood Watch schemes (which might involve up to 40 households on the same road) the researchers felt that a smaller group would be much more effective. This was partly because there would be less risk of a diffusion of responsibility, and also that smaller scale surveillance was more practical. Thus the six or so households closest to the victim's home were approached and asked to pay particular attention to anything suspicious occurring around the target house. If they agreed to cooperate, then they were "rewarded" by having their own home's security uprated. This proved to be an effective tactic, and most households agreed to help. In a way this method of increased and targeted surveillance by neighbours mirrored what might occur naturally in well established and closely knit traditional communities, but which was rare on estates like Kirkholt.

In the first report on the project (Forrester et al, 1988) the researchers were able to report considerable success with the initiative, with an overall reduction of 40% in the rate of burglaries only five months after the start of the programme. This was a much higher figure than most crime prevention initiatives achieve, and the scheme attracted a great deal of media attention. It was not possible to demonstrate that the decline in burglaries of the targeted homes was statistically greater than the overall reduction, but this is perhaps not surprising given that there was an overall increase in crime prevention awareness. (For example, those houses around a previously burgled house also had security upgrading, and neighbours were more vigilant overall.) However, the researchers could report that there were no repeat victimisations at all in the first five months of the project and no more than two in any subsequent month. This went against the trend in other areas of Rochdale where repeat victimisations remained at a high level. There was also no evidence that crime had been displaced to surrounding areas.

The Kirkholt Burglary Prevention Project shows what can be achieved in a relatively short period of time and with relatively few resources. There are a number of reasons why the scheme was successful, but perhaps prominent amongst these is the way in which the team were able to bring together people from many different agencies who worked jointly to produce a result. Each group achieved something by way of a reward, and so were more willing to cooperate. Perhaps as quasi-independent researchers, the team were better able to secure the cooperation of the many groups involved, but even so the project was an object lesson in how genuine interprofessional collaboration can achieve results. There were inevitably some difficulties along the way, but once all the local groups, the electricity and gas companies, the local council, victim support, and neighbours became involved there was a much greater likelihood of success. Prior to the initiative, the police would record and investigate each burglary, perhaps the crime prevention officer would give advice; victim support would be informed; the local electricity company would repair the meter; the council would replace the broken lock and so on. But such isolated responses had little success in terms of overall crime prevention, as there was little common purpose.

A coordinated approach may appear time-consuming for the police as there will inevitably be meetings to attend, disagreements over policy and other problems. However, in terms of dealing with a crime which causes great anxiety to its victims, the police could achieve greater respect for their work and an enhanced public image if they were seen to be more effective. It should also be noted that the way in which the police first handle victims can affect the way in which such people come to see the whole criminal justice process. Poor handling can produce alienation in victims, meaning that they are less willing to cooperate with the system, for example by not agreeing to appear as a witness in court (see Norris & Thompson, 1993). By blaming others (e.g. the local council) the police may be missing the point and will find it more difficult to secure help in the future. By genuinely involving all other agencies, the community itself will benefit, and paradoxically, the police may have fewer demands on their time to investigate further burglaries. Quantifying the exact savings in monetary terms is not easy (see Bailey & Lynch, 1988) but any initiative which achieves such a success rate (a reduction of 75% in the rate of burglary by the end of Phase II of the project) deserves closer attention.

It is interesting to note that during the research, residents on

Kirkholt began to take much more responsibility for security on the estate. For example, the Kirkholt Crime Prevention Group was established and provided a focus for residents who wanted to play a more active role in their estate. One consequence of such an initiative is that residents may be less likely to rely on the police to resolve all crime prevention matters, and the police in turn will be freer to target their own resources more effectively.

To date we have considered the practical steps which were taken to prevent crime as and when it was occurring. But of course one could argue that crime prevention should instead be considering the offenders rather than the offences. In other words, if one were to concentrate on the motivations for offending rather than on the offences themselves, "crime prevention" could be moved one stage further back. Trying to understand why people commit crime has been the focus for many psychologists and sociologists for a number of years (see e.g. West & Farrington, 1973; Moffitt, 1993). In Phase II of the Kirkholt project there was more consideration of offenders' motives and a greater involvement on the part of the local probation service. This led to increased understanding of offenders' behaviour, in particular the identification of drink and drug addictions, and problems caused by a high level of unemployment. Following this, focused groups were established by the probation service, whose main aims were the understanding and modifying of clients' behaviour.

A second important initiative in Phase II was the Kirkholt Schools Crime Prevention Project. Whilst it is quite common for community police officers to give talks to their local schools, this part of the project sought to go much further. In particular there was an attempt to channel what was called the "negative ingenuity" of young people into more positive outlets. In an innovative move, a theatre company was brought into each of the five schools on the estate. The company acted out scenes with a crime prevention theme, and then groups of children in each school worked on their own drama projects dealing with crime prevention. Following the visit of the theatre group, teachers worked with vulnerable children and discussed topics such as the type of community in which the children would like to live. A group was also established to deal with disaffected young people, allowing them to talk about crime and crime prevention. There was even a Crime Prevention Festival organised on the theme of "Unity For Our Community".

A third strand to Phase II was the establishment of the Kirkholt Credit Union. At first glance it may not appear obvious why such a scheme should be included in a crime prevention initiative. However, interviews with offenders had established that lack of money management skills was a primary motivation for offending. By establishing a community-based credit union, more effective money management could be encouraged and people who might have previously been refused banking facilities could be helped.

The overwhelming finding from both Phases I and II of the Kirkholt project was that crime (in this case burglary) can be reduced if a coordinated and innovative crime prevention strategy is adopted. Many of the ideas in the project have now been replicated elsewhere in Britain and in other countries (see Thurman, Giacomazzi & Bayer, 1993.) It would be naïve to suggest that the police have the resources and degree of expertise to introduce such initiatives entirely by themselves. However, by showing what can be achieved through interagency collaboration, it is hoped that the police will be more open to the idea of truly joint initiatives and less willing to fall back on negative stereotypes of members of other organisations. In the same way, the police themselves will need to acknowledge the stereotype which others may have of them, and make some attempt to remove suspicion and hostility. Negative images can take a great deal of time to break down, but unless a start is made in removing some of the psychological barriers to collaboration, the police will be perceived as failing in one of their stated primary duties, i.e. the prevention of crime.

INTERPROFESSIONAL COLLABORATION WITH SOCIAL WORKERS

Whilst crime prevention remains a high priority for any organisation, a great deal of police time is actually spent dealing with non-crime matters. Whilst the public may have come to believe that policing is almost all related to crime, the reality is somewhat different. As Punch (1979) pointed out many years ago, up to 50% of calls for police action are actually what might be called service calls, and have little to do with crime. Service calls could be anything from asking directions or advice to delivering messages. Alderson (1979) put the figure for these types of calls higher, claiming that service work took up to 80% of police officers' time. In reality, a great deal of "policing" involves social work of one kind or another, though the police prefer to play down this less glamorous or exciting side of their day-to-day work (see Shapland & Vagg, 1988; Stephens & Becker, 1994). In fact it is not always easy to separate out these two types of calls, as there is inevitably a considerable degree of overlap. If a police officer receives a call to deal with a domestic dispute between a married couple, this could be seen as a service call, but it may also defuse a situation which could escalate rapidly and become a crime.

If a significant amount of police time is spent on service, or what might be termed social service calls, then it might be assumed that the police would have frequent and productive interactions with social workers. In reality this is rarely the case. Whilst the need for interaction has long been recognised (see e.g. Treger, 1975) cooperation has not come naturally, and where collaboration has come about, this has rarely been easy or productive. Some of the possible general reasons for difficulty in interprofessional collaboration have been discussed earlier in the chapter, but there are additional difficulties specific to police–social work interactions. There tends to be a heavy reliance on stereotypes when it comes to visualising members of the other organisation (see Thomas, 1994, pp. 2–4 for some wonderful examples of this). We saw in Chapter 4 how stereotyping can lead to poor communication between individuals and organisations. Fielding (1988, p. 69) suggests that the stereotyping begins during police training. Cornick (1988) encapsulates the heart of the stereotypes in the following way:

"Recruitment into both agencies attracts very different people, and their . . . training . . . would seem to create further divisions. Police officers are likely to see social workers as wishy washy, indecisive and intellectual do-gooders, while many social workers . . . will view the police as omnipotent, inflexible, and with a rule book mentality." (p. 26)

Perhaps at the heart of the debate is the notion of care versus control (see Stephens & Becker, 1994). Traditionally, social work has been seen as the agency of care, whereas the police are seen as the agency of control. Whilst this is of course far too simplistic a view, it is nonetheless a dichotomy which is recognised by members of both professions, and serves as a first stumbling block to the establishment of effective interactions (see Fielding, 1984). For their part, many police officers cling to and espouse their cynical, machismo image, painting a picture of the thin blue line just about managing to hold back the almost inevitable destruction of society. This is a picture which does not mesh well with the traditional image of social work. As Thomas (1994) notes, in the 1970s:

"the police stereotyped the social worker as a naïve, perpetual student who covered up crimes, and got young offenders off charges; they epitomised the liberal 'do-gooder' movements which were at large and which questioned the traditional police approach to their work . . . In contrast, the social work view of police was one of apprehension and defensiveness, with more latent expressions of them as an insensitive 'force' rather than 'service', concerned only with simplistic law enforcement to the exclusion of more sophisticated and subtle thought." (p. 5)

As with policing, social work does not so easily fit into a distinct category in terms of care and control. As Fielding and Conroy (1994) point out, although social workers see themselves as employees in a truly caring profession, they have sweeping powers, including the ability to remove the mentally ill from society, and to remove children from their parents. These authors describe the public perception of social workers thus:

> "To many ordinary people the social services are not a benign agency, but a threatening force of bearded intellectuals and busybodies whose speech and reasoning are incomprehensible and whose decisions are capricious at best." (Fielding & Conroy, 1994, p. 194)

A description with which many would certainly not agree, though such portrayals show that it may be inappropriate to see social work as simply a caring profession. It also shows that police officers are not the only ones to suffer from the effects of negative stereotyping. Indeed some writers have noted that social workers come in for more public criticism than almost any other occupational group. As Pope and Greenhill (1978) note, the problem is that stereotypes which are not challenged become part of the socialisation process and the myths are then very difficult to remove. Only slowly might social workers come to realise that the police have something of value to offer (see Maguire, 1993).

As we will see later, there are a number of areas in which good police–social work cooperation is desirable or necessary. But perhaps nowhere is the interaction more important than in cases of child sexual abuse. Because of the nature of such cases, there is invariably involvement by both agencies, albeit approaching the problem from different angles. During the 1980s there was a very large increase in the number of such cases that were reported. This was crystallised in Cleveland in 1987 with a massive increase in diagnosed cases of child sex abuse, which culminated in a public inquiry. The inquiry identified a large number of factors which had caused the crisis, but among the reasons was a lack of cooperation between the various agencies. More specifically the inquiry suggested that different agencies and organisations lacked detailed knowledge about what others' responsibilities were, and this was coupled with very poor communication between agencies. Like other previous reports, the Cleveland inquiry advocated the development of better interagency cooperation (DHSS, 1988). There then followed various circulars designed to improve interagency working (see Home Office, 1991). Whilst these did lead to the establishment of joint initiatives between the various organisations, the fundamental gulf between agencies was never truly bridged.

Waterhouse and Carnie (1990) identified a number of barriers to good collaboration. These included competing aims and objectives, diffusion of responsibilities, difficulty in decision-making, and delay or reluctance in disseminating information. These authors found that the reality of interagency collaboration was not ideal, and could come in any of three forms. These were:

1 *Minimalist.* Here only the most basic information is exchanged, and that is done formally, with little discussion. This is really "going through the motions" but without any real commitment to the ideal of cooperation.
2 *Collaborative.* In this scenario there is a genuine free exchange of information on an informal and personal basis. There is collaboration in decision-making about the case, and both parties keep each other up to date on any developments.
3 *Integrated.* As the name implies, this was a genuinely integrated approach, involving joint interviewing, joint investigation, and joint appraisal of cases. Here the picture is one of a dedicated and specialist multi-disciplinary team, working with a common agenda.

There are thus large differences in the level of collaboration, despite a widespread recognition that better collaboration is needed. As Thomas (1994) notes, although collaboration sounds like a good idea, and many people are full of good intent, the reality is that there remains an antipathy towards genuine cooperation, and, in many cases, a deep suspicion of the real motives of the other agency. This has not perhaps been helped by the Criminal Justice Act, 1991, which gave the police more powers in child abuse cases – to the annoyance of some social workers. Some social work personnel have suggested that child sex abuse investigations are now more about obtaining good evidence to take to court rather than about protecting the child. They see this shift in emphasis as an encroachment on their duty to "put the child first" (see Bilton, 1993).

Earlier in this chapter, attention was drawn to the tendency for each side to blame the other for the lack of cooperation, making progress difficult. In theory at least one would expect that cooperation would have improved dramatically in recent years. As Thomas (1994) notes, there has been a decline in the amount of mud slinging since the 1970s, and there have been a large number of inquiries identifying poor interagency cooperation as a major fault in child abuse allegations. Coupled with this, both agencies received a great deal of criticism in the 1980s and '90s, and so might have been expected to draw closer together in facing a critical public, but this has not generally been the case. Thomas comments that despite an apparent improvement in interagency relations, there is still an underlying feeling of suspicion and lack of trust. Even when collaboration is improved, there is still uncertainty about whether there really can be a productive joint approach. Indeed Thomas suggests that some social workers feel that after working more closely with police officers, they are in danger of being overwhelmed by the police and losing their autonomy. For some social workers, working with the police has felt more like being controlled by the police.

Thomas (1994) identifies a number of important reasons why there are potential difficulties associated with increased collaboration. Most fall into three categories, around the areas of accountability, structural factors, and cultural differences.

Following a number of changes, public and local accountability for the police has diminished in recent years, and will continue to do so in the future. Local police committees no longer have the power formerly bestowed upon them. By comparison, social services departments have a clearer line of accountability. Local councils have social services committees which monitor the work of directors of social services and their staff. The Department of Health also gives guidance and formally identifies the duties of social workers. This can be important as a Director of Social Services may be called upon to resign following wrongful actions by his/her staff. However, it would be highly unusual for a Chief Constable to resign following criticism of his/her officers. (Indeed when the Derbyshire (UK) police force was severely criticised and refused its certificate of efficiency in 1993, the Chief Constable remained in post.)

A number of structural and cultural factors have already been identified earlier in this chapter. It is, however, important to recognise that there are a number of differences in demographic variables of the employees of each organisation. Police officers will on average have a lower level of education than the average social worker (although as noted in Chapter 8 this situation is changing). As Moore (1985) notes, it is also the case that people with different personalities will be attracted to different occupations. Once appointed, individuals will then be trained and socialised to develop a particular view of the world.

Police work is predominantly male-dominated, whilst social work is not. A police officer also has more powers than a social worker, and will tend to use those powers more frequently. The police organisation is described as having a semi-military structure, with a heavy emphasis on such matters as rank and discipline. By comparison, the social worker is effectively a council officer tied into the infrastructure of local government. Although we have seen that there are overlaps between the two professions, a great deal of day-to-day work is in fact different. Thus there will be inevitable differences in organisational culture and in training. To repeat what may be a stereotype, police training emphasises the arrest of wrongdoers, whilst social work is more concerned with understanding the reasons for offending.

Thomas also draws attention to questions of professionalism, and asks whether either occupation has truly reached what might be termed a professional status. He says:

> "both are still on the path to professionalism but fall short of it by virtue of lack of education, ad hoc training, or not having achieved public recognition for those traits and characteristics of a profession they do possess. Social work has been variously referred to as a semi-profession, meta-profession, bureau-profession or occupational profession, while the police have been termed as either managerial professionals or practical professionals." (Thomas, 1994, p. 16)

Perhaps the point about this is that members of an organisation who feel insecure about their professional or public image will seek to enhance their status by derogating members of other professions (see Chapter 4). In this case, police officers and social workers may both see their jobs as having sufficient overlap to make them feel threatened by members of the other organisation, and will therefore seek to enhance their own standing at the expense of the others. Consequently the informal police culture will contain anecdotes and uncomplimentary nicknames for social workers, with stories about such people repeated and embellished for internal consumption (see Fielding, 1988). Similarly social workers may continue to hold a negative view of the police and the social work office will resound to condemnation of the "typical" actions of one zealous police officer.

Occupational culture, through specialised jargon, in-jokes and common attitudes, can provide a great feeling of security and belonging. However, as we saw in Chapter 4, it can easily spill over into arrogance, animosity, and elitism: qualities almost guaranteed to drive a wedge between different occupations. One irony that Thomas alludes to is that as each occupation becomes more professional, the gulf between them may well widen.

Once again we seem to be coming back to the problems associated with a closed occupational culture (see Chapter 8). By virtue of their duties, police officers will come into contact with social workers, and yet members of this other profession will tend to be viewed as outsiders who are not to be trusted. Yet if cooperation were more evident, the police might well become more efficient and effective in a number of their primary roles. Having said that, it would be unfair to blame the police totally for a lack of cooperation. As was noted above, other occupations also have their own particular ways of working and are not always receptive to approaches from members of other organisations. Social workers might well experience difficulties in relating to other groups, such as members of the medical profession (see Bywaters, 1989). It is interesting to read a CCETSW document entitled *Sewing the Seams for a Seamless Service* (Weinstein, 1994). Despite the fact that the front cover contains a photograph of three people, one of whom is a uniformed police officer, the document makes virtually no mention of police officers in its text on interprofessional training.

Hey and Minty (1991) provide an interesting framework for identifying four different professional models. These are listed as:

1 The *practical professional*. This is typified by a common sense approach in one who believes that solutions can be found through trial and error.
2 The *expert professional*. This is someone who seems to know exactly what he/she is doing, and who keeps clients at arm's length.
3 The *managerialist model*. Here there is an assumption that the higher echelons of the organisation plan and develop policies, whilst the lower ranks carry out the work.
4 The *reflective practitioner*. This is exemplified by the worker who recognises that others (including those from other organisations) have a great deal of knowledge and experience and welcomes their contributions.

One can see that the best model in terms of likely interprofessional collaboration is the last of these. But as Hey notes, training rarely encourages this type of approach, preferring instead to emphasise one of the other three. Indeed one can see how different professions (e.g. medicine, the police) deliberately adopt one of these models and adhere to it rigidly.

So far we have discussed interagency collaboration as though it were an all or nothing activity. Yet there are inevitably varying degrees of collaboration. Thomas draws on the work of Davidson (1976) who described five different types of inter-agency relationships. These are:

1 *Communication*. This is where two organisations are actually talking to each other, sharing information up to a point, but still working separately.
2 *Cooperation*. Here work might be carried out collectively on small projects, or agencies would be working informally together on joint cases.

3 *Coordination*. Here there is more joint planning and direct involvement than in cooperation, but no sanctions are applied to those who refuse to work together.
4 *Federation*. In this case, the two work very closely together and may share offices and other facilities.
5 *Merger*. The final collaboration is one where each agency loses its own identity and becomes part of a larger body.

These are useful distinctions to make. Presently, where there is collaboration it is most likely to be at levels one and two, or occasionally, three. Both agencies might fear levels four and five, believing that it would end their feeling of autonomy. In reality there may be collaboration at more than one level at any one time. For example, senior managers may work together in a way that could be described as coordination, whilst on the ground, individual officers may well be working at the level of cooperation. Perhaps what would be ideal would be mutual interdependence, whereby members of each organisation know their own boundaries, and yet recognise that they are partly dependent on the other to achieve a satisfactory outcome to a particular case. Indeed Thomas suggests that only when interdependence is recognised will workers be motivated to establish genuine links with members of other organisations. As he notes: "Only when a degree of trust has been built up will the cocoons of professional and occupational cultures be discarded and organisational boundaries successfully spanned" (Thomas, 1994, p. 24). Thus relationships may be built up on an individual level, though this does not automatically mean that the two organisations are truly cooperating. It is possible for individuals to maintain their negative stereotype of most members of other organisations, whilst getting on well with one person at an individual level. When asked to explain this, the individual will no doubt refer to the fact that "well most of them are a waste of time, but this one's okay".

We can therefore see that interactions between the police and social workers have a disappointing track record, and that progress on cooperation is likely to be slow, given the many obstacles which have been identified. This is unfortunate but understandable, given the wide gulf which exists between the two agencies. Many public inquiries have identified a lack of cooperation as one causative factor when tragedies have occurred. Unfortunately, the differing philosophies, attitudes and world views of each organisation mean that difficulties will remain. That said, after identifying some of the factors highlighted above it is possible to start work on the building of bridges. As long as both organisations recognise that there is a need for each other's expertise and information, cooperation is more likely. To refer back to our earlier discussion, only when the rewards exceed the costs will cooperation become the norm.

There are an increasing number of areas in which the police will come into contact with social workers. Dealing with the mentally ill, child protection cases, domestic violence, disaster management, and juvenile offenders are just some of the areas where better cooperation would be beneficial, not least to the clients.

As police managers' minds are concentrated by performance indicators and other measures of their effectiveness, it is essential to recognise what can be achieved through better interagency cooperation. It is not enough simply to blame the other organisation for a lack of progress and then complain of one's lonely fight against difficult elements in society. A recognition of the tenets of social exchange theory (outlined earlier in this chapter) means that police officers will be better able to motivate others to help them, and to work collaboratively in solving a community problem. To some extent, the difficulties can be tackled by joint training initiatives (see Weinstein, 1994). However, these tend to be designed for those who are already specialising in certain areas, and are thus unlikely to break down the negative stereotypes held by the majority of members of each organisation. It is interesting that social work education, with its very heavy emphasis on anti-discriminatory practice, actually does very little to challenge the negative stereotypes which many social workers have of all police officers. On the other hand, even the more forward-thinking police trainers are no less guilty of perpetuating myths about members of certain other organisations. It is clear that a start needs to be made in breaking down some of the barriers which have built up over the years. Only then will both agencies begin to realise some of the potential benefits which a true collaboration would produce.

SUMMARY

This chapter has sought to consider the difficult questions which surround interactions between the police and other agencies. It has been recognised that collaboration is never easy, yet can be beneficial to the police in their day-to-day work. There are more and more areas in which the police could benefit from better cooperation from others, yet it is unfair for the police simply to blame others for the relative lack of progress. Social exchange theory presents one model which can account for some of the lack of cooperation. The police must acknowledge that if they want help from others there must be a genuine offer of something of equivalent value in return. It must be recognised that stereotypes are held on both sides, and that only by challenging these can progress be made.

FURTHER READING

Stephens, M. & Becker, S. (1994) *Police Force, Police Service: Care and Control in Britain*. Basingstoke: Macmillan.

Thomas, T. (1994) *The Police and Social Workers* (2nd edn). Aldershot: Arena.

Conclusion

It was acknowledged in the Introduction that this is a time of considerable change for many police forces. In Britain there have been a number of recent publications which have questioned the function, effectiveness and legitimacy of the police service. Throughout this book there has been an attempt to demonstrate the way in which applications of psychology can be greatly relevant to modern policing, especially at times of great change. The list of research topics which have relevance to police work is growing as the science of psychology itself grows, and this book has attempted merely to draw attention to some of the more important areas where this applies.

Perhaps the main theme which has recurred throughout the diverse topics covered in this volume is the way in which the police deal with other people. Whether or not the police are successful in their aims and objectives rests heavily on the help and support they receive from others in society. This applies not just to ordinary members of the public, but to many of the other agencies and institutions with whom the police must interact. Time and again psychologists and sociologists have written about the relative isolation of the police officer in society, and the closed occupational culture which dominates the police service (see e.g. Tournier, 1976). We have seen throughout this volume that the way in which the police treat and interact with other members of society is crucial in determining the level of support and respect which they command. Yet the selection, training and socialisation of police officers tend to serve largely to isolate them from the public from whom they are drawn and whom they are sworn to serve. Good communication skills are at the core of interactions with others, yet only slowly are police trainers incorporating the teaching of such skills into training programmes. Effective communication is crucial to many of the roles which police officers are expected to perform. As John F. Kennedy said, "Communication costs money, ignoring it costs even more". Good communication is important in day-to-day dealings with the public, but it is equally significant in the way in which the police relate to specific individuals, to other agencies, and to the media.

Only slowly have the police come to realise how important image is in winning over the public. They can no longer take for granted the support of the vast majority of the general public. Police forces are judged partly on the misdemeanours which a small number of officers commit, but equally important is the way in which each officer deals with general enquiries and routine calls. As was pointed out in Chapter 11, most people actually have very little contact with a police officer over the course of the average year. Thus when an interaction does take place it will be of great significance to the individual. It is all too easy for members of any occupational group to forget that the incident with which they are dealing will be very important and significant to the other person. Because police officers deal daily with some of the more distressing aspects of life, it is easy for them to forget that this is not "just another burglary" to the householder who has called in the police. To the householder this is a serious, rare and disturbing incident and he/she will expect that the distress be recognised by the officer who comes to take details. Even if the police do not solve the crime, the victim's opinion of them can be affected by the way in which the officer deals with this particular case. A short phone call to the victim some weeks after the crime may seem of little value to the harried police officer, but will be greatly appreciated by most householders.

The contact which many middle-class people have with the police may be limited to the occasional stop for speeding or some other motoring violation. Whilst no motorist likes being reported for a traffic offence, the way in which the officer handles the case will be crucial in determining that member of the public's opinion of "the police". An officer who both reports and insults an offending motorist will have made an enemy for many years to come. It is no good the same police officer complaining later that an appeal for witnesses to a serious traffic accident meets with no response. We have also seen that the police must be able to deal with the media appropriately if they wish to project a favourable image. They must recognise that the media have their own agenda, not least of which is to carry details of the more horrific crimes and to grab the public's attention with sensational headlines and photographs. The police must recognise that part of their job is to reassure a worried public that, although crime is increasing, the risk of becoming a victim of one of the more vicious attacks is actually quite remote.

Communication could also be seen as an underlying theme in the chapters which dealt with interviewing and interrogations. The way in which police officers handle victims and witnesses also carries messages to people who are generally not well treated by the criminal justice system. Indeed the plight of victims within this system is increasingly a cause for concern. A recent BBC television series, *Crime Limited*, focused predominantly on the victim and has shown how the system tends to forget the innocent victim, or the altruistic witness. The focus of much of the criminal justice system has been very much on the offender. It is understandably quite difficult for some victims to come to terms with this reality. As a recent episode of the aforementioned series pointed out, there are a whole range of people employed to serve the needs of offenders (e.g. social workers, probation officers, prison psychiatrists) yet little on which the victim can depend. Victim Support Schemes do help, yet such schemes tend to be run on a shoestring and to rely very heavily on the good nature of volunteers with relatively little training. Whilst appreciating that there are increasing pressures on police time, police officers should recognise that the victim needs to be treated in a sympathetic manner, and to believe that the police really do recognise his/her plight. In this volume we have suggested ways in which more information can be obtained from victims and witnesses using techniques such as the Cognitive Interview. This technique demonstrates one important way in which psychology and policing can be brought together in a productive symbiotic relationship.

This book has also recognised that the way in which suspects are questioned is slowly beginning to change, but there remain some causes for concern. Chapter 3 sought to challenge the widely held view that the guilty can be easily distinguished from the innocent in the interrogation situation. It is also important that police officers realise that it is possible for some innocent people to confess, simply because of the pressures exerted in the interrogation room. Recent legislation such as PACE has succeeded to some extent in removing some of the more oppressive tactics, but cases remain where police officers' methods have been questioned by the courts and confessions have been ruled as inadmissible. In one recent case in Leeds Crown Court, a man who had admitted the murder of a seven-year-old girl was acquitted because the judge ruled that the questioning was too oppressive and that the jury could not learn of his confession (see *The Guardian*, 22.11.93, p. 2).

The police are in something of a Catch 22 situation here. Performance indicators and other measures of efficiency are increasingly being introduced to police work; one consequence of this is that police officers are told that they should try to improve their detection rate. Yet they are also told that they must not try to elicit a confession from a reluctant suspect if that means exerting too much pressure on the person. Perhaps police tactics will change if courts continue to dismiss cases where there is even a suspicion of oppressive interviewing. The police must recognise that the tide of public opinion has changed, and that society is now much less willing to tolerate the sort of interrogation techniques which were common just a few years ago. It is understandable that some police officers feel that they are being asked to do their job with one hand tied behind their back, but those officers must recognise that convictions may be *more* likely if they stick to the more ethical forms of interviewing techniques.

In a previous publication (Ainsworth & Pease, 1987) it was argued that psychology had a vital role to play in the training of police officers. Since then there have been some signs of change in thinking but there is still (at least in Britain) a reluctance to accept that psychology has a major contribution to make in the education of police officers. Whilst there have been some positive moves, progress is still relatively slow, and attitudes are difficult to change. This book has spent some time considering the way in which stereotypes are used to simplify a complex world. It must be recognised that there are stereotypes about psychology and psychologists which are often not the most flattering! Whilst many police forces do now employ psychologists, their exact role and value is at times uncertain to a traditional organisation like the police service. Psychologists need to continue to demonstrate the value and relevance of their research findings and to disseminate such information in a comprehensible form (see Cohen, Sprafkin, Oglesby & Claiborn, 1976).

Respected academic journals have their place, but the technical language in such publications makes them virtually incomprehensible to the average non-psychologist reader. It is hoped that publications such as this current volume have served to unravel the intricate methodologies of most psychological research studies, and to put across important concepts and ideas in a more easily digestible form. This volume has shown a number of the areas in which this is important. For instance the Cognitive Interview Technique (Chapter 2) was developed from laboratory-based psychological research on memory processes. As Chapter 10 showed, when psychologists can use their skills in a way that can genuinely help in the investigation of crime, then police officers will be more willing to accept the contributions which they make. Psychology has made dramatic advances in its understanding of human behaviour in the last 20 years. For a profession such as policing, with its heavy reliance on understanding and predicting human behaviour, psychology does have a great deal to offer and will continue to do so. Some current areas of police concern (e.g. the reported rise in violent crimes, and the way in which the mentally ill should be handled) are subjects which have already been studied extensively by psychologists. Chapters 5 and 6 have summarised some of this accumulated knowledge. By understanding the reasons for behaviour of this kind, police officers will be better informed and feel more confident about dealing with what might previously have been seen as unpredictable and uncontrollable behaviour.

Psychologists may criticise some aspects of police procedures, and can demonstrate the dangers of certain approaches which police officers might take. Criticism is always easier after things have gone wrong, and, to paraphrase some words used earlier, one can predict virtually anything with hindsight. If psychologists point out that certain procedures are perilous then they must also suggest alternative methods which allow the police to fulfil their role, but which carry less inherent dangers. The use of techniques such as the Cognitive Interview is one example of how psychologists can suggest changes to current procedures which in the long run have benefit for the police.

We have seen throughout this book that the police's closed occupational culture means that any advice from "outsiders" is treated with suspicion or even contempt. However, once the benefits have been pointed out, there is more likely to be an acceptance of any techniques which might be helpful. In this way these same outsiders are seen less as interfering, ill-informed and ill-intentioned critics, and more as experts with valuable and relevant skills. There is always a danger that psychology can become trivialised, or that small parts of it can be taken out of context. We saw in Chapters 7 and 8 how psychological tests and psychological knowledge can be "bought in" and then inappropriately used by police personnel. Psychology may be seen as less valuable if it is taught by people within the organisation who have no formal training in the subject.

The police service has a habit of giving its own officers a small amount of training and then allowing them to put across their new knowledge to others who know even less. Neither the British Psychological Society nor the American Psychological Association would even contemplate letting anyone with just a few weeks training go out and teach psychology or use psychological tests. Yet in some cases, police officers do just that. In Britain there is about to be a major reorganisation of police training, following the appointment of a National Director. Among the changes will be an acknowledgement that training must become more professional with recognised standards of competence for both students and trainers. The recent document *The Future of Police Training* (Ryan, 1994) paints a promising picture of new developments in the organisation of training, but actually says very little about the place of subjects such as psychology in the training curriculum.

Policing will continue to be a difficult and demanding job in the foreseeable future. It is inevitably bound up with political ideologies and will always be the subject of great debate (see Reiner, 1992). However, it is hoped that police forces will increasingly recognise that those outside the organisation do have valuable contributions to make to day-to-day policing and to training. As both a theoretical and an applied discipline, psychology would seem to have the most to offer an organisation charged with the unenviable task of maintaining order in increasingly complex and demanding societies.

References

Ackroyd, S., Harper, R., Hughes, J. A., Shapiro, D. & Soothill, K. (1992) *New Technology and Practical Police Work*. Milton Keynes: Open University Press.

ACPO (Association of Chief Police Officers) (1990) *Strategic Policy Document. Setting the standards for policing: meeting community expectations.*

Adorno, T. W., Frenkel-Brunswick, E., Levinson, D. J. & Sanford, R. H. (1950) *The Authoritarian Personality*. New York: Harper & Row.

Ainsworth, P. B. (1993) Psychological Testing and Police Recruit Selection: difficulties and dilemmas. Paper presented to the *European Conference on Law and Psychology*, Oxford, England.

Ainsworth, P. B. & Armitage, S. (1989) Viewing of Videos and Violent Behaviour. Paper presented to the *British Psychological Society Conference*, St Andrews, Scotland.

Ainsworth, P. B. & Pease, K. (1987) *Police Work*. Leicester: BPS/Routledge.

Ajzen, I & Fishbein, M. (1980) *Understanding Attitudes and Predicting Social Behaviour*. Englewood Cliffs, NJ: Prentice-Hall.

Alderson, J. (1979) *Policing Freedom*. Plymouth: MacDonald & Evans.

American Psychiatric Association (1987) *Diagnostic and Statistical Manual of Mental Disorders*, Third Edition, Revised [DSM-III-R]. Washington DC: American Pschiatric Association.

American Psychiatric Association (1994) *Diagnostic and Statistical Manual of Mental Disorders*, Fourth Edition [DSM-IV]. Washington DC: American Psychiatric Association.

Anastasi, A. (1988) *Psychological Testing* (6th edn). New York: Macmillan.

Anderson, C. A. & Anderson, D. C. (1984) Ambient temperature and violent crime: tests of the linear and curvilinear hypotheses. *Journal of Personality and Social Psychology*, **45**, 91–97.

Arnold, M. (1974) How Mitchell–Stans jury reached acquittal verdict. *New York Times*, 5.5.74.

Aronson, E. (1992) *The Social Animal*. San Francisco: Freeman.

Audit Commission (1990) *Effective policing: performance review in police forces*. Police Paper 8. London: HMSO.

Ault, R. L. & Reese, J. T. (1980) A psychological assessment of crime profiling. *FBI Law Enforcement Bulletin*, **49**, 22–25.

Baehr, M. E. & Oppenheim, A. B. (1979) Job analysis in Police Selection Research. In C. D. Spielberger, *Police Selection and Evaluation*. Washington, DC: Hemisphere.

Bailey, F. L. & Rothblatt, H. B. (1971) *Successful Techniques for Criminal Trials*. Rochester: Lawyers Cooperative Publishing.

Bailey, S. & Lynch, I (1988) *The Cost of Crime*. Newcastle: Northumbria Police.

Baldwin, J. (1990) Police interviews on tape. *New Law Journal*, May, 662–663.

Baldwin, J. (1993) Police interview techniques: establishing truth or proof. *British Journal of Criminology*, **33** (3), 325–352.

Bales, R. F. (1950) *Interaction Process Analysis: A Method for the Study of Small Groups*. Reading, MA: Addison Wesley.

Bandura, A. (1973) *Aggression: A Social Learning Analysis*. Englewood Cliffs, NJ: Prentice-Hall.

Bandura, A., Ross, D. & Ross, S. A. (1963) Imitation of film-mediated aggressive models. *Journal of Abnormal and Social Psychology*, **66**, 3–11.

Baron, R. A. (1971) Aggression as a function of magnitude of victim's pain cues, level of prior anger arousal, and aggressor–victim similarity. *Journal of Personality and Social Psychology*, **18**, 48–54.

Baron, R. A. (1972) Aggression as a function of ambient temperature and prior anger arousal. *Journal of Personality and Social Psychology*, **21**, 183–189.

Baron, R. A. (1979) Aggression, empathy, and race: effects of victim's pain cues, victim's race, and level of instigation on physical aggression. *Journal of Applied Social Psychology*, **9**, 103–114.

Baron, R. A. (1990) Countering the effects of destructive criticism: the relative efficacy of four interventions. *Journal of Applied Psychology*, **75**, 25–45.

Baron, R. A. & Bell, R. L. (1975) Aggression and heat: mediating effects of prior provocation and exposure to an aggressive model. *Journal of Personality and Social Psychology*, **31**, 825–832.

Baron, R. A. & Byrne, D. (1994) *Social Psychology: Understanding Human Interaction*. (7th edn) Boston, MA: Allyn & Bacon.

Baron, R. A., Russell, G. W. & Arms, R. L. (1985) Negative ions and behavior: impact on mood, memory, and aggression among Type A and Type B persons. *Journal of Personality and Social Psychology*, **48**, 746–754.

Beaumont, K. (1994) Introducing the Quality of Service Concept to officers and staff of Cumbria Constabulary. Unpublished MA dissertation, University of Manchester.

Beck, A. T. (1967) *Depression: Clinical, Experimental and Theoretical Aspects*. New York: Harper & Row.

Belson, W. A. (1979) *Television Violence and the Adolescent Boy*. London: Saxon House.

Benn, D. (1972) Self-perception theory. In L. Berkowitz, *Advances in Experimental Social Psychology*, vol. 6. New York: Academic Press.

Bennett, R. (1984) Becoming blue: a longitudinal study of police recruit occupational socialisation. *Journal of Police Science and Administration*, **12**, 1, 47–58.

Bennett, T. (1990) *Evaluating Neighbourhood Watch*. Aldershot: Gower.

Bennett, T. & Wright, R. (1984) *Burglars on Burglary: Prevention and the Offender*. Aldershot: Gower.

Berkowitz, L. (1968) Impulse, aggression and the gun. *Psychology Today* (September), 18–22.

Berkowitz, L. (1969) The frustration–aggression hypothesis revisited. In L. Berkowitz (ed.), *Roots of Aggression*. New York: Atherton.

Berkowitz, L. (1989) The frustration–aggression hypothesis: an examination and reformulation. *Psychological Bulletin*, **106**, 59–73.

Bilton, K. (1993) *Child Protection Practice and the Memorandum of good*

practice on video recorded inteviews with children: A discussion paper.
London: British Association of Social Workers.

Bittner, E. (1967) The Police on Skid Row: A study of peace-keeping. *American Sociological Review*, **32**, 5, 699–715.

Blackburn, R. (1993) *The Psychology of Criminal Conduct: Theory, Research and Practice*. Chichester: Wiley.

Blanck, P. D. (1993) Interpersonal expectations in the courtroom: studying judges' and juries' behaviour. In P. D. Blanck, *Interpersonal Expectations*. New York: Cambridge University Press.

Blau, T. (1994) *Psychological Services for Law Enforcement*. Chichester: Wiley.

Boon, J. & Davies, G. (1993) Criminal Profiling. *Policing*, **9** (8), 1–13.

Bourlet, A. (1990) *Police Intervention in Marital Violence*. Milton Keynes: Open University Press.

Breakwell, G. M. (1989) *Facing Physical Violence*. Leicester: BPS/Routledge.

Brewer, M. B. (1979) Ingroup bias in the minimal intergroup situation: a cognitive motivational analysis. *Psychological Bulletin*, **86**, 307–324.

Brewer, M. B. & Silver, M. (1978) In-group bias as a function of task characteristics. *European Journal of Social Psychology*, **8**, 393–400.

Bromet, E. J. (1990) Methodological issues in the assessment of traumatic events. *Journal of Applied Social Pychology*, **20**, 1719–1724.

Brown, J. & Campbell, E. (1993) *Stress and Policing: Sources and Strategies*. Chichester: Wiley.

Brown, M. K. (1981) *Working the Street*. New York: Russell Sage Foundation.

Brown, R. (1986) *Social Psychology* (2nd edn). New York: Free Press.

Brown, R. & McNeil, D. (1966) The "tip-of-the-tongue" phenomenon. *Journal of Verbal Learning and Verbal Behaviour*, **5**, 325–337.

Bull, R. (1986) An Evaluation of Police Recruit Training in Human Awareness. In J. C. Yuille, *Police Selection and Training*. Dordrecht: Martinus Nijhoff.

Bull, R., Bustin, B., Evans, P. & Gahagan, D. (1984) *Psychology for Police Officers*. Chichester: Wiley.

Bull, R. & Horncastle, P. (1988) Evaluating training: the London Metropolitan Police's recruit training in human awareness/policing skills. In P. Southgate, *New Directions in Police Training*. London: HMSO.

Burbeck, E. & Furnham, A. (1985) Police officer selection: a critical review of the literature. *Journal of Police Science and Administration*, **13**, 58–69.

Burns, M. J. (1981) The mental retracing of prior activities: evidence for reminiscence in ordered retrieval. *Dissertation Abstracts International*, **42**, 2108B.

Buss, A. H. (1966) Instrumentality of aggression, feedback, and frustration as determinants of physical aggression. *Journal of Personality and Social Psychology*, **3**, 153–156.

Butler, A. J. P. (1992) *Police Management* (2nd edn). Aldershot: Dartmouth.

Bywaters, P. (1989) Social work and nursing: sisters or rivals. In *Social Work and Health Care*, ed. R. Taylor and J. Ford. London: Jessica Kingsley.

Calhoun, J. B. (1962) Population density and social pathology. *Scientific American*, **206**, 139–148.

Campbell, P. (1976) Offender profiling. *Psychology Today* (September), 271–277.

Canter, D. (1989) Offender profiling. *The Psychologist*, **2**, 2–16.

Canter, D. (1994) *Criminal Shadows: Inside the Mind of the Serial Killer*. London: HarperCollins.

Canter, D. & Heritage, R. (1990) A multi-variate model of sexual offence behaviour. *Journal of Forensic Psychiatry*, **1** (2), 185–212.

Castello, R. M., Schneider, S. L. & Schoenfeld, L. S. (1993) Applicants' fraud in Law Enforcement. *Psychological Reports*, **73** (1) 179–183.

Chatterton, M. (1979) The supervision of patrol work under the fixed points system. In S. Holdaway, *The British Police*. London: Edward Arnold.

Clark, S. & Morley, M. (1988) *Murder in Mind*. London: Boxtree.

Cohen, R., Sprafkin, R. P., Oglesby, S. & Claiborn, W. L. (1976) *Working with Police Agencies*. New York: Human Sciences Press.

Copson, G. (1993) *Offender Profiling*. ACPO Crime Subcommittee on Offender Profiling. London: ACPO.

Cornick, B. (1988) Proceeding together. *Community Care*, 17 March, 25–27.

Crawford, A., Jones, T., Woodhouse, T. & Young, J. (1990) *Second Islington Crime Survey*. Middlesex Polytechnic, Centre for Criminology.

Dabbs, J. M., Jr, Frady, R. L., Carr, T. S. & Besch, N. F. (1987) Saliva testosterone and criminal violence in young adult prison inmates. *Psychosomatic Medicine*, **49**, 174–182.

Davidson, S. (1976) Planning and coordination of services in multi-organisational contexts. *Social Service Review*, **50**, 117–137.

Davies, A. (1992) Rapists' behaviour: a three aspect model as a basis for analysis and the identification of serial crime: *Forensic Science International*, **55**, 173–194.

Dawkins, R. (1986) *The Selfish Gene*. New York: McGraw-Hill.

Dean, C. W. (1976) Summation of critical issues for social scientists working with police agencies. In R. Cohen et al, *Working with Police Agencies*. New York: Human Sciences Press.

DeAngelis, T. (1989) Mania, depression and genius. *APA Monitor*, January, 1–24.

Denkers, F. (1986) The Panacea of Training and Selection. In J. C. Yuille, *Police Selection and Training*. Dordrecht: Martinus Nijhoff.

Dent, H. & Flin, R. (1992) *Children as Witnesses*. Chichester: Wiley.

Devons, E. (1978) Serving as a juryman in Britain. In J. Baldwin & A. K. Bottomley, *Criminal Justice: Selected Readings*. London: Martin Robertson.

DHSS (1988) *Report of the Inquiry into Child Abuse in Cleveland 1987*, Cm 412. London: HMSO.

Diamond, E. L., Scheiderman, N., Schwartz, D., Smith, J. C., Vorp, R. & Pasin, R. D. (1984) Harassment, hostility, and Type A as determinants of cardiovascular reactivity during competition. *Journal of Behavioral Medicine*, **7**, 171–189.

Dix, M. C. & Layzell, A. D. (1983) *Road Users and the Police*. London: Croom Helm.

Dollard, J., Doob, L. W., Miller, N. E., Mowrer, O. H. & Sears, R. R. (1939) *Frustration and Aggression*. New Haven, CT: Yale University Press.

Dominick, J. R. (1978) Crime and law enforcement on prime-time television. In C. Winick (ed.), *Deviance and Mass Media*. London: Sage.

Douglas, M. (1986) *Risk*. London: Routledge & Kegan Paul.

Duncan, B. L. (1976) Different social perceptions and attribution of intergroup violence: testing the lower limits of stereotyping of blacks, *Journal of Personality & Social Psychology*, **34**, 590–598.

Eagley, A. & Chaiken, S. (1993) *The Psychology of Attitudes*. San Diego, CA: Harcourt Brace Jovanovich.

Earle, H. (1973) *Police Recruit Training: Stress vs Non Stress*. Springfield, IL: Charles Thomas.

Ekblom, P. (1988) *Getting the Best out of Crime Analysis*. Home Office Crime

Prevention Unit Paper 10. London: Home Office.

Ekman, P. (1985) *Telling Lies*. New York: Norton.

Evans, G. W. (1979) Behavioral and physiological consequences of crowding in humans. *Journal of Applied Social Psychology*, **9**, 27–46.

Evans, G. W. et al (1989) Residential density and psychological health: the mediating effects of social support. *Journal of Personality & Social Psychology*, **57**, 994–999.

Fellows, N. (1986) *Killing Time*. Oxford: Lion.

Feshbach, S. (1984) The function of aggression and the regulation of aggressive drive. *Psychological Review*, **71**, 257–272.

Feshbach, S. & Price, J. (1984) Cognitive competencies and aggressive behavior: a developmental study. *Aggressive Behavior*, **10**, 185–200.

Festinger, L. (1957) *A Theory of Cognitive Dissonance*. Evanston, IL: Row, Peterson.

Fielding, N. (1984) *Probation Practice*. Aldershot: Gower.

Fielding, N. (1988) Socialisation of recruits into the police role. In P. Southgate, *New Directions in Police Training*. London: HMSO.

Fielding, N. G. & Conroy, S. (1994) Against the grain: cooperation in child sexual abuse investigations. In M. Stephens & S. Becker, *Police Force, Police Service*. Basingstoke: Macmillan.

Fisher, R. P. & Cutler, B. L. (1991) The relationship between consistency and accuracy of eyewitness testimony. Unpublished manuscript, Florida International University.

Fisher, R. P. & Geiselman, R. E. (1992) *Memory Enhancing Techniques for Investigative Interviewing*. Springfield IL: Charles C. Thomas.

Fisher, R. P., Geiselman, R. E. & Raymond, D. S. (1987) Critical analysis of police interview techniques. *Journal of Police Science and Administration*, **15**, 177–185.

Fiske, S. T. & Neuberg, S. L. (1990). A continuum of impression formation, from category-based to individuating processes. *Advances in Experimental Social Psychology*, **23**, 1–74.

Forrester, D., Chatterton, M. & Pease, K. (1988) *The Kirkholt Burglary Prevention Project, Rochdale*. Crime Prevention Unit Paper 13. London: Home Office.

Forrester, D., Frenz, S., O'Connell, M. & Pease, K. (1990) *The Kirkholt Burglary Prevention Project Phase II*. Crime Prevention Unit Paper 23. London: Home Office.

Freud, S. (1930/1963) Why war? In P. Rieff (ed.), *Freud: Character and Culture*. New York: Collier Books.

Friedman, R. R. (1992) *Community Policing: Comparative Perspectives*. Hemel Hempstead: Harvester Wheatsheaf.

Garberth, V. J. (1983) *Practical Homicide Investigation*. New York: Elsevier.

Geen, R. G. (1990) *Human Aggression*. Milton Keynes: Open University Press.

Geiselman, R. E. & Callot, R. (1990) Reverse versus forward recall of script-based texts. *Applied Cognitive Psychology*, **4**, 141–144.

Geiselman, R. E., Fisher, R. P., MacKinnon, D. P. & Holland, H. L. (1986) Enhancement of eyewitness testimony with the Cognitive Interview. *American Journal of Psychology*, **99**, 385–401.

George, R. (1991) A field and experimental evaluation of three methods of interviewing witnesses/victims of crime. Unpublished manuscript, Polytechnic of East London.

Goldstein, A. P., Carr, E. G., Davidson, W. S. & Wehr, P. (1979) *In Response to Aggression*. New York: Pergamon.

Graber, D. (1980) *Crime News and the Public*. New York: Praeger.

Graef, R. (1990) *Talking Blues: the Police in their Own Words*. London: Fontana.

Groth, A. N. (1979) *Men Who Rape: The Psychology of the Offender*. New York: Plenum.

Groth, A. N., Burgess, A. W. & Holmstrom, L. L. (1977) Rape, power, anger and sexuality. *American Journal of Psychiatry*, **134**, 1239–1248.

Gudjonsson, G. (1992) *The Psychology of Interrogations, Confessions and Testimony*. Chichester: Wiley.

Gudjonsson, G. H. & MacKeith, J. A. C. (1982) False confessions: psychological effects of interrogation. In A. Trankel (ed.), *Reconstructing the Past: The Role of Psychologists in Criminal Trials*. Deventer, Holland: Kluwer.

Halgin, R. P. & Whitbourne, S. K. (1993) *Abnormal Psychology*. Orlando, FL: Harcourt Brace Jovanovich.

Hall, S., Clarke, J., Jefferson, T., Critcher, C. & Roberts, B. (1978) *Policing the Crisis: Mugging, Law and Order and the State*. London: Macmillan.

Hans, V. P. & Vidmar, N. (1986) *Judging the Jury*. New York: Plenum.

Hare, R. D. (1983) Diagnosis of antisocial personality disorder in two prison populations. *American Journal of Psychiatry*, **140**, 887–890.

Hare, R. D., McPherson, L. M. & Forth, A. E. (1988) Male psychopaths and their criminal careers. *Journal of Consulting and Clinical Psychology*, **56**, 710–714.

Harris, R. (1973) *The Police Academy: An Inside View*. New York: Wiley.

Hastie, R. (1993) *Inside the Juror*. Cambridge: Cambridge University Press.

Hazelwood, R. R. (1983) The behaviour oriented interview of rape victims: the key to profiling. *FBI Law Enforcement Bulletin*, January, 1–8.

Hazelwood, R. R. (1987) Analyzing the rape and profiling the offender. In R. R. Hazelwood & A. W. Burgess, *Practical Aspects of Rape Investigation*. New York: Elsevier.

Hazelwood, R. R. & Burgess, A. W. (1987) *Practical Aspects of Rape Investigation: A Multidisciplinary Approach*. New York: Elsevier.

Hazelwood, R. R. & Warren, J. (1989) The serial rapist. *FBI Law Enforcement Bulletin*, **59**, 1–8.

Hebenton, W. & Thomas, T. (1992) The police and social services departments in England and Wales; the exchange of personal information. *Journal of Social Welfare and Family Law*, **2**, 114–126.

Hey, A. & Minty, B. (1991) Interprofessional and interagency work. Theory, practice and training for the nineties. In M. C. Pietroni, *Right or Privilege?* London: CCETSW.

Hoffman, L. R. (1965) Group problem solving. In L. Berkowitz (ed.), *Advances in Experimental Social Psychology* (vol. 2). Orlando FL: Academic Press.

Holdaway, S. (1991) *Recruiting a Multiracial Police Force*. London: HMSO.

Holdaway, S. (1994) Recruitment, race and the police subculture. In M. Stephens & S. Becker, *Police Force, Police Service*. Basingstoke: Macmillan.

Home Office (1983) *Manpower, efficiency and effectiveness in the police service*. Circular 114/83. London: HMSO.

Home Office (1988) Circular 106/1988. *Applications for increases in police force establishments*. London: HMSO.

Home Office (1991) Circular 84/1991. London: HMSO.

Home Office (1993) *Inquiry into police responsibilities and rewards*. Cm. 2280-1. London: HMSO.

Home Office, DOH, DES and Welsh Office (1991) *Working Together under the Children Act 1989*. London: HMSO.

Horton, C. & Smith, D. (1988) *Evaluating Police Work*. London: Policy Studies Institute.

Hough, M. & Mayhew, P. (1983) *The British Crime Survey: First Report*. Home Office Research Study No. 76. London: HMSO.

Hough, M. & Mayhew, P. (1985) *Taking Account of Crime: Key Findings from the 1984 British Crime Survey*. London: HMSO.

Hovland, C. L. & Weiss, W. (1951) The influence of source credibility on communication effectiveness. *Public Opinion Quarterly*, 1, 635–650.

Howard, J. & Rothbart, M. (1980) Social categorisation and memory for in-group and out-group behaviour. *Journal of Personality and Social Psychology*, **38**, 301–310.

Humphrey, C., Pease, K. & Carter, P. (1993) *Changing Notions of Accountability in the Probation Service*. London: Institute of Chartered Accountants.

Hurd, G. (1979) The television presentation of the police. In S. Holdaway (ed.), *The British Police*. London: Edward Arnold.

Hyman, H. M. & Tarant, C. M. (1975) Aspects of American trial jury history. In R. J. Simon (ed.), *The Jury System in America: a Critical Overview*. Newbury Park, CA: Sage.

Irving, B. L. & McKenzie, I. K. (1989) *Police Interrogation: the Effects of the Police and Criminal Evidence Act*. London: The Police Foundation.

Jefferson, T. & Grimshaw, R. (1984) *Controlling the Constable: Police Accountability in England and Wales*. London: Muller.

Joint Consultative Committee of the Police Staff Associations (1990) *Operational Policing Review*. Surbiton: Police Federation.

Jones, B. (1992) *Voices from an Evil God*. London: Blake.

Jones, S. (1986) *Policewomen and Equality*. Basingstoke: Macmillan.

Kadane, J. B. (1993) Sausages and the law: juror decisions in the much larger justice system. In R. Hastie (ed.), *Inside the Juror*. Cambridge: Cambridge University Press.

Kalven, H. & Zeisel, H. (1966) *The American Jury*. Boston: Little Brown.

Kassin, S. M. & Wrightsman, L. S. (1985) Confession evidence. In S. M. Kassin & L. S. Wrightsman (eds), *The Psychology of Evidence and Trial Procedure* (pp. 67–94). London: Sage.

Keith, M. (1993) *Race, Riots and Policing: Law and Disorder in a Multiracist Society*. London: UCL Press.

Kennedy, L. (1986) Foreword. In N. Fellows (ed.), *Killing Time* (pp. 6–8). Oxford: Lion.

Kiesler, C. A. & Kiesler, S. B. (1969) *Conformity*. Reading, MA: Addison Wesley.

Klein, M. W. (1969) Violence in American juvenile gangs. In D. J. Mulvihill and M. M. Tumin, *Crimes of Violence: A Staff Report Submitted to the National Commission on the Causes and Prevention of Violence*, (vol. 13). Washington, DC: United States Government Printing Office, 1427–1460.

Konecni, V. J. & Ebbesen, E. B. (1982) *The Criminal Justice System: A Social Psychological Analysis*. San Francisco: Freeman.

Kosslyn, S. (1981) The medium and the message in mental imagery: a theory. *Psychological Review*, **88**, 46–66.

Krueger, J. (1992) On the overestimation of between-group differences. In W. Stroebe & M. Hewstone, *European Review of Social Psychology* (vol. 3). Chichester: Wiley.

Labuc, S. (1991) Can future performance be predicted? *PRSU Bulletin*, September.

Laing, R. D. (1964) Is schizophrenia a disease? *International Journal of Social Psychiatry*, **10**, 184–193.

Lambert, J. L. (1986) *Police Powers and Accountability*. London: Croom Helm.

Lang, A. R., Goeckner, D. J., Adesso, V. J. & Marlatt, G. A. (1975) Effects of alcohol on aggression in male social drinkers. *Journal of Abnormal Psychology*, **84**, 508–518.

Latané, B. & Darley, J. M. (1968) Group inhibition of bystander intervention in emergencies. *Journal of Personality and Social Psychology*, **10**, 215–221.

Latts, M. G. & Geiselman, R. E. (1991) Interviewing survivors of rape. *Police and Criminal Psychology*, **7**, 8–17.

Lerner, M. J. (1970) The desire for justice and reactions to victims. In J. Macaulay & L. Berkowitz (eds), *Altruism and Helping Behavior*. Orlando, FL: Academic Press.

Levens, B. R. & Dutton, D. G. (1980) *The Social Service Role of Police*. Ottowa: Research Division, Solicitor General.

Lewis, D. O., Moy, E., Jackson, L. D., Aaronson, R., Restifo, N., Serra, S. & Simos, A. (1985) Biopsychological characteristics of children who later murder: a prospective study. *American Journal of Psychiatry*, **142**, 1161–1167.

Loeber, R. & Dishion, T. J. (1984) Boys who fight at home and school: family conditions influencing cross-setting consistency. *Journal of Consulting and Clinical Psychology*, **52**, 759–768.

Loftus, E. (1979) *Eyewitness Testimony*. Cambridge, MA: Harvard University Press.

Loftus, E. F. (1981) Metamorphosis: alterations in memory produced by mental bonding of new information into old. In J. Long & A. Baddeley (eds), *Attention and Performance* (vol. IX). Hillsdale, NJ: Earlbaum.

Loftus, E. F. & Palmer, J. C. (1974) Reconstruction of automobile destruction: an example of the interaction between language and thought. *Journal of Verbal Learning and Verbal Behavour*, **13**, 585–589.

Loo, R. & Meredith, C. (1986) Recruit selection in the RCMP. In J. C. Yuille (ed.), *Police Selection and Training*. Dordrecht: Martinus Nijhoff.

Lorenz, K. (1966) *On Aggression*. New York: Harcourt Brace Jovanovich.

Lorr, M. & Strack, S. (1994) Personality profiles of police candidates. *Journal of Clinical Psychology*, **50** (2), 200–207.

Maguire, E. R. (1993) The professionalization of police in child sexual abuse cases. *Journal of Child Sex Abuse*, **2** (3), 107–116.

Manning, P. K. (1981) Careers in criminal justice. In N. Morris, *Encyclopedia of Crime and Justice*. New York: Garland.

Manolias, M. (1988) Training for stress. In P. Southgate, *New Directions in Police Training*. London: HMSO.

Marshall, W. L. (1989) Intimacy, loneliness and sexual offenders. *Behavioural Research in Therapy*, **27** (5), 491–503.

Mason, P. (1992) *Reading The Bill: An Analysis of the Thames Television Police Drama*. Bristol University: Centre for Criminal Justice.

Matthews, R. W., Paulus, P. B. & Baron, R. A. (1979) Physical aggression after being crowded. *Journal of Nonverbal Behavior*, **4**, 5–17.

Mayhew, P., Maung, N. A. & Mirrlees-Black, C. (1993) *The 1992 British Crime Survey*. Home Office Research Study 132. London: HMSO.

Mayhew, P., Mirrlees-Black, C. & Maung, N. A. (1994) *Trends in Crime: Findings from the 1994 British Crime Survey*. London: HMSO.

McAndrew, F. T. (1993) *Environmental Psychology*. Pacific Grove: Brooks Cole.

McConville, M. & Shepherd, D. (1992) *Watching Police, Watching Communities*. London: Routledge.

McGue, M., Pickens, R. W. & Svikis, D. S. (1992) Sex and age effects on the inheritance of alcohol problems. A twin study. *Journal of Abnormal Psychology*, **101**, 3–17.

Measham, F., Newcombe, R. & Parker, H. (1994) The normalisation of drug use amongst young people in North West England. *British Journal of Sociology*. **45** (2), 287–312.

Milgram, S. (1965) Some conditions of obedience and disobedience to authority. *Human Relations*, **18**, 57–76.

Milgram, S. (1976) Psychological maps of Paris. In H. H. Proshansky et al (eds), *Environmental Psychology: People and Their Physical Settings*. New York: Holt Rinehart & Winston.

Milgram, S. (1977) *The Individual in a Social World*. Reading, MA: Addison Wesley.

Miller, G. R. & Stiff, J. B. (1993) *Deceptive Communication*. London: Sage.

Moffitt, T. E. (1993) Adolescence-limited and life-course-persistent antisocial behavior: a developmental taxonomy. *Psychological Review*, **100**, 674–701.

Moore, J. (1985) *The ABC of Child Abuse Work*. London: Gower.

Moos, R. (1976) *The Human Context*. New York: Wiley.

Moston, S. (1990) The ever so gentle art of police interrogation. Paper presented to the *British Psychological Society Annual Conference*, Swansea University, 5 April.

Moston, S. (1991) *Investigative Interviewing* (vol. 1). London: Metropolitan Police/ACPO.

Moston S., Stephenson, G. M. & Williamson, T. M. (1992) The effects of case characteristics on suspect behaviour during police questioning. *British Journal of Criminology*, **32**, 23–40.

Moston S., Stephenson, G. M. & Williamson, T. M. (1993) The incidence, antecedents and consequences of the use of the right to silence during police questioning. *Criminal Behaviour and Mental Health*, **3**, 30–47.

Mueller, C. W. (1983) Environmental stressors and aggressive behavior. In R. G. Geen and E. I. Donnerstein (eds), *Aggression: Theoretical and Empirical Reviews*, vol. 2: *Issues in Research* (pp. 51–76). New York: Academic Press.

Mulvihill, D. J. & Tumin, M. M. (1969) *Crimes of Violence: A Staff Report Submitted to the National Commission on the Causes and Prevention of Violence*. Washington, DC: United States Government Printing Office.

Munsterberg, H. (1908) *On the Witness Stand*. New York: Doubleday.

Newman, O. (1972) *Defensible Space*. New York: Macmillan.

Niederhoffer, A. (1967) *Behind the Shield: the Police in Urban Society*. New York: Doubleday.

Norris, F. H. & Thompson, M. P. (1993) The victim in the system: the influence of police responsiveness on victim alienation. *Journal of Traumatic Stress*, **6** (4), 515–532.

Ofshe, R. (1989) Coerced confessions: the logic of seemingly irrational action. *Cultic Studies Journal*, **6**, 1–15.

Ohbuchi, K. & Saito, M. (1986) Power imbalance, its legitimacy, and aggression. *Aggressive Behavior*, **12**, 33–40.

Olweus, D., Mattsson, A., Schalling, D. & Low, H. (1980) Testosterone, aggression, physical, and personality dimensions in normal adolescent males. *Psychosomatic Medicine*, **42**, 253–269.

Orne, M. (1979) The use and misuse of hypnosis in court. *International Journal of Clinical and Experimental Hypnosis*, **27**, 311–341.

Orne, M. T., Soskis, D. A., Dinges, D. E. & Orne, E. C. (1984) Hypnotically induced testimony. In G. Wells & E. Loftus (eds), *Eyewitness Testimony: Psychological Perspectives*. New York: Cambridge University Press.

Osherow, N. (1988) Making sense of the nonsensical: an analysis of Jonestown. In E. Aronson, *Readings About the Social Animal*. New York: Freeman.

Oxford, T. (1991) Spotting a liar. *Police Review*, 328–329.

Patterson, G. R. (1980) Mothers: the unacknowledged victims. *Monographs of the Society for Research in Child Development*, 45.

Peach, Sir Leonard (1993) *Annual Report of the Police Complaints Authority (1993)*. London: HMSO.

Pearson, G. (1983) *Hooligan: A History of Respectable Fears*. London: Macmillan.

Penrod, S. (1979) Study of attorney and "scientific" jury selection models. Unpublished doctoral dissertation, Harvard University.

Peters, D. L. (1988) Eyewitness memory arousal in a natural setting. In M. Gruneberg, P. Morris & R. Sykes (eds), *Practical Aspects of Memory: Current Research and Issues*. New York: Wiley.

Phillips, R. G. (1984) State and local law enforcement training needs. *FBI Law Enforcement Bulletin*. January.

Pictroni, M. C. (1991) *Right or Privilege? Post Qualifying Training with Special Reference to Child Care*. London: CCETSW.

Pihl, R. O., Zacchia, C. & Zeichner, A. (1982) Predicting levels of aggression after alcohol intake in men social drinkers: a preliminary investigation. *Journal of Studies on Alcohol*, **43**, 599–602.

Police Complaints Authority (1993) Annual Report by Sir Leonard Peach. London.

Policy Studies Institute (1983) *Police and People in London*. London: PSI.

Pontius, A. A. (1984) Specific stimulus-evoked violent action in psychotic trigger reaction: a seizure-like imbalance between frontal lobe and limbic system? *Perceptual and Motor Skills*, **59**, 299–333.

Pope, D. & Greenhill, N. (1978) Social work and the police. *Social Work Today*, 14 February.

Punch, M. (1979) The secret social service. In S. Holdaway, *The British Police* (pp. 102–117). London: Edward Arnold.

Pylshyn, Z. W. (1981) The imagery debate: analogue media versus tacit knowledge. *Psychological Review*, **88**, 16–45.

Raine, A. (1993) *The Psychopathology of Crime: Criminal Behaviour as a Clinical Disorder*. London: Sage.

Rand Corporation (1975) *The Criminal Investigation Process* (vols 1–3). Santa Monica, CA: Rand Corporation Technical Report R-1777-DOJ.

Reiner, R. (1992) *The Politics of the Police* (2nd edn). Hemel Hempstead: Wheatsheaf.

Reiner, R. (1994) The dialectics of Dixon: the changing image of the TV cop. In M. Stephens & S. Becker, *Police Force, Police Service: Care and Control in Britain*. Basingstoke: Macmillan.

Reiner, R. & Spencer, S. (1993) *Accountable Policing: Effectiveness Empowerment and Equity*. London: IPPR.

Reisser, M. (1980) *Handbook of Investigative Hypnosis*. Los Angeles: LEHI.

Reisser, M. (1986) Critical issues for the police psychologist in training police. In J. C. Yuille, *Police Selection and Training*. Dordrecht: Martinus Nijhoff.

Renson, G. J., Adams, J. E. & Tinklenberg, J. R. (1978) Buss–Durkee assessment and validation with violent versus nonviolent chronic alcohol abusers. *Journal of Consulting and Clinical Psychology*, **46**, 360–361.

Report of the Inquiry into the Care and Treatment of Christopher Clunis (1994). (Chair Jean Richie, QC). London: HMSO.

Ressler, R. K. & Shachtman, T. (1992) *Whoever Fights Monsters*. London: Simon & Schuster.

Robins, L. N. (1966) *Deviant Children Grow Up: A Sociological and Psychiatric Study of Sociopathic Personality*. Baltimore: Williams & Wilkins.

Robins, L. N., Helzer, J. E., Weissman, M. M., Orvaschel, H., Gruneberg, E., Burke, J. D. & Regier, D. A. (1984). Lifetime prevalence of specific psychiatric disorders in three sites. *Archives of General Psychiatry*, **41**, 949–958.

Rosenhan, D.L. (1973) On being sane in insane places. *Science*, **179**, 250–258.

Rotter, J. B. (1966) Generalized expectancies for internal versus external control of reinforcement. *Psychological Monographs*, **80** (1, whole No. 609).

Rotton, J. & Frey, J. (1985) Air pollution, weather, and violent crimes: concomitant time-series analysis of archival data. *Journal of Personality and Social Psychology*, **49**, 1207–1220.

Rotton, J., Frey, J., Barry, T., Milligan, M. & Fitzpatrick, M. (1979) The air pollution experience and physical aggression. *Journal of Personality and Social Psychology*, **9**, 397–412.

Rowett, C. (1986) Violence in social work. *Institute of Criminology Occasional Paper No 14*, Cambridge University.

Royal Commission on the Police (1962) *Final Report*, Cmnd. 1728. London: HMSO.

Ruback, R. B. & Innes, C. A. (1990) The relevance and irrelevance of psychological research: the example of prison crowding. *American Psychologist*, September, 683–693.

Rushton, J. P., Fulker, D. W., Neale, M. C., Nias, D. K. B. & Eysenck, H. J. (1986) Altruism and aggression: the heritability of individual differences. *Journal of Personality and Social Psychology*, **50**, 1192–1198.

Ryan, P. J. (1994) *The Future of Police Training*. Bramshill: Police College.

Salasin, S. E. (1981) *Evaluating Victim Services*. Beverly Hills, CA: Sage.

Saunders, A. (1993) Controlling the discretion of the individual officer. In R. Reiner & S. Spencer, *Accountable Policing: Effectiveness, Empowerment and Equity*. London: IPPR.

Scarman, Rt. Hon., Lord (1981) *The Brixton Disorders 10–12 April 1981: Report of an Enquiry by the Rt. Hon. Lord Scarman*. Cmnd 8427. London: HMSO.

Schachter, S. (1959) *The Psychology of Affiliation*. Stanford, CA: Stanford University Press.

Schreiber, F. R. (1973) *Sybil*. Chicago: Henry Regnery.

Scully, D. & Marolla, J. (1983) *Incarcerated Rapists: Exploring a Sociological Model* Washington, DC: NIMH.

Seligman, M. E. P. (1975) *Helplessness: On Depression, Development and Death*. San Francisco: W. H. Freeman.

Sewell, J. D. (1983) The development of a critical life events scale for law enforcement. *Journal of Police Science and Administration*, **11** (1), 113–114.

Shapland, J. & Vagg, J. (1988) *Policing by the Public*. London: Tavistock.

Sheehy, Sir Patrick (1993) *Inquiry into Police Responsibilities and Rewards.* London: HMSO.

Shepherd, E. (1991) Ethical Interviewing. *Policing,* **7**, 42–60.

Shepherd, E. (1993) Resistance in interviews: the contribution of police perceptions and behaviour. In E. Shepherd (ed.), *Aspects of Police Interviewing.* Leicester: British Psychological Society.

Sherif, M., Harvey, O. J., Hood, W. R. & Sherif, C. W. (1961) *Intergroup Conflict and Cooperation: The Robbers Cave Experiment.* Norman: University of Oklahoma Book Exchange.

Sherrod, D. R. (1974) Crowding, perceived control and behavioral aftereffects. *Journal of Applied Social Psychology,* **4**, 171–186.

Simon, B. (1992) The perception of ingroup and outgroup homogeneity: reintroducing the social context. In W. Stroebe & M. Hewstone (eds), *European Review of Social Psychology* (vol. 3). Chichester: Wiley.

Simon, R. J. (1967) *The Jury and the Defence of Insanity.* Boston: Little Brown.

Skolnik, J. H. (1975) *Justice Without Trial* (2nd edn). New York: Wiley.

Skolnik, J. H. & Bayley, D. H. (1987) Theme and variation in community policing. In N. Morris and M. Tonry (eds), *Crime and Justice* (pp. 1–37). Washington DC: National Institute of Justice.

Smith, D. J. & Gray, J. (1983) *Police and People in London.* London: PSI.

Smith, V. L. & Ellsworth, P. C. (1987) The social psychology of eyewitness accuracy: misleading questions and communicator's expertise. *Journal of Applied Psychology,* **72**, 294–300.

Sommer, R. (1969) *Personal Space.* Englewood Cliffs, NJ: Prentice-Hall.

Southgate, P. (1988) *New Directions in Police Training.* London: HMSO.

Southgate, P. & Crisp, D. (1992) *Public Satisfaction with Police Services,* Research and Planning Unit Paper 73. London: HMSO.

Sparks, R. (1992) *Television and the Drama of Crime: Moral Tales and the Place of Crime in Public Life.* Milton Keynes: Open University Press.

Spielberger, C. D. (1979) *Police Selection and Evaluation: Issues and Techniques.* Washington, DC: Hemisphere.

Spivey, W. (1994) Stranger rape: some characteristics of offences, offenders, and victims. Unpublished MSc dissertation, University of Manchester.

Stephens, M. & Becker, S. (1994) *Police Force, Police Service: Care and Control in Britain.* Basingstoke: Macmillan.

Stephenson, G. M. & Moston, S. M. (1993) Attitudes and assumptions of police officers when questioning criminal suspects. In E. Shepherd, *Aspects of Police Interviewing. Issues in Criminological and Legal Psychology,* No.18. Leicester: British Psychological Society.

Stradling, S. & Harper, K. (1988) The Tutor Constable attachment, the management of encounters and the development of discretionary judgement. In P. Southgate, *New Directions in Police Training.* London: HMSO.

Stradling, S. G., Tuohy, A. P. & Harper, K. J. (1990) Judgmental asymmetry in the exercise of police discretion. *Applied Cognitive Psychology,* **4**, 409–421.

Stratton, J. G. (1984) *Police Passages.* Manhattan Beach, CA: Glennon.

Straus, M. A. (1980) A sociological perspective on the causes of family violence. In M. R. Green (ed.), *Violence and the Family.* Washington, DC: American Association for the Advancement of Science.

Strodtbeck, F. & Lipinski, R. M. (1985) Becoming first among equals: moral considerations in jury foreman selection. *Journal of Personality & Social Psychology,* **49**, 927–936.

Sutherland, E. H. & Cressey, D. R. (1974) *Principles of Criminology* (9th edn). New York: Lippincott.

Swanson, C. R., Chamelin, N. C. & Territo, L. (1988) *Criminal Investigation* (4th edn). New York: McGraw-Hill.

Sykes, R. E., Fox, J. E. & Clark, J. P. (1976) Socio-legal theory of police discretion. In A. Niederhoffer & A. S. Blumberg (eds), *The Ambivalent Force: Perspectives on the Police*. Hinsdale, IL: Dryden Press.

Szasz, T. (1961) *The Myth of Mental Illness*. New York: Harper & Row.

Tajfel, H. (1971) Social categorisation and inter-group behaviour. *European Journal of Social Psychology*, **1**, 149–178.

Tajfel, H. (1978) *Differentiation between Social Groups*. New York: Academic Press.

Tajfel, H. (1981) *Human Groups and Social Categories: Studies in Social Psychology*; Cambridge: Cambridge University Press.

Tajfel, H. & Turner, J. C. (1986) The social identity theory of intergroup behavior. In S. Worchel & G. W. Austin, *Psychology of Intergroup Relations* (2nd edn). Chicago: Nelson-Hall.

Taylor, M. & Pease, K. (1988) Psychological testing and police recruit selection. *Eurocriminology*, **2**, 57–72.

Taylor, S. P. & Epstein, S. (1967) Aggression as a function of the interaction of the sex of the aggressor and the sex of the victim. *Journal of Personality*, **35**, 474–475.

Taylor, S. P. & Gammon, C. B. (1975) Effects of type and use of alcohol on human physical aggression. *Journal of Personality and Social Psychology*, **32**, 169–175.

Taylor, S. P. & Leonard, K. E. (1983) Alcohol and human physical aggression. In R. G. Geen and E. Donnerstein (eds), *Aggression: Theoretical and Empirical Reviews*, vol. 2: *Issues in Research* (pp. 77–101). New York: Academic Press.

Thomas, T. (1994) *The Police and Social Workers* (2nd edn). Aldershot: Ashgate.

Thurman, O. C., Giacomazzi, A. & Bayer, P. (1993) Cops, kids and community policing: an assessment of a community demonstration project. *Crime and Delinquency*, **39** (4) 555–564.

Toch, H. (1969) *Violent Men: An Inquiry into the Psychology of Violence*. Chicago: Aldine.

Tournier, R. E. (1976) Social isolation and the quality of law enforcement. In R. Cohen et al, *Working with Police Agencies*. New York: Human Sciences Press.

Treger, H. C. (1975) *The Police Social Work Team*. Springfield, IL: Thomas.

Trower, P., Bryant, B. & Argyle, M. (1978) *Social Skills and Mental Health*. London: Methuen.

Tulving, E. (1983) *Elements of Episodic Memory*. Oxford: Clarendon Press.

Tuohy, A. P., Wrennall, M. J., McQueen, R. A. & Stradling, S. (1993) Effect of socialization factors on decisions to prosecute. *Law and Human Behaviour*, **17**, 2, 167–181.

Van Maanen, J. (1974) Working the street: a developmental view of police behaviour. In H. Jacob, *The Potential for Reform of Criminal Justice*. Beverly Hills, CA: Sage.

Van Maanen, J. (1975) Police socialisation: a longitudinal examination of job attitudes in an urban police department. *Administration Science Quarterly*, **20**, 207–208.

Vrij, A. & Winkel, F. W. (1993) Objective and subjective indicators of deception. *Issues in Criminological and Legal Psychology*, **20**, 51–57.

Waddington, P. A. (1984) Citizen or slag. *Police*, XVI (6).

Waddington, P. A. (1988) *Arming an Unarmed Police*. London: Police Foundation.

Wallace, W. (1994) The value of assessment centres as a determining element in the police promotion process. Unpublished MA dissertation, University of Manchester.

Waterhouse, L. & Carnie, J. (1990) Investigating child sexual abuse: towards inter-agency cooperation. *Adoption and Fostering*, **14**, 4, 7–12.

Weatheritt, M. (1993) Measuring police performance: accounting or accountability. In R. Reiner & S. Spencer, *Accountable Policing: Effectiveness, Empowerment and Equity*. London: IPPR.

Weinstein, J. (1994) *Sewing the Seams for a Seamless Service*. London: CCETSW.

Wells, G. L. & Loftus, E. F. (1984) *Eyewitness Testimony: Psychological Perspectives*. Cambridge: Cambridge University Press.

West, D. J. & Farrington, D. P. (1973) *Who Becomes Delinquent?* London: Heinemann.

White, S., Evans, P., Mihill, C. & Tysoe, M. (1992) *Hitting the Headlines: a Practical Guide to the Media*. Leicester: British Psychological Society.

Williamson, T. M. (1990) Strategic changes in police interrogation. Unpublished PhD thesis, University of Kent.

Wilson, J. (1975) *Thinking about Crime*. New York: Basic Books.

Witkin, H. A., Mednick, S. A., Schulsinger, F., Bakkestrom, E., Christiansen, K. O., Goodenough, D. R., Hirschhorn, K., Lundsteen, C., Owen, D. R., Philip, J., Rubin, D. B. & Stocking, M. (1976) Criminality in XYY and XXY men. *Science*, **193**, 547–555.

Wolfgang, M. & Ferracuti, F. (1967) *The Subculture of Violence: Toward an Integrated Theory of Criminality*. London: Tavistock.

Wolfgang, M. & Strohm, R. B. (1956) The relationship between alcohol and criminal homicide. *Quarterly Journal of Studies on Alcohol*, **17**, 411–425.

Wolpe, J. (1958) *Psychotherapy by Reciprocal Inhibition*. Stanford, CA: Stanford University Press.

Wolpe, J. (1969) Basic principles and practices of behavior therapy of neuroses. *American Journal of Psychotherapy*, **25**, 362–368.

Wood, W. & Kallgren, C. A. (1988) Communicator attributes and persuasion: recipients' access to attitude-relevant information in memory. *Personality and Social Psychology Bulletin*, **14**, 172–182.

Wrightsman, L. S. (1991) *Psychology and the Legal System* (2nd edn). Belmont, CA: Brookes/Cole.

Young, J. (1987) The tasks facing a realist criminology. *Contemporary Crises*, **11**, 337–356.

Yuille, J. C. (1986) *Police Selection and Training*. Dordrecht: Martinus Nijhoff.

Zeisel, H. & Diamond, S. S. (1976) The jury selection in the Mitchell–Stans conspiracy trial. *American Bar Foundation Research Journal*, **1**, 151–174.

Zillmann, D., Baron, R. A. & Tamborini, R. (1981) Social costs of smoking: effects of tobacco smoke on hostile behavior. *Journal of Applied Social Psychology*, **11**, 548–561.

Zimbardo, P. (1966) The psychology of imprisonment. In J. C. Brigham & L. S. Wrightsman, *Contemporary Issues in Social Psychology*. Belmont, CA: Brookes/Cole.

Index